POPULAR CULTURE
A BROADVIEW TOPICS READER

A Note to Students

The *Popular Culture* companion website provides a set of explanatory notes that go beyond the footnotes in the bound book. These notes are designed to be of particular help to students who have limited familiarity with North American culture, and/or students who have learned English as an additional language—though the extra notes may offer support to any student. Words and phrases for which additional notes are provided on the website are marked with a small asterisk in these pages. The notes themselves may either be consulted online or be printed out and kept handy as you read.

The website also features interactive exercises to improve your grammar and other writing skills.

Visit the website here:
https://sites.broadviewpress.com/popularculture/

POPULAR CULTURE
A BROADVIEW TOPICS READER

Editors

Laura Buzzard
Don LePan
Nora Ruddock
Alexandria Stuart

broadview press

BROADVIEW PRESS – www.broadviewpress.com
Peterborough, Ontario, Canada

Founded in 1985, Broadview Press remains a wholly independent publishing house. Broadview's focus is on academic publishing; our titles are accessible to university and college students as well as scholars and general readers. With over 600 titles in print, Broadview has become a leading international publisher in the humanities, with world-wide distribution. Broadview is committed to environmentally responsible publishing and fair business practices.

Library and Archives Canada Cataloguing in Publication

Title: Popular culture : a Broadview topics reader / editors, Laura Buzzard, Don LePan, Nora Ruddock, Alexandria Stuart.
Other titles: Popular culture (Peterborough, Ont.)
Names: Buzzard, Laura, editor. | LePan, Don, 1954- editor. | Ruddock, Nora, 1978- editor. | Stuart, Alexandria, 1970- editor.
Description: Includes bibliographical references and index.
Identifiers: Canadiana 20190183462 | ISBN 9781554814909 (softcover)
Subjects: LCSH: Popular culture.
Classification: LCC HM621 .P67 2019 | DDC 306—dc23

Broadview Press handles its own distribution in North America:
PO Box 1243, Peterborough, Ontario K9J 7H5, Canada
555 Riverwalk Parkway, Tonawanda, NY 14150, USA
Tel: (705) 743-8990; Fax: (705) 743-8353
email: customerservice@broadviewpress.com

Distribution is handled by Eurospan Group in the UK, Europe, Central Asia, Middle East, Africa, India, Southeast Asia, Central America, South America, and the Caribbean. Distribution is handled by Footprint Books in Australia and New Zealand.

Broadview Press acknowledges the financial support of the Government of Canada for our publishing activities.

Canada

Design and typeset by Alexandria Stuart
Cover design by Lisa Brawn

PRINTED IN CANADA

CONTENTS

CLAIMING BLACKNESS

LANGUAGE AND CULTURE

FORMING THE SELF

POWER IN SPORTS

CONTENTS BY GENRE AND RHETORICAL CATEGORY

Academic Writing / Blog Posts and Online Media / Cause and Effect / Classification / Comparison and Contrast / Definition / Description / Journalism / Memoir, Biography, and Personal Experience / Narration / Poetry and Lyric Essays / Satire / Speeches and Lectures

Journalism

Memoir, Biography, and Personal Experience

Narration

Poetry and Lyric Essays

Satire

Speeches and Lectures

SUGGESTED PAIRINGS

Though it is by no means an exhaustive list of such combinations, the following list identifies pieces in this book that the editors suggest may be of interest to consider together:

PREFACE

When seeking to engage students who are new to the humanities—some of whom may well be reluctant or uncomfortable to find themselves in a writing course—teachers of introductory composition often turn to the subject of popular culture. This focus not only allows students to delve into a topic most are already interested in, but also encourages them to consider how they already use communication and interpretation skills in their daily lives. For reasons such as these, it was no surprise that, when we asked academics what should be the subject of the second book in our series of Broadview Topics Readers, many expressed interest in a reader on popular culture.

As we selected the contents of this book and prepared the headnotes, footnotes, and discussion questions for each reading, we have tried to keep in mind an audience of students new to postsecondary study and to the study (if not the experience) of popular culture. We hope that familiar cultural touchstones—advertising, superhero films, hip hop music, social media, and so on—will provide an accessible bridge into the discussion of other matters central to the humanities, from issues of genre and writing style to the dynamics of race, class, gender, and other axes of identity.

We have aimed to keep the book as slim and inexpensive for students as possible while still providing instructors with a diverse range of materials to choose from. A variety of analytical and persuasive essays are a central part of the anthology—but the reader will also find personal essays, occasional pieces, lectures, a lyric essay, and so on. Op-ed pieces are included, as are film and television reviews and other examples of print and online journalism. We have included some scholarly pieces meant to provide students with a critical framework—such as two selections from Barthes's *Mythologies*—but we have also been careful to keep the emphasis on popular culture itself, as opposed to works of critical theory that may be overwhelming to students in an introductory composition class. We have also aimed to keep the length of individual pieces manageable for first-year students; selections range from two pages to a little over fifteen pages in length. The emphasis is on the popular culture of the twenty-first century, but a few twentieth-century classics of continuing relevance are also included.

Given the importance of visual media to popular culture we have also included a color insert of visual material including advertisements, art works, and journalistic photography. Some of the selected images are mentioned specifically in one or more of the written pieces, while others have been chosen because they relate strongly to themes present in the anthology; all, we hope, are of interest in themselves as cultural artifacts. Discussion questions for each image are available on the anthology's companion website.

Another feature of the anthology is the inclusion of paired or grouped selections. In some cases, the pairings are of pieces that take directly opposing points of view on the same topic; such is the case with the two pieces on the NFL. In others, they treat a topic from complementary viewpoints. Although it is by no means exhaustive, a listing of selections (including images) that may usefully be taught together is provided in this anthology's prefatory material.

We have also aimed for what seems to us to be an appropriate balance so far as gender and race are concerned. Roughly half the pieces in this anthology are by women; more than half are by writers of color.

One issue in assembling almost any anthology is whether or not to excerpt. If the book is to be essentially an anthology of essays, does the integrity of the form demand that all essays selected for inclusion be included in their entirety? Should selections taken from full-length books be excluded on the grounds of their provenance? To both these questions we have answered in the negative. If an anthology such as this is to do the best possible job of presenting the widest possible range within a manageable compass, both practical and pedagogical concerns seem to us to justify the occasional decision to excerpt a very long essay, or to reprint a selection from a full-length book.

After consulting with instructors, we have arranged the contents of this volume by thematic subgroup, rather than chronologically or by rhetorical category. An alternative table of contents follows in which materials are listed by genre and rhetorical category. In this alternative listing, individual selections are likely to appear several times; many persuasive essays also employ description or narration, many lectures are also scholarly works, and so on.

The apparatus for the anthology is designed to provide substantial help to students, and to do so in ways that help them to engage actively with the material. Introductory headnotes are designed to fill in the context, not to provide a summary of each piece. Footnotes are there to assist students in understanding material that may be unfamiliar—but in every case the aim is to provide explanatory background rather than interpretation. Questions at the end of each selection are designed to help students engage with the content of the pieces as well as to develop their writing and critical thinking skills.

We have also provided a set of additional notes on the anthology's companion website—notes designed to be of particular help to English as an Additional Language (EAL) students and/or students who have little familiarity with North American history, politics, and culture. Phrases such as "canary in the coal mine" or "buy the farm" are not likely to require glossing for the student who has just graduated from a high school in Chicago or Toronto or San Francisco, but may seem obscure or confusing to a student who has recently arrived in the United States or Canada for the first time. And, of course, students will always arrive at university with different vocabularies and bodies of background knowledge. These notes, then, offer additional support to any student who may wish to consult them. Words and phrases for which additional notes are provided are marked with a small asterisk in these pages. Students wishing to consult these additional notes may find them on the anthology's companion website; these notes may be read online or printed out and kept handy as the student reads the relevant selections.

•   •   •

We are indebted to a good many people for suggestions and advice, and would like to thank the following for the guidance they have provided to us along the way: Jennifer B. Waters, Arizona State University and Mesa Community College; Mark Dowdy, San Jose State University; Carl Della Badia, College of Western Idaho; Dan Roche, Le Moyne College; Anu Chatterjee, University of Cincinnati Clermont College; Jennifer Wiley, Pima Community College; Sheela S. Free, San Bernardino Valley College; Gaines Hubbell, University of Alabama, Huntsville; Dinty W. Moore, Ohio University.

•   •   •

We welcome the comments and suggestions of all readers—instructors or students—about any and all aspects of this book, from the selections themselves to the book's organization and ancillary material (both within these pages and on the companion website); please feel free to email the publishers at broadview@broadviewpress.com. We hope you will enjoy this book as it stands—but we also hope you will join us in thinking of possible improvements for future editions.

Laura Buzzard
Don LePan
Nora Ruddock
Alexandria Stuart

15 October 2019

THE COSTS OF
ADVERTISING

ROLAND BARTHES

from MYTHOLOGIES
SOAP-POWDERS AND DETERGENTS[1]

*Roland Barthes was a pioneer in semiology, the study of signs.
For him, a sign is any unit that communicates meaning, such as
a word, gesture, or image; by treating its components as signs, an
interpreter can examine any work of art or advertising, any event
or behavior, much as one might analyze a written or spoken work.
In his book* Mythologies *(1957), Barthes considers how cultural
artifacts and practices—wine, Einstein's brain, a cruise, wrestling—
reveal the way society constructs meaning, how its ideologies and
power structures are sustained and created. "Toys," another essay
from* Mythologies, *appears elsewhere in this anthology.*

❧

The first World Detergent Congress (Paris, September 1954) had the effect
of authorizing the world to yield to *Omo*[2] euphoria: not only do detergents
have no harmful effect on the skin, but they can even perhaps save miners
from silicosis.[3] These products have been in the last few years the object of
such massive advertising that they now belong to a region of French daily
life which the various types of psychoanalysis would do well to pay some
attention to if they wish to keep up to date. One could then usefully contrast
the psycho-analysis of purifying fluids (chlorinated, for example) with that

---

1   *Mythologies: Soap-Powders and Detergents*   Translated by Annette Lavers, 1972;
Soaps are made of mainly natural ingredients (fats mixed with sodium or potassium salts),
whereas detergents are mainly synthetic. Detergents are generally preferred for laundry, as
they don't react to the minerals found in water, but they can also be toxic and damaging to
the environment.

2   *Omo*   One of the Unilever brands of laundry detergent.

3   *silicosis*   Also called "black lung," silicosis is a potentially fatal lung disease that
afflicts miners. The lungs are scarred by the inhalation of silica dust in the mines; silicosis
also leads to increased risk of tuberculosis and lung cancer. It was thought to be helpful to
wash the silica dust off the miners' clothes so they would not bring it home with them.

of soap-powders (*Lux, Persil*[4]) or that of detergents (*Omo*). The relations between the evil and the cure, between dirt and a given product, are very different in each case.

Chlorinated fluids, for instance, have always been experienced as a sort of liquid fire, the action of which must be carefully estimated, otherwise the object itself would be affected, "burnt." The implicit legend of this type of product rests on the idea of a violent, abrasive modification of matter: the connotations are of a chemical or mutilating type: the product "kills" the dirt. Powders, on the contrary, are separating agents: their ideal role is to liberate the object from its circumstantial imperfection: dirt is "forced out" and no longer killed; in the *Omo* imagery, dirt is a diminutive enemy, stunted and black, which takes to its heels from the fine immaculate linen at the sole threat of the judgment of *Omo*. Products based on chlorine and ammonia are without doubt the representatives of a kind of absolute fire, a savior but a blind one. Powders, on the contrary, are selective, they push, they drive dirt through the texture of the object, their function is keeping public order not making war. This distinction has ethnographic correlatives: the chemical fluid is an extension of the washerwoman's movements when she beats the clothes, while powders rather replace those of the housewife pressing and rolling the washing against a sloping board.

But even in the category of powders, one must in addition oppose against advertisements based on psychology those based on psychoanalysis[5] (I use this word without reference to any specific school). "Persil Whiteness" for instance, bases its prestige on the evidence of a result; it calls into play vanity, a social concern with appearances, by offering for comparison two objects, one of which is whiter than the other. Advertisements for *Omo* also indicate the effect of the product (and in superlative fashion, incidentally), but they chiefly reveal its mode of action; in doing so, they involve the consumer in a kind of direct experience of the substance, make him the accomplice of a liberation rather than the mere beneficiary of a result; matter here is endowed with value-bearing states.

Omo uses two of these, which are rather novel in the category of detergents: the deep and the foamy. To say that *Omo* cleans in depth (see the Cinéma-Publicité advertisement[6]) is to assume that linen is deep, which no

4   *Lux, Persil*   Brands of laundry soap. Persil was the first "self-activated" soap that combined bleach with the soap flakes, rendering sun-drying unnecessary.

5   *psychology*   Scientific study of the human mind; *psychoanalysis*   Method of psychiatric therapy, originated by Sigmund Freud; treatment involves analysis of conscious and unconscious elements in the patient's mind, using techniques of association and dream interpretation.

6   *Cinéma-Publicité advertisement*   Advertisement placed in advance of a film shown in the movie theater.

one had previously thought, and this unquestionably results in exalting it, by establishing it as an object favorable to those obscure tendencies to enfold and caress which are found in every human body. As for foam, it is well known that it signifies luxury. To begin with, it appears to lack any usefulness; then, its abundant, easy, almost infinite proliferation allows one to suppose there is in the substance from which it issues a vigorous germ, a healthy and powerful essence, a great wealth of active elements in a small original volume. Finally, it gratifies in the consumer a tendency to imagine matter as something airy, with which contact is effected in a mode both light and vertical, which is sought after like that of happiness either in the gustatory category (foie gras, entremets,[7] wines), in that of clothing (muslin, tulle), or that of soaps (filmstar in her bath). Foam can even be the sign of a certain spirituality, inasmuch as the spirit has the reputation of being able to make something out of nothing, a large surface of effects out of a small volume of causes (creams have a very different "psychoanalytical" meaning, of a soothing kind: they suppress wrinkles, pain, smarting, etc.). What matters is the art of having disguised the abrasive function of the detergent under the delicious image of a substance at once deep and airy which can govern the molecular order of the material without damaging it. A euphoria, incidentally, which must not make us forget that there is one plane on which *Persil* and *Omo* are one and the same: the plane of the Anglo-Dutch trust Unilever.[8]

(1957)

Questions

1. What, according to Barthes, is the "psychoanalysis" of bleach ("chlorinated fluids")? What kind of language surrounds these products? How does it differ from the language surrounding soap-powders?

2. Barthes cautions that we must not "forget that there is one plane on which *Persil* and *Omo* are one and the same: the plane of the Anglo-Dutch trust Unilever." What is the significance of this statement?

3. How does Barthes deconstruct the appeal of "foamy" products? Why do they appeal to us?

---

7 *foie gras* Creamy spread made of fattened duck livers, considered a delicacy in France; *entremets* Dish served between courses, most often a dessert; modern entremets are usually layered mousse cakes.

8 *Unilever* Large multinational corporation that sells food, cleaning agents, and personal care products.

4. Barthes describes the effects of soap and detergent advertising on the mind (and on society in general) as euphoric. Do you agree that a kind of intoxicating pleasure can be found in products and in the advertisement of products? Why or why not? What might be the social consequences of such euphoric states?

5. Find a present-day advertisement that markets a soap or detergent to a North American audience. What (if any) aspects of Barthes's analysis can be applied to this advertisement?

NAOMI KLEIN

from NO LOGO

THE SWOOSH

In her enormously influential 1999 bestseller No Logo: Taking Aim at the Brand Bullies, *leading social activist Naomi Klein addresses corporate branding in the context of economic and cultural globalization. Klein divides her book into sections, beginning with "No Space," which outlines the history and growth of branding; "No Choice," which catalogues the methods large corporations use to secure economic and cultural dominance; and "No Jobs," which describes how workers are impacted as manufacturing jobs are moved to the least regulated countries. In the last portion of the book, "No Logo," she presents examples of what she considers a burgeoning global movement of resistance to corporate branding and labor practices. "Branding," she writes, "is a balloon economy: it inflates with astonishing rapidity but it is full of hot air. It shouldn't be surprising that this formula has bred armies of pin-wielding critics, eager to pop the corporate balloon and watch the shreds fall to the ground." In the selection reproduced here, she discusses attempts to pop "the most inflated of all the balloon brands."*

❧

Nike CEO Phil Knight has long been a hero of the business schools. Prestigious academic publications such as *The Harvard Business Review* have lauded his pioneering marketing techniques, his understanding of branding and his early use of outsourcing. Countless MBA candidates and other students of marketing and communications have studied the Nike formula of "brands, not products." So when Phil Knight was invited to be a guest speaker at the Stanford University Business School—Knight's own alma mater—in May 1997, the visit was expected to be one in a long line of Nike love-ins. Instead, Knight was greeted by a crowd of picketing students, and when he approached the microphone he was taunted with chants of "Hey Phil, off the stage. Pay your workers a living wage." The Nike honeymoon had come to a grinding halt.

No story illustrates the growing distrust of the culture of corporate branding more than the international anti-Nike movement—the most publicized and tenacious of the brand-based campaigns. Nike's sweatshop scandals have been the subject of over 1,500 news articles and opinion columns. Its Asian factories have been probed by cameras from nearly every major media organization, from CBS to Disney's sports station, ESPN. On top of all that, it has been the subject of a series of Doonesbury[1] cartoon strips and the butt of Michael Moore's documentary *The Big One*. As a result, several people in Nike's PR department work full time dealing with the sweatshop controversy—fielding complaints, meeting with local groups and developing Nike's response—and the company has created a new executive position: vice president for corporate responsibility. Nike has received hundreds and thousands of letters of protest, faced hundreds of both small and large groups of demonstrators, and is the target of a dozen critical Web sites.

For the last two years, anti-Nike forces in North America and Europe have attempted to focus all the scattered swoosh bashing on a single day. Every six months they have declared an International Nike Day of Action, and brought their demands for fair wages and independent monitoring directly to Nike's customers, shoppers at flagship Nike Towns in urban centers or the less glamorous Foot Locker outlets in suburban malls. According to Campaign for Labor Rights, the largest anti-Nike event so far took place on October 18, 1997: eighty-five cities in thirteen countries participated. Not all the protests have attracted large crowds, but since the movement is so decentralized, the sheer number of individual anti-Nike events has left the company's public-relations department scrambling to get its spin onto dozens of local newscasts. Though you'd never know it from its branding ubiquity, even Nike can't be everywhere at once.

Since so many of the stores that sell Nike products are located in malls, protests often end with a security guard escorting participants into the parking lot. Jeff Smith, an activist from Grand Rapids, Michigan, reported that "when we asked if private property rights ruled over free speech rights, the [security] officer hesitated and then emphatically said YES!" (Though in the economically depressed city of St. John's, Newfoundland, anti-Nike campaigners reported that after being thrown out of a mall, "they were approached by a security guard who asked to sign their petition.")[2] But there's plenty that can be done on the sidewalk or in the mall parking lot. Campaigners have dramatized Nike's

---

1   *Doonesbury*   Comic strip launched in 1970 by American cartoonist Gary Trudeau and known for its commentary on current political and social issues.

2   [Klein's note]   Memo, 4 May 1998, from Maquila Solidarity Network, "Nike Day of Action Canada Report & Task Force Update."

labor practices through what they call "sweatshop fashion shows," and "The Transnational Capital Auction: A Game of Survival" (the lowest bidder wins), and a global economy treadmill (run fast, stay in the same place). In Australia, anti-Nike protestors have been known to parade around in calico bags painted with the slogan "Rather wear a bag than Nike." Students at the University of Colorado in Boulder dramatized the difference between the legal minimum wage and a living wage by holding a fundraising run in which "participants pay an entrance fee of $1.60 (daily wages for a Nike worker in Vietnam) and the winner will receive $2.10 (the price of three square meals in Vietnam)."[3] Meanwhile, activists in Austin, Texas, made a giant papier-mâché Nike sneaker piñata, and a protest outside a Regina, Saskatchewan, shopping center featured a deface-the-swoosh booth. The last stunt is something of a running theme in all the anti-Nike actions: Nike's logo and slogan have been jammed so many times—on T-shirts, stickers, placards, banners and pins—that the semiotic[4] bruises have turned them black and blue.

Tellingly, the anti-Nike movement is at its strongest inside the company's home state of Oregon, even though the area has reaped substantial economic benefits from Nike's success (Nike is the largest employer in Portland and a significant local philanthropist). Phil Knight's neighbors, nonetheless, have not all rushed to his defense in his hour of need. In fact, since the *Life* magazine soccer-ball story[5] broke, many Oregonians have been out for blood. The demonstrations outside the Portland Nike Town are among the largest and most militant in the country, sometimes sporting a menacing giant Phil Knight puppet with dollar signs for eyes or a twelve-foot Nike swoosh dragged by small children (to dramatize child labor). And in contravention of the principles of nonviolence that govern the anti-Nike movement, one protest in Eugene, Oregon, led to acts of vandalism including the tearing-down of a fence surrounding the construction of a new Nike Town, gear pulled off shelves at an existing Nike store and, according to one eyewitness, "an entire rack of clothes ... dumped off a balcony into a fountain below."[6]

Local papers in Oregon have aggressively (sometimes gleefully) followed Knight's sweatshop scandals, and the daily paper *The Oregonian* sent a

5

---

3   [Klein's note]   "Nike protest update," *Labor Alerts*, 18 October 1997.

4   *semiotic*   Related to symbols and other signs (units that communicate meaning, such as words, gestures, and images).

5   *Life magazine soccer-ball story*   "Six Cents an Hour," an influential 1996 article detailing the egregious mistreatment experienced by child laborers who make soccer balls for Nike and other major companies in India and Pakistan.

6   [Klein's note]   "Nike Mobilization: Local Reports," *Labor Alerts*, Campaign for Labor Rights, 26 October 1998.

reporter to Southeast Asia to do its own lengthy investigation of the factories. Mark Zusman, editor of the Oregon newspaper *The Willamette Week*, publicly admonished Knight in a 1996 "memo": "Frankly, Phil, it's time to get a little more sophisticated about this media orgy ... Oregonians already have suffered through the shame of Tonya Harding, Bob Packwood and Wes Cooley.[7] Spare us the added humiliation of being known as the home of the most exploitative capitalist in the free world."[8]

Even Nike's charitable donations have become controversial. In the midst of a critical fundraising drive to try to address a $15 million shortfall, the Portland School Board was torn apart by a debate about whether to accept Nike's gift of $500,000 in cash and swooshed athletic gear. The board ended up accepting the donation, but not before looking their gift horse publicly in the mouth. "I asked myself," school board trustee Joseph Tam told *The Oregonian*, "Nike contributed this money so my children can have a better education, but at whose expense? At the expense of children who work for six cents an hour? ... As an immigrant and as an Asian I have to face this moral and ethical dilemma."[9]

Nike's sponsorship scandals have reached far beyond the company's home state. In Edmonton, Alberta, teachers, parents and some students tried to block Nike from sponsoring a children's street hockey program because "a company which profits from child labor in Pakistan ought not to be held up as a hero to Edmonton children."[10] At least one school involved in the city-wide program sent back its swooshed equipment to Nike headquarters. And when Nike approached the City of Ottawa Council in March 1998 to suggest building one of its swooshed gymnasium floors in a local community center, it faced questions about "blood money." Nike withdrew its offer and gave the court to a more grateful center, run by the Boys and Girls Clubs. The dilemma of accepting Nike sponsorship money has also exploded on university campuses.

---

7   *Tonya Harding*   American figure skater (b. 1970) who was banned from the sport after being implicated in an attack on her rival Nancy Kerrigan;   *Bob Packwood*   Republican Senator (b. 1932) who resigned his seat in 1995 under allegations of sexual assault and harassment;   *Wes Cooley*   Republican Senator and member of the House of Representatives (1932–2015) who was convicted in 1996 of lying in campaign materials about his military service record.

8   [Klein's note]   Mark L. Zusman, "Editor's Notebook," *Willamette Week*, 12 June 1996.

9   [Klein's note]   *Oregonian*, 16 June 1996.

10   [Klein's note]   Campaign for Labor Rights Web site, regional reports.

At first, much of the outrage stemmed from the fact that when the sweatshop scandal hit the papers, Nike wasn't really acting all that sorry about it. While Kathie Lee Gifford[11] and the Gap had at least displayed contrition when they got caught with their sweatshops showing, Phil Knight had practically stone-walled: denying responsibility, attacking journalists, blaming rogue contractors and sending out flacks* to speak for the company. While Kathie Lee was cry-ing on TV, Michael Jordan* was shrugging his shoulders and saying that his job was to shoot hoop, not play politics. And while the Gap agreed to allow a particularly controversial factory in El Salvador to be monitored by local human-rights groups, Nike was paying lip service to a code of conduct that its Asian workers, when interviewed, had never heard of.

But there was a critical difference between Nike and the Gap at this stage. Nike didn't panic when its scandals hit the middle-American mall, because the mall, while it is indeed where most Nike products are sold, is not where Nike's image was made. Unlike the Gap, Nike has drawn on the inner cities, merging, as we've seen, with the styles of poor black and Latino youth to load up on imagery and attitude. Nike's branding power is thoroughly intertwined with the African-American heroes who have endorsed its products since the mid-eighties: Michael Jordan, Charles Barkley, Scottie Pippen, Michael Johnson, Spike Lee, Tiger Woods, Bo Jackson—not to mention the rappers who wear Nike gear on stage. While hip-hop style was the major influence at the mall, Phil Knight must have known that as long as Nike was King Brand with Jordan fans in Compton and the Bronx, he could be stirred but not shaken. Sure, their parents, teachers and church leaders might be tut-tutting over sweatshops, but as far as Nike's core demographic of thirteen- to seventeen-year-old kids was concerned, the swoosh was still made of Teflon.

By 1997, it had become clear to Nike's critics that if they were serious about taking on the swoosh in an image war, they would have to get at the source of the brand's cachet—and as Nick Alexander of the multicultural *Third Force* magazine wrote in the summer of that year, they weren't even close. "Nobody has figured out how to make Nike break down and cry. The reason is that nobody has engaged African Americans in the fight.... To gain significant support from communities of color, corporate campaigns need to make con-nections between Nike's overseas operations and conditions here at home."[12]

10

---

11   *Kathie Lee Gifford*   American performer (b. 1953) best known as the co-host of *Live! with Regis and Kathie Lee*. In 1996, a media frenzy surrounded the use of sweatshop labor to manufacture her clothing line.

12   [Klein's note]   Nick Alexander, "Sweatshop Activism: Missing Pieces," *Z Magazine*, September 1997, 14–17.

The connections were there to be made. It is the cruelest irony of Nike's "brands, not products" formula that the people who have done the most to infuse the swoosh with cutting-edge meaning are the very people most hurt by the company's pumped-up prices and nonexistent manufacturing base. It is inner-city youth who have most directly felt the impact of Nike's decision to manufacture its products outside the US, both in high unemployment rates and in the erosion of the community tax base (which sets the stage for the deterioration of local public schools).

Instead of jobs for their parents, what the inner-city kids get from Nike is the occasional visit from its marketers and designers on "bro-ing" pilgrimages. "Hey, bro, what do you think of these new Jordans—are they fresh or what?" The effect of high-priced cool hunters whipping up brand frenzy on the cracked asphalt basketball courts of Harlem, the Bronx and Compton* has already been discussed: kids incorporate the brands into gang-wear uniforms; some want the gear so badly they are willing to sell drugs, steal, mug, even kill for it. Jessie Collins, executive director of the Edenwald-Gun Hill Neighborhood Center in the northeast Bronx, tells me that it's sometimes drug or gang money, but more often it's the mothers' minimum-wage salary or welfare checks that are spent on disposable status wear. When I asked her about the media reports of kids stabbing each other for their $150 Air Jordans she said dryly, "It's enough to beat up on your mother for ... $150 is a hell of a lot of money."[13]

Shoe-store owners like Steven Roth of Essex House of Fashion are often uncomfortable with the way so-called street fashions play out for real on the postindustrial streets of Newark, New Jersey, where his store is located:

> I do get weary and worn down from it all. I'm always forced to face
> the fact that I make my money from poor people. A lot of them are on
> welfare. Sometimes a mother will come in here with a kid, and the kid
> is dirty and poorly dressed. But the kid wants a hundred-twenty-buck
> pair of shoes and that stupid mother buys them for him. I can feel that
> kid's inner need—this desire to own these things and have the feelings
> that go with them—but it hurts me that this is the way things are.[14]

It's easy to blame the parents for giving in, but that "deep inner need" for designer gear has grown so intense that it has confounded everyone from community leaders to the police. Everyone pretty much agrees that brands like Nike are playing a powerful surrogate role in the ghetto, subbing for everything from self-esteem to African-American cultural history to political power. What they

---

13 [Klein's note]   Personal interview, 6 October 1997.

14 [Klein's note]   [Donald] Katz, *Just Do It[: The Nike Spirit in the Corporate World* (Holbrook: Adams Media Corporation), 1994], 271.

are far less sure about is how to fill that need with empowerment and a sense of self-worth that does not necessarily come with a logo attached. Even broaching the subject of brand fetishism to these kids is risky. With so much emotion invested in celebrity consumer goods, many kids take criticism of Nike or Tommy as a personal attack, as grave a transgression as insulting someone's mother to his face.

Not surprisingly, Nike sees its appeal among disadvantaged kids differently. By supporting sports programs in Boys and Girls Clubs, by paying to repave urban basketball courts and by turning high-performance sports gear into street fashions, the company claims it is sending out the inspirational message that even poor kids can "Just Do It."* In its press material and ads, there is an almost messianic quality to Nike's portrayal of its role in the inner cities: troubled kids will have higher self-esteem, fewer unwanted pregnancies and more ambition—all because at Nike "We see them as athletes." For Nike, its $150 Air Jordans are not a shoe but a kind of talisman with which poor kids can run out of the ghetto and better their lives. Nike's magic slippers will help them fly—just as they made Michael Jordan fly.

A remarkable, subversive accomplishment? Maybe. But one can't help thinking that one of the main reasons black urban youth can get out of the ghetto only by rapping or shooting hoops is that Nike and the other multinationals are reinforcing stereotypical images of black youth and simultaneously taking all the jobs away. As US Congressman Bernie Sanders and Congresswoman Marcy Kaptur stated in a letter to the company, Nike has played a pivotal part in the industrial exodus from urban centers. "Nike has led the way in abandoning the manufacturing workers of the United States and their families.... Apparently, Nike believes that workers in the United States are good enough to purchase your shoe products, but are no longer worthy enough to manufacture them."[15]

And when the company's urban branding strategy is taken in conjunction with this employment record, Nike ceases to be the savior of the inner city and turns into the guy who steals your job, then sells you a pair of overpriced sneakers and yells, "Run like hell!" Hey, it's the only way out of the ghetto, kid. Just do it.

That's what Mike Gitelson thought, anyway. A social worker at the Bronx's Edenwald-Gun Hill Neighborhood Center, he was unimpressed with the swoosh's powers as a self-help guru* in the projects and "sick of seeing kids wearing sneakers they couldn't afford and which their parents couldn't afford."[16] Nike's critics on college campuses and in the labor movement may

15   [Klein's note]   Letter dated 24 October 1997.
16   [Klein's note]   Personal interview.

15

be fueled largely by moral outrage, but Mike Gitelson and his colleagues simply feel ripped off. So rather than lecturing the kids on the virtues of frugality, they began telling them about how Nike made the shoes that they wanted so badly. Gitelson told them about the workers in Indonesia who earned $2 a day, he told them that it cost Nike only $5 to make the shoes they bought for between $100 and $180, and he told them about how Nike didn't make any of its shoes in the US—which was part of the reason their parents had such a tough time finding work. "We got really angry," says Gitelson, "because they were taking so much money from us here and then going to other countries and exploiting people even worse.... We want our kids to see how it affects them here on the streets, but also how here on the streets affects people in Southeast Asia." His colleague at the center, youth worker Leo Johnson, lays out the issue using the kids' own lingo. "Yo, dude," he tells his preteen audiences, "you're being suckered if you pay $100 for a sneaker that costs $5 to make. If somebody did that to you on the block, you know where it's going."[17]

The kids at the center were upset to learn about the sweatshops but they were clearly most pissed off that Phil Knight and Michael Jordan were playing them for chumps. They sent Phil Knight a hundred letters about how much money they had spent on Nike gear over the years—and how, the way they figured it, Nike owed them big time. "I just bought a pair of Nikes for $100," one kid wrote. "It's not right what you're doing. A fair price would have been $30. Could you please send me back $70?" When the company answered the kids with a form letter, "That's when we got really angry and started putting together the protest," Gitelson says.

20   They decided the protest would take the form of a "shoe-in" at the Nike Town at Fifth Avenue and Fifty-seventh Street. Since most of the kids at the center are full-fledged swooshaholics,* their closets are jam-packed with old Air Jordans and Air Carnivores that they would no longer even consider wearing. To put the obsolete shoes to practical use, they decided to gather them together in garbage bags and dump them on the doorstep of Nike Town.

When Nike executives got wind that a bunch of black and Latino kids from the Bronx were planning to publicly diss their company, the form letters came to an abrupt halt. Up to that point, Nike had met most criticism by attacking its critics as members of "fringe groups," but this was different: if a backlash took root in the inner cities, it could sink the brand at the mall. As Gitelson puts it, "Our kids are exactly who Nike depends upon to set the trends for them so that the rest of the country buys their sneakers. White middle-class adults who are

---

17 [Klein's note] David Gonzalez, "Youthful Foes Go Toe to Toe with Nike," *New York Times*, 27 September 1997, B1.

fighting them, well, it's almost okay. But when youth of color start speaking out against Nike, they start getting scared."[18]

The executives in Oregon also knew, no doubt, that Edenwald was only the tip of the iceberg. For the past couple of years, debates have been raging in hip-hop scenes about rappers "label whoring for Nike and Tommy" instead of supporting black-owned clothing companies like FUBU (For Us By Us). And rapper KRS-One planned to launch the Temple of Hip Hop, a project that promised to wrest the culture of African-American youth away from white record and clothing labels and return it to the communities that built it. It was against this backdrop that, on September 10, 1997—two weeks before the shoe-in protest was scheduled to take place—Nike's chief of public relations, Vada Manager, made the unprecedented move of flying in from Oregon with a colleague to try to convince the center that the swoosh was a friend of the projects.

"He was working overtime to put the spins on us," says Gitelson. It didn't work. At the meeting, the center laid out three very concrete demands:

1. Those who work for Nike overseas should be paid a living wage, with independent monitoring to ensure that it is happening.
2. Nike sneakers should be sold less expensively here in America with no concessions to American workforce (i.e. no downsizing, or loss of benefits).
3. Nike should seriously re-invest in the inner city in America, especially New York City since we have been the subject of much of their advertising.[19]

Gitelson may have recognized that Nike was scared—but not *that* scared. Once it became clear that the two parties were at an impasse, the meeting turned into a scolding session as the two Nike executives were required to listen to Edenwald director Jessie Collins comparing the company's Asian sweatshops with her experience as a young girl picking cotton in the sharecropping[20] South. Back in Alabama, she told Manager, she earned $2 a day, just like the

---

18 [Klein's note] Personal interview.

19 [Klein's note] Minutes from 10 September meeting between Nike executives and the Edenwald-Gun Hill Neighborhood Center.

20 *sharecropping* Sharecroppers are farmers who give a portion of their crops to landlords as rent for the land they work. This system of labor, which largely replaced slavery in the South after Emancipation, often kept Black workers in a situation of increasing debt to white landowners.

Indonesians. "And maybe a lot of Americans can't identify with those workers' situation, but I certainly can."[21]

Vada Manager returned to Oregon defeated and the protest went off as planned, with two hundred participants from eleven community centers around New York. The kids—most of whom were between eleven and thirteen years old—hooted and hollered and dumped several clear garbage bags of smelly old Nikes at the feet of a line of security guards who had been brought in on special assignment to protect the sacred Nike premises. Vada Manager again flew to New York to run damage control, but there was little he could do. Local TV crews covered the event, as did an ABC news team and *The New York Times*.

25   In a harsh bit of bad timing for the company, the *Times* piece ran on a page facing another story about Nike. Graphically underlining the urgency of the protest, this story reported that a fourteen-year-old boy from Crown Heights had just been murdered by a fifteen-year-old boy who beat him and left him on the subway tracks with a train approaching. "Police Say Teenager Died for His Sneakers and Beeper,"[22] the headline read. And the brand of his sneakers? Air Jordans. The article quoted the killer's mother saying that her son had got mixed up with gangs because he wanted to "have nice things." A friend of the victim explained that wearing designer clothes and carrying a beeper had become a way for poor kids to "feel important."

The African-American and Latino kids outside Nike Town on Fifth Avenue—the ones swarmed by cameras and surrounded by curious onlookers—were feeling pretty important, too. Taking on Nike "toe to toe," as they said, turned out to be even more fun than wearing Nikes. With the Fox News camera pointed in his face, one of the young activists—a thirteen-year-old boy from the Bronx—stared into the lens and delivered a message to Phil Knight: "Nike, we made you. We can break you."

What is perhaps most remarkable about the Nike backlash is its durability. After four solid years in the public eye, the Nike story still has legs (so too, of course, does the Nike brand). Still, most corporate scandals are successfully faced down with a statement of "regret" and a few glossy ads of children playing happily under the offending logo. Not with Nike. The news reports, labor studies and academic research documenting the sweat behind the swoosh have yet to slow down, and Nike critics remain tireless at dissecting the steady stream of materials churned out by Nike's PR machine. They were unmoved by Phil Knight's presence on the White House Task Force on Sweatshops—despite

---

21 [Klein's note] Personal interview.
22 *Beeper* Pager, a device that beeps when a person calls it; the beeper's owner typically then phones the person who called the beeper.

his priceless photo op standing beside President Clinton at the Rose Garden press conference. They sliced and diced the report Nike commissioned from civil-rights leader Andrew Young, pointing out that Young completely dodged the question of whether Nike's factory wages are inhumanely exploitative, and attacking him for relying on translators provided by Nike itself when he visited the factories in Indonesia and Vietnam. As for Nike's other study-for-hire—this one by a group of Dartmouth business students who concluded that workers in Vietnam were living the good life on less than $2 a day—well, everyone pretty much ignored that one altogether.

Finally, in May 1998, Phil Knight stepped out from behind the curtain of spin doctors and called a press conference in Washington to address his critics directly. Knight began by saying that he had been painted as a "corporate crook, the perfect corporate villain for these times." He acknowledged that his shoes "have become synonymous with slave wages, forced overtime and arbitrary abuse." Then, to much fanfare, he unveiled a plan to improve working conditions in Asia. It contained some tough new regulations on factory air quality and the use of petroleum-based chemicals. It promised to provide classes inside some Indonesian factories and promised not to hire anyone under eighteen years old in the shoe factories. But there was still nothing substantial in the plan about allowing independent outside monitors to inspect the factories, and there were no wage raises for the workers. Knight did promise, however, that Nike's contractors would no longer be permitted to appeal to the Indonesian government for a waiver on the minimum wage.

It wasn't enough. That September the San Francisco human-rights group Global Exchange, one of the company's harshest critics, released an alarming report on the status of Nike's Indonesian workers in the midst of the country's economic and political crisis. "While workers producing Nike shoes were low paid before their currency, the rupiah, began plummeting in late 1997, the dollar value of their wages has dropped from $2.47/day in 1997 to 80 cents/day in 1998." Meanwhile, the report noted that with soaring commodity prices, workers "estimated that their cost of living had gone up anywhere from 100 to 300 per cent."[23] Global Exchange called on Nike to double the ages of its Indonesian workforce, an exercise that would cost it $20 million a year—exactly what Michael Jordan is paid annually to endorse the company.

Not surprisingly, Nike did not double the wages, but it did, three weeks later, give 30 per cent of the Indonesian workforce a 25 per cent raise.[24] That,

30

---

23 [Klein's note] "Wages and Living Expense for Nike Workers in Indonesia," report released by Global Exchange, 23 September 1998.

24 [Klein's note] "Nike Raises Wages for Indonesian Workers," *Oregonian*, 16 October 1998.

too, failed to silence the crowds outside the superstores, and five months later Nike came forward again, this time with what vice president of corporate responsibility Maria Eitel called "an aggressive corporate responsibility agenda at Nike."[25] As of April 1, 1999, workers would get another 6 per cent raise. The company had also opened up a Vietnamese factory near Ho Chi Minh City to outside health and safety monitors, who found conditions much improved. Dara O'Rourke of the University of California at Berkeley reported that the factory had "implemented important changes over the past 18 months which appear to have significantly reduced worker exposures to toxic solvents, adhesives and other chemicals." What made the report all the more remarkable was that O'Rourke's inspection was a genuinely independent one: in fact, less than two years earlier, he had enraged the company by leaking a report conducted by Ernst & Young that showed that Nike was ignoring widespread violations at that same factory.

O'Rourke's findings weren't all glowing. There were still persistent problems with air quality, factory overheating and safety gear—and he had visited only the one factory.[26] As well, Nike's much-heralded 6 per cent pay raise for Indonesian workers still left much to be desired; it amounted to an increase of one cent an hour and, with inflation and currency fluctuation, only brought wages to about half of what Nike paychecks were worth before the economic crisis. Even so, these were significant gestures coming from a company that two years earlier was playing the role of the powerless global shopper, claiming that contractors alone had the authority to set wages and make the rules.

The resilience of the Nike campaign in the face of the public-relations onslaught is persuasive evidence that invasive marketing, coupled with worker abandonment, strikes a wide range of people from different walks of life as grossly unfair and unsustainable. Moreover, many of those people are not interested in letting Nike off the hook simply because this formula has become the standard one for capitalism-as-usual. On the contrary, there seems to be a part of the public psyche that likes kicking the most macho and extreme of all the sporting-goods companies in the shins—I mean *really* likes it. Nike's critics have shown that they don't want this story to be brushed under the rug with a reassuring bit of corporate PR; they want it out in the open, where they can keep a close eye on it.

---

25 [Klein's note] "Nike to Improve Minimum Monthly Wage Package for Indonesian Workers," Nike press release, 19 March 1999.

26 [Klein's note] Steven Greenhouse, "Nike Critic Praises Gains in Air Quality at Vietnam Factory," *New York Times*, 12 March 1999.

In large part, this is because Nike's critics know the company's sweatshop scandals are not the result of a series of freak accidents: they know that the criticisms leveled at Nike apply to all the brand-based shoe companies contracting out to a global maze of firms. But rather than this serving as a justification, Nike—as the market leader—has become a lightning rod for this broader resentment. It has been latched on to as the essential story of the extremes of the current global economy: the disparities between those who profit from Nike's success and those who are exploited by it are so gaping that a child could understand what is wrong with this picture and indeed it is children and teenagers who most readily do.

So, when does the total boycott of Nike products begin? Not soon, apparently. A cursory glance around any city in the world shows that the swoosh is still ubiquitous; some athletes still tattoo it on their navels, and plenty of high-school students still deck themselves out in the coveted gear. But at the same time, there can be little doubt that the millions of dollars that Nike has saved in labor costs over the years are beginning to bite back, and take a toll on its bottom line. "We didn't think that the Nike situation would be as bad as it seems to be," said Nikko stock analyst Tim Finucane in *The Wall Street Journal* in March 1998.[27] Wall Street really had no choice but to turn on the company that had been its darling for so many years. Despite the fact that Asia's plummeting currencies meant that Nike's labor costs in Indonesia, for instance, were a quarter of what they were before the crash, the company was still suffering. Nike's profits were down, orders were down, stock prices were *way* down, and after an average annual growth of 34 per cent since 1995, quarterly earnings were suddenly down by 70 per cent. By the third quarter, which ended in February 1999, Nike's profits were once again up 70 per cent—but by the company's own account, the recovery was not the result of rebounding sales but rather of Nike's decision to cut jobs and contracts. In fact, Nike's revenues and future orders were down in 1999 for the second year in a row.[28]

Nike has blamed its financial problems on everything *but* the human-rights campaign. The Asian currency crisis was the reason Nikes weren't selling well in Japan and South Korea; or it was because Americans were buying "brown shoes" (walking shoes and hiking boots) as opposed to big white sneakers. But the brown-shoe excuse rang hollow. Nike makes plenty of brown shoes—it has a line of hiking boots, and it owns Cole Haan (and recently saved millions

---

27 [Klein's note] Shanthi Kalathil, "Being Tied to Nike Affects Share Price of Yue Yuen," *Wall Street Journal*, 25 March 1998.

28 [Klein's note] "Third quarter brings 70 per cent increase in net income for sneaker giant," Associated Press, 19 March 1999.

by closing down the Cole Haan factory in Portland, Maine, and moving production to Mexico and Brazil).[29] More to the point, Adidas staged a massive comeback during the very year that Nike was free-falling. In the quarter when Nike nose-dived, Adidas sales were up 42 per cent, its net income was up 48 per cent, to $255 million, and its stock price had tripled in two years. The German company, as we have seen, turned its fortunes around by copying Nike's production structure and all but Xeroxing its approach to marketing and sponsorships. In 1997–98, Adidas even redesigned its basketball shoes so they looked just like Nikes: big, white and ultra high tech. But unlike Nikes, they sold briskly. So much for the brown-shoe theory.

Over the years Nike has tried dozens of tactics to silence the cries of its critics, but the most ironic by far has been the company's desperate attempt to hide behind its product. "We're not political activists. We are a footwear manufacturer," said Nike spokeswoman Donna Gibbs, when the sweatshop scandal first began to erupt.[30] A footwear manufacturer? This from the company that made a concerted decision in the mid-eighties not to be about boring corporeal stuff like footwear—and certainly nothing as crass as manufacturing. Nike wanted to be about sports, Knight told us, it wanted to be about the idea of sports, then the idea of transcendence through sports; then it wanted to be about self-empowerment, women's rights, racial equality. It wanted its stores to be temples, its ads a religion, its customers a nation, its workers a tribe. After taking us all on such a branded ride, to turn around and say, "Don't look at us, we just make shoes" rings laughably hollow.

Nike was the most inflated of all the balloon brands, and the bigger it grew, the louder it popped.

(1999)

Questions

1. Summarize in no more than two paragraphs the case against Nike as Klein presents it.

2. On 8 March 2000, Nike released a point-by-point response to the allegations Klein makes in this piece. Find Nike's response online. Briefly summarize one of the points Nike Makes. Does this point effectively refute any part of Klein's argument? Why or why not?

---

29 [Klein's note]   "Cole Haan Joins Ranks of Shoe Companies Leaving Maine," Associated Press, 23 April 1999.

30 [Klein's note]   Zusman, "Editor's Notebook."

3. In Klein's view, why is it particularly pernicious for Nike to have drawn on the ethos of Black inner-city culture in shaping the image of its brand?

4. To what extent does it trouble you to buy products that were made under exploitive conditions? To what degree are your purchasing decisions likely to be altered by information such as that provided by Klein?

5. Legible clothing makes a statement about the values and self-image of the wearer. But it also provides free advertising. Do you wear legible clothing? Why?

6. How would you describe the tone of Klein's writing? With particular reference to paragraphs 26–28, comment on how this tone is created.

7. Identify and research a boycott campaign currently underway. What is being boycotted and why? What effects, if any, is the boycott having? Would you consider participating in the boycott? Why or why not?

8. *No Logo* was first published in 1999. What (if any) of Klein's points seem dated to you? What (if any) are applicable today?

9. Activist and football star Colin Kaepernick was the face of a major 2018 ad campaign conducted by Nike; see the color insert of this anthology for an image of a billboard from the campaign.

   a. What do you think this billboard is meant to achieve? Who is its audience?

   b. To what extent do Klein's objections to Nike's branding in the 1990s apply to the 2018 ad?

   c. On the whole, do you see this advertisement's likely cultural impact as positive, negative, or some of both? Why?

VIRGIE TOVAR

THE BOPO-WASHING[1] OF
WEIGHT WATCHERS
(& THE WEIGHT LOSS INDUSTRY)

The twenty-first century has seen the popularization of the body positivity and fat acceptance movements. Both of these movements have in common the position that the discrimination fat people face in Western society is deeply harmful to psychological health. Many in these movements also argue that fatphobia makes it more difficult for fat people to achieve good physical health, due to factors such as discrimination by doctors and nurses, eating disorders caused by internalized shame, and workplace discrimination leading to lower incomes. (Fat and body positivity activists differ in their views as to the precise relationship between fat and health. Some argue that it is misleading to focus on body weight as an indicator of health, while others argue that, even if high proportions of body fat are associated with specific health risks, shaming and other forms of discrimination are not effective ways to improve health.)

Prominent fat activist Virgie Tovar writes a regular column, titled "Take the Cake," for the online magazine Ravishly; *the following "Take the Cake" piece was posted in January 2019.*

❧

I was bouncily heading into the mall to meet a friend for a lipstick and perfume play date at Sephora, when an ad caught my eye. It was just inside of GNC.[2]

It was a simple image—a smiling woman in jeans against a blue backdrop with text that began: "Who cares what the size is ...?" There was more, but my feet were taking me to makeup faster than I could finish reading.

---

1   *BoPo-Washing*   Covering with a veneer of body positivity. The term derives from "whitewashing," which refers to covering up an undesirable truth (or, more specifically, to casting white actors to play characters of color so as to make white audiences more comfortable).

2   *GNC*   Chain of stores that sells nutritional supplements and other health products.

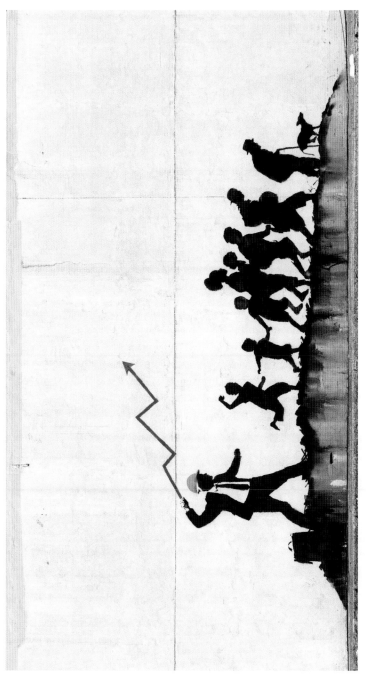

Banksy, street art on Coney Island Avenue, 2018. The identity of England-based celebrity artist Banksy is unknown. Banksy is best known for politically provocative graffiti but also produces film, installation art, and controversial stunts (such as, perhaps most famously, selling a painting that shredded itself after being purchased).

(See the anthology's companion website for discussion questions related to images in this color insert.)

Virgie Tovar, photograph of GNC Total Lean advertisement, 2019. Tovar, a body positivity activist and critic of weight-based discrimination, analyzes this advertisement in her article "The BoPo-Washing of Weight Watchers (& The Weight Loss Industry)," included in this anthology.

Andria Lo, portrait of Virgie Tovar, 2019.

Eric Risberg, photograph of Nike billboard, 2018. NFL star Colin Kaepernick became a divisive figure in 2016 when, as a protest against racism and police brutality toward African Americans, he refused to stand during the American national anthem. No NFL team would sign him after his season of protest. In 2018, Kaepernick became the face of a major Nike advertising campaign with the tag line "Believe in something, even if it means sacrificing everything." His endorsement outraged supporters of Donald Trump, many of whom burned their sneakers and boycotted the brand.

Rebecca Belmore, *Mixed Blessings*, 2011. Canadian Anishinaabekwe artist Rebecca Belmore (b. 1960) is internationally respected for her work in a vast range of media including performance, sculpture, sound sculpture, and installation pieces. Belmore, who is a member of Lac Seul First Nation in northwestern Ontario, Canada, often takes up colonization and its impact as a theme in her art. The hoodie worn by the figure in the sculpture pictured here (photographed by Toni Hafkenscheid) reads horizontally "FUCKIN INDIAN"; vertically, it reads "FUCKIN ARTIST."

Tracey Emin, *My Bed*, 1998. In this landmark installation piece, English artist Tracey Emin (b. 1963) displays her actual bed surrounded by the objects accumulated after she spent several days in the bed binging on alcohol during a period of extreme depression. Some were shocked by the work's confessional content (items surrounding the bed include condoms, stained underwear, and empty alcohol bottles), and its selection as a finalist for the prestigious Turner Prize in 1999 was a subject of intense controversy.

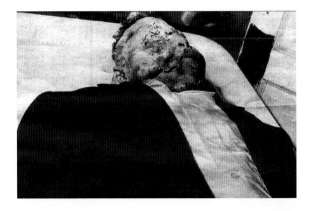

(Left) Photograph of Emmett Till taken by his mother; and (above) photograph of the body of Emmett Till before his funeral, from the *Chicago Defender*, 1955. When Emmett Till was fourteen years old, he was murdered and mutilated by a white mob after a white woman falsely accused him of attempting to flirt with her. Till became an icon of the Civil Rights Movement when his mother, Mamie Till-Mobley, held a public open-casket funeral to display the brutality of the violence committed against him: as she later explained, "The whole nation had to bear witness to this." Tens of thousands of people viewed Till's body, and photographs showing his mutilation were printed in *The American Negro: A Magazine of Protest*, *Jet* magazine, and the *Chicago Defender*, all publications with a predominantly Black readership. (No publications with a predominantly white readership printed images of Till's body.) The photographs prompted many African Americans to take a more active role in the Civil Rights Movement.

Pedro Pardo, *Climbing the Border Fence*, 2018. In 2018, caravans of people fleeing violence and poverty traveled from Central America to the United States border, where many planned to seek asylum. This photograph was taken the day after one caravan reached the border and asylum seekers learned they faced a months-long wait before they could begin the claim process; the family pictured is attempting to climb the fence separating Mexico and America.

Andres Kudacki, photograph of Serena Williams, 2018. This image shows renowned tennis player Serena Williams moments after winning a point during the fourth round of the US Open tennis tournament.

My brain registered that I needed to have a feminist moment with this text. So I did an actual break and reverse into ye olde* General Nutrition Center. I hadn't stepped foot inside a GNC since I was a child procuring vitamins with my grandfather, a former bodybuilder who had a daily weight training regimen well into his sixties. The sales person asked me if I needed help with anything and I chirped a quick "nope" as I pulled out my phone and took a picture.

The full text reads: "Who cares what the size is? Get back in your favorite jeans." It was advertising GNC's "Total Lean," a line of meal replacement shakes and bars that accompany a weight-loss program. In the rhetorical question that the ad presented, I saw the ripple effect of body justice, fat activism and body positivity (BoPo). I heard the rallying cries from my early introduction to fat activism: "Health at every size!" and "Every body is a good body!"

How had a fat feminist idea—like not caring about the size of your jeans— 5
made it to the aisles of GNC?

I had just seen a similar stab at faux weight-neutrality in the news.

Recently Weight Watchers rebranded as a wellness-focused company. The new move toward just "WW" is about becoming "the world's partner in wellness," said president and CEO Mindy Grossman. "No matter what your goal is—to lose weight, eat healthier, move more, develop a positive mindset, or all of the above—we will deliver science-based solutions that fit into people's lives." The rebrand includes several new features, including a focus on mindfulness, rewards for tracking weight and meals, and a new line of food products that have no artificial sweeteners, flavors, colors or preservatives.

From 2012 to 2016 Weight Watchers' sales dropped by 37 percent. This timeline corresponds with the rise of fat activism and body positivity. In August 2017 *The New York Times* reported on the company's decline, implying a significant query: How does a weight loss company sell weight loss products to people who don't want to be fat but also don't want to say they don't want to be fat or identify as being on a diet?

This question lives at the heart of what I'm going to call "BoPo-washing." BoPo-washing is the new paradigm of companies using weight-neutral or body positive language in order to peddle products.

While digging into bottomless breadsticks at Olive Garden post-Sephora, I   10
postulated on WW's and GNC's strategy with my friend.

We are in the midst of an important civil rights moment focused on ending fat discrimination and weight-based bigotry. There's a growing number of books, films, activists, university courses and professionals focused on changing the conversation around food, body size, fashion and plus size representation. For many, these things have changed hearts and minds, pushing us to reconsider how we think of our bodies and the bodies of others. For the weight-loss industry, however, these things have done little more than signal that it's become passé to *overtly* sell products meant to promote weight-loss. The keyword here is "overtly." Let's talk more about that.

The rebranding of WW and Total Lean's shift in brand messaging signals that we're witnessing an important cultural phenomenon—when a form of bigotry (in this case, fatphobia) goes from overt to covert. This process happens when any justice or civil rights movement hits a tipping point and becomes visible on a grand scale. In the past fifty years we have seen this process take place with a number of marginalized identities, but I'd like to talk about what happened when a resurgence of feminism in the 1960s and 1970s began demanding gender equality for women.

Before Trump and #MeToo, we had entire swaths of the population who denied that sexism was a real problem in our country anymore. Why? Because how we publicly talked about women as a culture had changed a lot, but how we felt about women as a culture hadn't. Feminists fought for the idea that women were not inferior to men and should be seen and treated as equals. In the same way that fat activists fight for the idea that fat people are not inferior to thin people and should be seen and treated as equals. While many people took to changing how they thought about women, many others only changed how they spoke about women in public. They knew they faced censure from their bosses or disparaging looks from acquaintances. So, they changed how they *spoke,* but not how they *felt or thought.*

Further, these forms of oppression and stigma go much deeper than they appear. Sexism isn't just about gender.

15   In the same way that fatphobia isn't just about body size. It's connected to the cultural commitment to hierarchy of all kinds. We cannot get rid of sexism or fatphobia without seriously taking stock of the matrix that has allowed them to thrive for so long. It's safe to say that most people feel they have a lot to lose if we start following the breadcrumbs* back to the heart of these kinds of problems. The truth is that it's very hard to fix a big problem, and many people are committed to not fixing things no matter how much others are suffering because they believe they benefit from the way things are (in some cases, they are correct).

Fatphobia has deep roots in core American values—like conformity (the idea that people should act the same and believe the same things and that people who don't do that are bad) and bootstrapping (the idea that anyone can pull themselves up by their bootstraps, and if someone doesn't have something—like a thin body—it's because they didn't try hard enough and therefore deserve no compassion).

The language shift that WW and GNC are undertaking acts as the canary in the coal mine.* This shift is not signaling the end of dieting. It's signaling a growing chasm between how we *talk* about fat bodies and how we still *feel* about fat bodies in this culture.

So when GNC rhetorically asks "who cares what the size is?" they're parroting a core tenet of fat activism and body justice—the tenet of weight neutrality. The idea behind weight neutrality is that we can more effectively promote justice and wellness when we stop trying to control our weight and stop using weight as an indicator of morality, attractiveness or health. It is therefore misleading to use a weight-neutral sentiment in order to sell a product or service designed to promote weight-loss. True weight neutrality would mean Weight Watchers—and, yes, WW—closing its doors forever. It would mean the end of Total Lean. It would mean the end of a lot of things that we have come to understand as normal parts of everyday life—like fat shaming, food policing, weight challenges, and a system of values that rewards people for being thin.

Until that end comes, I think it's safe to say that weight loss companies will churn out more double-speak advertising and rebrands that their CEO can't even explain.

And I'll be here encouraging you not to fall for it.   20

(2019)

Questions

1. Examine the author's tone and use of first-person point of view. Does this make this piece of writing more or less accessible to the reader? What does it suggest about the intended audience of the piece?

2. Tovar introduces the term "BoPo-washing" (paragraph 9).

    a. What is BoPo-washing?

    b. According to Tovar, how does BoPo-washing benefit companies such as GNC and WW?

    c. According to Tovar, how does BoPo-washing harm the body positivity movement?

3. In your culture, what messages do you receive about fatness? How do these messages affect you personally?

4. Tovar claims that "[f]atphobia has deep roots in core American values" (paragraph 16). What core values does she identify, and how are these linked to fatphobia? Can you think of any other values not mentioned by Tovar that are linked to fatphobia in North America?

5. Tovar's photograph of the GNC advertisement she discusses is included in this anthology's color insert.

    a. Summarize Tovar's criticism of this ad.

    b. What (if anything) about this ad supports Tovar's view that it is an example of "Bo-Po Washing"? What (if anything) contradicts her view?

    c. Who would be likely to find this ad persuasive, and who would not? Why?

6. Tovar discusses "an important cultural phenomenon—when a form of bigotry (in this case, fatphobia) goes from overt to covert" (paragraph 12). What forms of bigotry do you see as "overt" in your community? What forms do you see as "covert"?

7. Read the selection from Naomi Klein's *No Logo* also reprinted in this anthology. What parallels (if any) do you see between the branding of Nike and the rebranding of WW and GNC? What (if any) differences do you see?

8. A photograph of Tovar is included in this anthology's color insert. Consider her self-presentation in this photograph; what values and political commitments does it suggest?

EMILY NUSSBAUM

THE PRICE IS RIGHT: WHAT ADVERTISING DOES TO TV

Mad Men, *a highly popular television show about the world of New York advertising firms in the 1960s, ran from 2007 to 2015 on the American basic cable network AMC. In this essay, a television critic for* The New Yorker *magazine is prompted by the conclusion of that program to consider the role advertising itself plays in shaping television and popular culture. The article was published in the 12 October 2015 issue of* The New Yorker.

&

Ever since the finale of "Mad Men," I've been meditating on its audacious last image. Don Draper,* sitting cross-legged and purring "Ommmm," is achieving inner peace at an Esalen[1]-like retreat. He's as handsome as ever, in khakis and a crisp white shirt. A bell rings, and a grin widens across his face. Then, as if cutting to a sponsor, we move to the iconic Coke ad from 1971—a green hillside covered with a racially diverse chorus of young people, trilling, in harmony, "I'd like to teach the world to sing." Don Draper, recently suicidal, has invented the world's greatest ad. He's back, baby.

The scene triggered a debate online. From one perspective, the image looked cynical: the viewer is tricked into thinking that Draper has achieved Nirvana,* only to be slapped with the source of his smile. It's the grin of an adman who has figured out how to use enlightenment to peddle sugar water, co-opting the counterculture as a brand. Yet, from another angle, the scene looked idealistic. Draper has indeed had a spiritual revelation, one that he's expressing in a beautiful way—through advertising, his great gift. The night the episode aired, it struck me as a dark joke. But, at a discussion a couple of days later, at the New York Public Library, Matthew Weiner, the show's creator, told the novelist A.M. Homes that viewers should see the hilltop ad as "very pure," the product of "an enlightened state." To regard it otherwise, he warned, was itself the symptom of a poisonous mind-set.

---

1   *Esalen*   New Age educational facility.

The question of how television fits together with advertising—and whether we should resist that relationship or embrace it—has haunted the medium since its origins. Advertising is TV's original sin. When people called TV shows garbage, which they did all the time, until recently, commercialism was at the heart of the complaint. Even great TV could never be good art, because it was tainted by definition. It was there to sell.

That was the argument made by George W.S. Trow in this magazine, in a feverish manifesto called "Within the Context of No Context." That essay, which ran in 1980, became a sensation, as coruscating denunciations of modernity so often do. In television, "the trivial is raised up to power," Trow wrote. "The powerful is lowered toward the trivial." Driven by "demography"—that is, by the corrupting force of money and ratings—television treats those who consume it like sales targets, encouraging them to view themselves that way. In one of several sections titled "Celebrities," he writes, "The most successful celebrities are products. Consider the real role in American life of Coca-Cola. Is any man as well-loved as this soft drink is?"

5   Much of Trow's essay, which runs to more than a hundred pages, makes little sense. It is written in the style of oracular[2] poetry, full of elegant repetitions, elegant repetitions that induce a hypnotic effect, elegant repetitions that suggest authority through their wonderful numbing rhythms, but which contain few facts. It's élitism in the guise of hipness. It is more nostalgic than *Mad Men* ever was for the era when Wasp* men in hats ran New York. It's a screed against TV written at the medium's low point—after the energy of the sitcoms of the seventies had faded but before the innovations of the nineties—and it paints TV fans as brainwashed dummies.

And yet there's something in Trow's manifesto that I find myself craving these days: that rude resistance to being sold to, the insistence that there is, after all, such a thing as selling out. Those of us who love TV have won the war. The best scripted shows are regarded as significant art—debated, revered, denounced. TV showrunners are embraced as heroes and role models, even philosophers. At the same time, television's business model is in chaos, splintered and re-forming itself, struggling with its own history. Making television has always meant bending to the money—and TV history has taught us to be cool with any compromise. But sometimes we're knowing about things that we don't know much about at all.

Once upon a time, TV made sense, economically and structurally: a few dominant network shows ran weekly, with ads breaking them up, like choruses between verses. Then came pay cable, the VCR, the DVD, the DVR, and the

---

2   *oracular*   Prophetic.

Internet. At this point, the model seems to morph every six months. Oceanic flat screens give way to palm-size iPhones. A cheap writer-dominated medium absorbs pricey Hollywood directors. You can steal TV; you can buy TV; you can get it free. Netflix, a distributor, becomes a producer. On Amazon, customers vote for which pilots will survive. Shows cancelled by NBC jump to Yahoo, which used to be a failing search engine. The two most ambitious and original début series this summer came not from HBO or AMC but from a pair of lightweight cable networks whose slogans might as well be "Please underestimate us": Lifetime, with *UnREAL*, and USA Network, with *Mr. Robot*. That there is a summer season at all is a new phenomenon. This fall, as the networks launch a bland slate of pilots, we know there are better options.

A couple of months ago, at a meeting of the Television Critics Association, the C.E.O. of FX,[3] John Landgraf, delivered a speech about "peak TV," in which he lamented the exponential rise in production: three hundred and seventy-one scripted shows last year, more than four hundred expected this year—a bubble, Landgraf said, that would surely deflate. He got some pushback: Why now, when the door had cracked open to more than white-guy antiheroes, was it "too much" for viewers? But just as worrisome was the second part of Landgraf's speech, in which he wondered how the industry could fund so much TV. What was the model, now that the pie had been sliced into slivers? When Landgraf took his job, in 2005, ad buys made up more than fifty per cent of FX's revenue, he said. Now that figure was thirty-two per cent. When ratings drop, ad rates drop, too, and when people fast-forward producers look for new forms of access: through apps, through data mining, through deals that shape the shows we see, both visibly and invisibly. Some of this involves the ancient art of product integration, by which sponsors buy the right to be part of the story: these are the ads that can't be fast-forwarded.

This is both a new crisis and an old one. When television began, it was a live medium. Replicating radio, it was not merely supported by admen; it was run by them. In TV's early years, there were no showrunners: the person with ultimate authority was the product representative, the guy from Lysol or Lucky Strike.[4] Beneath that man (always a man) was a network exec. A layer down were writers, who were fungible, nameless figures, with the exception of people like Paddy Chayefsky, machers[5] who often retreated when they grew frustrated by the industry's censorious limits. The result was that TV writers developed a complex mix of pride and shame, a sense that they were hired

---

3   *FX* Basic cable network known for the quality of its original programming.

4   *Lucky Strike* Cigarette brand. Though Lucky Strike is a real company, Draper's firm advertises for it in *Mad Men*.

5   *machers* People with influence, but lacking substance.

hands, not artists. It was a working-class model of creativity. The shows might be funny or beautiful, but their creators would never own them.

10   Advertisements shaped everything about early television programs, including their length and structure, with clear acts to provide logical inlets for ads to appear. Initially, there were rules governing how many ads could run: the industry standard was six minutes per hour. (Today, on network, it's about fourteen minutes.) But this didn't include the vast amounts of product integration that were folded into the scripts. (Product placement,* which involves props, was a given.) Viewers take for granted that this is native to the medium, but it's unique to the U.S.; in the United Kingdom, such deals were prohibited until 2011. Even then, they were barred from the BBC, banned for alcohol and junk food, and required to be visibly declared—a "P" must appear onscreen.

In *Brought to You By: Postwar Television Advertising and the American Dream*, Lawrence R. Samuel describes early shows like NBC's *Coke Time*, in which Eddie Fisher sipped the soda. On an episode of *I Love Lucy* called "The Diet," Lucy and Desi smoked Philip Morris cigarettes. On *The Flintstones*, the sponsor Alka-Seltzer ruled that no character get a stomach ache, and that there be no derogatory presentations of doctors, dentists, or druggists. On *My Little Margie*, Philip Morris reps struck the phrase "I'm real cool!," lest it be associated with their competitors Kool cigarettes. If you were a big name—like Jack Benny, whom Samuel calls "the king of integrated advertising"—"plugola"* was par for the course. (Benny once mentioned Schwinn bikes, then looked directly into the camera and deadpanned, "Send three.") There were only a few exceptions, including Sid Caesar, who refused to tout brands on *Your Show of Shows*.

Sponsors were a conservative force. They helped blacklist* writers suspected of being Communists, and, for decades, banned plots about homosexuality and "miscegenation."[6] In Jeff Kisseloff's oral history *The Box*, from 1995, Bob Lewine, of ABC, describes pitching Sammy Davis, Jr.,[7] in an all-black variety show: Young & Rubicam execs walked out, so the idea was dropped. This tight leash affected even that era's version of prestige TV. In *Brought to You By*, Samuel lists topics deemed off limits as "politics, sex, adultery, unemployment, poverty, successful criminality and alcohol"—now the basic food groups of cable. In one notorious incident, the American Gas Association sponsored CBS's anthology series *Playhouse 90*. When an episode called "Portrait of a Murderer" ended, it created an unfortunate juxtaposition: after the killer was executed, the show cut to an ad with the slogan "Nothing but gas does so

---

6   *miscegenation* Conception of children by or marriage between people of different races.

7   *Sammy Davis, Jr.* African American actor, dancer, and musician (1925–90).

many jobs so well." Spooked, American Gas took a closer look at an upcoming project, George Roy Hill's *Judgment at Nuremberg*. The company objected to any mention of the gas chambers—and though the writers resisted, the admen won.

This sponsor-down model held until the late fifties, around the time that the quiz-show scandals[8] traumatized viewers: producers, in their quest to please ad reps, had cheated. Both economic pressures and the public mood contributed to increased creative control by networks, as the old one-sponsor model dissolved. But the precedent had been established: when people talked about TV, ratings and quality were existentially linked, the business and the art covered by critics as one thing. Or, as Trow put it, "What is loved is a hit. What is a hit is loved."

Kenya Barris's original concept for the ABC series *Black-ish*, last year's smartest network-sitcom début, was about a black writer in a TV writers' room. But then he made the lead role a copywriter at an ad agency, which allowed the network to cut a deal with Buick, so that the show's hero, Dre, is seen brainstorming ads for its car. In *Automotive News*, Buick's marketing manager, Molly Peck, said that the company worked closely with Barris. "We get the benefit of being part of the program, so people are actually watching it as opposed to advertising where viewers often don't watch it."

Product integration is a small slice of the advertising budget, but it can take on outsized symbolic importance, as the watermark of a sponsor's power to alter the story—and it is often impossible to tell whether the mention is paid or not. *The Mindy Project* celebrates Tinder. An episode of *Modern Family* takes place on iPods and iPhones. On the ABC Family drama *The Fosters*, one of the main characters, a vice-principal, talks eagerly about the tablets her school is buying. "Wow, it's so light!" she says, calling the product by its full name, the "Kindle Paperwhite e-reader," and listing its useful features. On last year's most charming début drama, the CW's *Jane the Virgin*, characters make trips to Target, carry Target bags, and prominently display the logo.

Those are shows on channels that are explicitly commercialized. But similar deals ripple through cable television and the new streaming producers. FX cut a deal with MillerCoors, so that every character who drinks or discusses a beer is drinking its brands. (MillerCoors designs retro bottles for *The Americans*.) According to *Ad Age*, Anheuser-Busch struck a deal with *House of Cards*, trading supplies of booze for onscreen appearances; purportedly, Samsung struck another, to be the show's "tech of choice." Unilever's

15

Choco Taco paid for integration on Comedy Central's *Workaholics*, aiming to be "the dessert for millennials." On NBC, Dan Harmon's avant-garde comedy, *Community*, featured an anti-corporate plot about Subway paid for by Subway. When the show jumped to Yahoo, the episode "Advanced Safety Features" was about Honda. "It's not there were just a couple of guys driving the car; it was the whole episode about Honda," Tom Peyton, an assistant V.P. of marketing at Honda, told *Ad Week*. "You hold your breath as an advertiser, and I'm sure they did too—did you go too far and commercialize the whole thing and take it away from it?—but I think the opposite happened.... Huge positives."

Whether that bothers you or impresses you may depend on whether you laughed and whether you noticed. There's a common notion that there's good and bad integration. The "bad" stuff is bumptious—unfunny and in your face. "Good" integration is either invisible or ironic, and it's done by people we trust, like Stephen Colbert or Tina Fey. But it brings out my inner George Trow. To my mind, the cleverer the integration, the more harmful it is. It's a sedative designed to make viewers feel that there's nothing to be angry about, to admire the ad inside the story, to train us to shrug off every compromise as necessary and normal.

Self-mocking integration used to seem modern to me—the irony of a post-*Simpsons* generation—until I realized that it was actually nostalgic: Jack Benny did sketches in which he playfully "resisted" sponsors like Lucky Strike and Lipton tea. Alfred Hitchcock, on *Alfred Hitchcock Presents*, made snide remarks about Bristol-Myers. The audience had no idea that those wisecracks were scripted by a copywriter who had submitted them to Bristol-Myers for approval.

A few weeks ago, Stephen Colbert began hosting CBS's *Late Show*. In his first show, he pointed to a "cursed" amulet. He was under the amulet's control, Colbert moaned, and thus had been forced to "make certain"—he paused— "regrettable compromises." Then he did a bit in which he slavered over Sabra hummus and Rold Gold pretzels. Some critics described the act as satire, but that's a distinction without a difference. Colbert embraced "sponsortunities" when he was on Comedy Central, too, behind the mask of an ironic persona; it's likely one factor that made him a desirable replacement for Letterman, the worst salesman on late-night TV.

20   During this summer of industry chaos, one TV show did make a pungent case against consumerism: *Mr. Robot*, on USA Network. A dystopian thriller with Occupy-inflected politics,[9] the series was refreshing, both for its melancholy beauty and for its unusually direct attack on corporate manipulation. *Mr.*

---

9   *Occupy-inflected politics*   Reference to the Occupy Wall Street movement against economic inequality.

Robot was the creation of a TV newcomer, Sam Esmail, who found himself in an odd position: his anti-branding show was itself rebranding an aggressively corporate network, known for its "blue sky"[10] procedurals—a division of NBCUniversal, a subsidiary of Comcast.

Mr. Robot tells the story of Elliott Alderson, corporate cog by day, hacker by night, a mentally unstable junkie who is part of an Anonymous-like[11] collective that conspires to delete global debt. In one scene, Elliott fantasizes about being conventional enough for a girlfriend: "I'll go see those stupid Marvel movies with her. I'll join a gym. I'll heart things on Instagram." He walks into his boss's office with a Starbucks vanilla latte, the most basic of beverages. This sort of straightforwardly hostile namecheck is generally taboo, both to avoid offending potential sponsors and to leave doors open for their competitors. Esmail says he fought to get real brands in the story, citing *Mad Men* as precedent, as his phone calls with the network's lawyers went from "weekly to daily."

Were any of these mentions paid for? Not in the first season—although Esmail says that he did pursue integrations with brands, some of which turned him down and some of which he turned down (including tech companies that demanded "awkward language" about their features). He's open to these deals in Season 2. "If the idea is to inspire an interesting debate over capitalism, I actually think (depending on how we use it) it can help provoke that conversation even more," he said. As long as such arrangements are "organic and not forced," they're fine with him—what's crucial is not the money but the verisimilitude that brands provide. Only one major conflict came up, Esmail said, in the finale, when Elliott's mysterious alter ego screams in the middle of Times Square, "I'm no less real than the fucking meat patty in your Big Mac." Esmail and USA agreed to bleep "Big Mac"—"to be sensitive to ad sales," Esmail told me—but they left it in for online airings. Esmail said he's confident that the network fought for him. "Maybe Comcast has a relationship with McDonald's?" he mused. (USA told me that the reason was "standards and practices.")[12]

"Are you asking me how I feel about product integration?" Matt Weiner said. "I'm for it." Everything on TV is an ad for something, he pointed out, down to Jon Hamm's beautifully pomaded hair—and he argued that a paid integration is far less harmful than other propaganda embedded in television, such

---

10 *blue sky* Optimistic and pleasantly escapist.

11 *Anonymous-like* Anonymous is an Internet-based anarchic collective of activists.

12 *standards and practices* Network "Standards and Practices" departments govern legal and ethical issues surrounding the content of the network's programs.

as how cop shows celebrate the virtues of the state. We all have our sponsors. Michelangelo painted for the Pope! What's dangerous about modern TV isn't advertisers, Weiner told me; it's creatives not getting enough of a cut of the proceeds.

Weiner used to work in network television, in a more restrictive creative environment, until he got his break, on *The Sopranos*. Stepping into HBO's subscription-only chamber meant being part of a prestige brand: no ads, that gorgeous hissing logo, critical bennies.[13] The move to AMC, then a minor cable station, was a challenge. Weiner longed for the most elegant model, with one sponsor—the approach of *Playhouse 90*. But getting ads took hustle, even in a show about them. Weiner's description of the experience of writing integrations is full of cognitive dissonance. On the one hand, he said, wistfully, he didn't realize at first that he could say no to integrations. Yet he was frustrated by the ones he couldn't get, like attaching Revlon to Peggy's "Basket of Kisses" plot about lipstick. Such deals were valuable—"money you don't leave on the floor"—but it was crucial that the audience not know about them, and that there be few.

The first integration on *Mad Men*, for Jack Daniel's,* was procured before Weiner got involved; writing it into the script made him feel "icky." (Draper wouldn't drink Jack Daniel's, Weiner told me.) Pond's cold cream was a more successful fit. But he tried to impose rules: the sponsor could see only the pages its brand was on; dialogue would mention competitors; and, most important, the company couldn't run ads the night its episode was on the air. Unilever cheated, Weiner claimed—and AMC allowed it. The company filmed ads mimicking the *Mad Men* aesthetic, making the tie with the show visible. If viewers knew that Pond's was integrated, they wouldn't lose themselves in the story, Weiner worried.

In the end, he says, he did only three—Heineken was the third (an integration procured after Michelob backed out). I naïvely remarked that Jaguar couldn't have paid: who would want to be the brand of sexual coercion? "You'd be surprised," he said. Jaguar didn't buy a plug, but the company loved the plot—and hired Christina Hendricks to flack the car,* wearing a bright-red pantsuit.

Weiner had spent the Television Critics Association convention talking up *Mr. Robot* and he told me that he was "stunned" by Esmail's show, which he called American TV's "first truly contemporary anti-corporate message." Then again, he said, "show business in general has been very good at co-opting the people that bite the hands that feed them." NBCUniversal was wise to buy into

---

13 *critical bennies* Critical "buzz." ("Bennies" is a slang term for benzedrine, an amphetamine.)

Esmail's radical themes, he said, because these are ideas that the audience is ready for—"even the Tea Party* knows we don't want to give the country over to corporations."

Weiner made clear that Coke hadn't paid for any integration; he mentioned it a few times. Finally, I asked, Why not? *Mad Men* ended in a way that both Coke and viewers could admire. Why not take the money? Two reasons, he said. First, Coca-Cola could "get excited and start making demands." But, really, he didn't want to "disturb the purity of treating that ad as what it was." Weiner is proud that *Mad Men* had a lasting legacy, influencing how viewers saw television's potential, how they thought about money and power, creativity and the nature of work. He didn't want them to think that Coke had bought his finale.

There is no art form that doesn't run a three-legged race with the sponsors that support its production, and the weaker an industry gets (journalism, this means you; music, too) the more ethical resistance flags. But readers would be grossed out to hear that Karl Ove Knausgaard[14] had accepted a bribe to put the Talking Heads into his childhood memories. They'd be angry if Stephen Sondheim[15] slipped a Dewar's jingle into *Company*. That's not priggishness or élitism. It's a belief that art is powerful, that storytelling is real, that when we immerse ourselves in that way it's a vulnerable act of trust. Why wouldn't this be true for television, too?

Viewers have little control over how any show gets made; TV writers and directors have only a bit more—their roles mingle creativity and management in a way that's designed to create confusion. Even the experts lack expertise, these days. But I wonder if there's a way for us to be less comfortable as consumers, to imagine ourselves as the partners not of the advertisers but of the artists—to crave purity, naïve as that may sound. I miss *Mad Men*, that nostalgic meditation on nostalgia. But embedded in its vision was the notion that television writing and copywriting are and should be mirrors, twins. Our comfort with being sold to may look like savvy, but it feels like innocence. There's something to be said for the emotions that Trow tapped into, disgust and outrage and betrayal—emotions that can be embarrassing but are useful when we're faced with something ugly.

30

---

14 *Karl Ove Knausgaard*   Author of *My Struggle*, a six-volume autobiography that has been much discussed in the literary world.

15 *Stephen Sondheim*   Songwriter known for acclaimed musicals such as *Company* and *West Side Story*.

Perhaps this makes me sound like a drunken twenty-two-year-old waving a battered copy of Naomi Klein's *No Logo*.[16] But that's what happens when you love an art form. In my imagination, television would be capable of anything. It could offend anyone; it could violate any rule. For it to get there, we might have to expect of it what we expect of any art.

(2015)

Questions

1. To what extent do you value TV shows as "significant art"? Explain.

2. In this article, Nussbaum condemns the use of product integration as a means of financing TV shows. List all the arguments you can think of for and against the use of product integration—both those given in the article and any others you can think of. After considering these arguments, do you agree or disagree with Nussbaum?

3. Nussbaum describes "Weiner's description of the experience of writing integrations" as being "full of cognitive dissonance" (paragraph 24). Where is this cognitive dissonance displayed? What is its cause?

4. Nussbaum writes that "[m]aking television has always meant bending to the money—and TV history has taught us to be cool with any compromise" (paragraph 6). Consider the short history of TV production that Nussbaum offers. How have history and economics come together to shape the current role advertising plays in TV production?

5. Do your own research to find an example of product integration in a recent film or TV show (preferably one you have seen).

   a. How does the example you found function as an advertisement? How might it affect a viewer's perception of the product being advertised?

   b. How (if at all) does the product integration impact the scene's artistic quality? (Does it, for example, interfere with—or add to—the scene's tone, character development, thematic content, and/or plot?)

---

16 *No Logo* Influential 1999 book critiquing corporate branding. A selection from *No Logo*, "The Swoosh," appears elsewhere in this anthology.

TECHNOLOGY AND
THE GOOD LIFE

ETHAN KROSS, PHILIPPE VERDUYN, EMRE
DEMIRALP, JIYOUNG PARK, DAVID SEUNGJAE LEE,
NATALIE LIN, HOLLY SHABLACK, JOHN JONIDES,
OSCAR YBARRA

from FACEBOOK USE PREDICTS DECLINES IN SUBJECTIVE WELL-BEING[1] IN YOUNG ADULTS

Ethan Kross is a social psychologist at the University of Michigan. Together with Philippe Verduyn, a researcher at the University of Leuven, as well as other colleagues at the University of Michigan, Kross conducted the study printed below, which examines how Facebook use influences young adults' self-reported happiness over time. It was originally published in PLoS ONE, *an online science journal.*

❧

ABSTRACT

Over 500 million people interact daily with Facebook. Yet, whether Facebook use influences subjective well-being over time is unknown. We addressed this issue using experience-sampling, the most reliable method for measuring in-vivo[2] behavior and psychological experience. We text-messaged people five times per day for two-weeks to examine how Facebook use influences the two components of subjective well-being: how people feel moment-to-moment and how satisfied they are with their lives. Our results indicate that Facebook

---

1   *Subjective Well-Being*   Refers to how people experience their quality of life and includes both emotional reactions (affective well-being) and cognitive judgments (cognitive well-being).

    NB   **To distinguish notes added for this anthology from the authors' note numbers referring to their list of references at the end of the article, subscript numbers have been used here for the latter.**

2   *experience-sampling*   Method of gathering experimental data by requiring participants to provide regular updates about their behavior and feelings; *in vivo*   Occurring within a complete, live organism.

use predicts negative shifts on both of these variables over time. The more people used Facebook at one time point, the worse they felt the next time we text-messaged them; the more they used Facebook over two-weeks, the more their life satisfaction levels declined over time. Interacting with other people "directly" did not predict these negative outcomes. They were also not moderated by the size of people's Facebook networks, their perceived supportiveness, motivation for using Facebook, gender, loneliness, self-esteem, or depression. On the surface, Facebook provides an invaluable resource for fulfilling the basic human need for social connection. Rather than enhancing well-being, however, these findings suggest that Facebook may undermine it.

Introduction

Online social networks are rapidly changing the way human beings interact. Over a billion people belong to Facebook, the world's largest online social network, and over half of them log in daily.[1] Yet, no research has examined how interacting with Facebook influences subjective well-being over time. Indeed, a recent article that examined every peer-reviewed publication and conference proceeding on Facebook between 1/2005 and 1/2012 (412 in total) did not reveal a single study that examined how using this technology influences subjective well-being over time.[2, [See also Supporting Information 1 at the end of the article.]

Subjective well-being is one of the most highly studied variables in the behavioral sciences. Although significant in its own right, it also predicts a range of consequential benefits including enhanced health and longevity.[3-5] Given the frequency of Facebook usage, identifying how interacting with this technology influences subjective well-being represents a basic research challenge that has important practical implications.

This issue is particularly vexing because prior research provides mixed clues about how Facebook use should influence subjective well-being. Whereas some cross-sectional research reveals positive associations between online social network use (in particular Facebook) and well-being,[6] other work reveals the opposite.[7,8] Still other work suggests that the relationship between Facebook use and well-being may be more nuanced and potentially influenced by multiple factors including number of Facebook friends, perceived supportiveness of one's online network, depressive symptomatology,* loneliness, and self-esteem.[9,10,11]

5   So, how does Facebook usage influence subjective well-being over time? The cross-sectional approach[3] used in previous studies makes it impossible to

---

3   *cross-sectional approach*   Approach to gathering experimental data by observing an entire group at a specific time.

know. We addressed this issue by using experience-sampling, the most reliable method for measuring in-vivo behavior and psychological experience over time.[12] We text-messaged participants five times per day for 14-days. Each text-message contained a link to an online survey, which participants completed using their smartphones. We performed lagged analyses[4] on participants' responses, as well as their answers to the Satisfaction With Life Questionnaire (SWLS),[13] which they completed before and immediately following the 14-day experience-sampling period, to examine how interacting with Facebook influences the two components of subjective well-being: how people feel ("affective" well-being) and how satisfied they are with their lives ("cognitive" well-being).[14,15] This approach allowed us to take advantage of the relative timing of participants' natural Facebook behavior and psychological states to draw inferences about their likely causal sequence.[16-19]

METHODS

Participants

Eighty-two people (M_{age} = 19.52, SD_{age} = 2.17;[5] 53 females; 60.5% European American, 28.4% Asian, 6.2% African American, and 4.9% other) were recruited for a study on Facebook through flyers posted around Ann Arbor, Michigan. Participants needed a Facebook account and a touch-screen smartphone to qualify for the study. They received $20 and were entered into a raffle to receive an iPad2 for participating.

Ethics Statement

The University of Michigan Institutional Review Board approved this study. Informed written consent was obtained from all participants prior to participation.

Materials and Procedure

PHASE 1
Participants completed a set of questionnaires, which included the SWLS (M = 4.96, SD = 1.17), Beck Depression Inventory[20] (M = 9.02, SD = 7.20), the Rosenberg Self-Esteem Scale[21] (M = 30.40, SD = 4.96), and the Social Provision Scale[22] (M = 3.55, SD = .34), which we modified to assess perceptions of Facebook support. We also assessed participants' motivation for using

---

4   *lagged analyses*   Identification of patterns in data collected over time.

5   *M* Mean; *SD* Standard Deviation, a number indicating the extent of difference within a group.

Facebook by asking them to indicate whether they use Facebook "to keep in touch with friends (98% answered yes)," "to find new friends (23% answered yes)," "to share good things with friends (78% answered yes)," "to share bad things with friends (36% answered yes)," "to obtain new information (62% answered yes)," or "other: please explain (17% answered yes)." Examples of other reasons included chatting with others, keeping in touch with family, and facilitating schoolwork and business.

PHASE 2

Participants were text-messaged 5 times per day between 10am and midnight over 14-days. Text-messages occurred at random times within 168-minute windows per day. Each text-message contained a link to an online survey, which asked participants to answer five questions using a slider scale: (1) How do you feel right now? (*very positive* [0] to *very negative* [100]; $M = 37.47$, $SD = 25.88$); (2) How worried are you right now? (*not at all* [0] to *a lot* [100]; $M = 44.04$, $SD = 30.42$); (3) How lonely do you feel right now? (*not at all* [0] to *a lot* [100]; $M = 27.61$, $SD = 26.13$); (4) How much have you used Facebook since the last time we asked? (*not at all* [0] to *a lot* [100]; $M = 33.90$, $SD = 30.48$); (5) How much have you interacted with other people "directly" since the last time we asked? (*not at all* [0] to *a lot* [100]; $M = 64.26$, $SD = 31.11$). When the protocol for answering these questions was explained, interacting with other people "directly" was defined as face-to-face or phone interactions. An experimenter carefully walked participants through this protocol to ensure that they understood how to answer each question and fulfill the study requirements.

10

Participants always answered the affect question first. Next the worry and loneliness questions were presented in random order. The Facebook use and direct social interaction questions were always administered last, again in random order. Our analyses focused primarily on affect (rather than worry and loneliness) because this affect question is the way "affective well-being" is typically operationalized.

PHASE 3

Participants returned to the laboratory following Phase 2 to complete another set of questionnaires, which included the SWLS ($M = 5.13$, $SD = 1.26$) and the Revised UCLA Loneliness Scale[23] ($M = 1.69$, $SD = .46$). Participants' number of Facebook friends ($M = 664.25$, $SD = 383.64$) was also recorded during this session from participants' Facebook accounts.[See Supporting Information 2 at the end of the article.]

RESULTS

Attrition and compliance

Three participants did not complete the study. As the methods section notes, participants received a text message directing them to complete a block of five questions once every 168 minutes on average (the text message was delivered randomly within this 168-minute window). A response to any question within a block was considered "compliant" if it was answered *before* participants received a subsequent text-message directing them to complete the next block of questions. Participants responded to an average of 83.6% of text-messages (range: 18.6%–100%). Following prior research,[24] we pruned the data[6] by excluding all of the data from two participants who responded to <33% of the texts, resulting in 4,589 total observations. The results did not change substantively when additional cutoff rates were used.

Analyses overview

We examined the relationship between Facebook use and affect using multilevel analyses to account for the nested data structure.[7] Specifically, we examined whether T_2[8] affect (i.e., How do you feel *right now?*) was predicted by T_{1-2} Facebook use (i.e., How much have you used Facebook *since the last time we asked?*), controlling for T_1 affect at level-1 of the model (between-day lags were excluded). Note that although this analysis assesses Facebook use at T_2, the question refers to usage between T_1 and T_2 (hence the notation T_{1-2}). This analysis allowed us to explore whether Facebook use during the time period separating T_1 and T_2 predicted changes in affect over this time span.…

The relationship between mean Facebook use and life satisfaction was assessed using OLS regressions[9] because these data were not nested. Both

---

6   *pruned the data*   Removed unnecessary data.

7   *multilevel analyses*   Methods of analyzing data which recognize that there are multiple sources which may explain variations in data. Multilevel analyses are used specifically in research where data may be classified and organized at several levels;   *nested data structure*   Describes data that is obtained from multiple observations of individuals in particular groups, e.g., students in a particular class, or data that is obtained through repeated observation of the same individual over time.

8   T_2 Refers to "Time $_2$," the moment when the participant receives an online survey to assess "Time $_{1-2}$," the period of Facebook usage beginning from the completion of the previous survey. "Time $_1$" is thus the moment a survey is completed.

9   *OLS regressions*   Ordinary Least Squares regressions, models that calculate the relationship between a dependent variable and an independent variable in order to estimate the boundaries of the variables.

unstandardized (B) and standardized (β) OLS regression coefficients[10] are reported. [Supporting Information 3]

Facebook use and well-being

AFFECTIVE WELL-BEING

15   We examined whether people's tendency to interact with Facebook during the time period separating two text messages influenced how they felt at T_2, controlling for how they felt at T_1. Nested time-lag analyses indicated that the more people used Facebook the worse they subsequently felt, $B = .08$, $\chi^2 = 28.90$, $p < .0001$.[11] ... The reverse pathway (T_1 Affect predicting T_{1-2} Facebook use, controlling for T_{0-1} Facebook use) was not significant, $B = -.005$, $\chi^2 = .05$, $p = .82$, indicating that people do not use Facebook more or less depending on how they feel. [See Supporting Information 4 and 5 at the end of the article.]···

COGNITIVE WELL-BEING

To examine how Facebook use influenced "cognitive well-being," we analyzed whether people's average Facebook use over the 14-day period predicted their life satisfaction at the end of the study, controlling for baseline life satisfaction and average emotion levels over the 14-day period. The more participants used Facebook, the more their life satisfaction levels declined over time, $B = -.012$, $\beta = -.124$, $t(73) = -2.39$,[12] $p = .02$....

ALTERNATIVE EXPLANATIONS

An alternative explanation for these results is that any form of social interaction undermines well-being. Because we also asked people to indicate how frequently they interacted with other people "directly" since the last time we text messaged them, we were able to test this idea. Specifically, we repeated each of the aforementioned analyses substituting "direct" social interaction for Facebook use. In contrast to Facebook use, "direct" social interaction did not predict changes in cognitive well-being, $B = -.006$, $\beta = -.059$, $t(73) = 1.04$, $p = .30$, and predicted *increases* (not decreases) in affective well-being, $B = -.15$, $\chi^2 = 65.30$, $p<.0001$. Controlling for direct social interaction did not

---

10 *OLS regression coefficients* Numerical indications of the relationship between two variables.

11 χ^2 Chi squared, used in statistical tests to determine the probability that a set of data reflects a significant relationship between variables; p Probability, here an indication of the likelihood of getting the same experimental results as the ones observed if there were no relationship between the variables being studied.

12 t Variable used in t-tests to calculate the significance of the differences between two sets of data.

substantively alter the significant relationship between Facebook use and affective well-being, $B = .05$, $\chi^2 = 10.78$, $p < .01$.

Another alternative explanation for these results is that people use Facebook when they feel bad (i.e., when they are bored, lonely, worried or otherwise distressed), and feeling bad leads to declines in well-being rather than Facebook use per se. The analyses we reported earlier partially address this issue by demonstrating that affect does not predict changes in Facebook use over time and Facebook use continues to significantly predict declines in life satisfaction over time when controlling for affect. However, because participants also rated how lonely and worried they felt each time we text messaged them, we were able to test this proposal further.

We first examined whether worry or loneliness predicted changes in Facebook use over time (i.e., T_1 worry [or T_1 loneliness] predicting T_{1-2} Facebook use, controlling for T_{0-1} Facebook use). Worry did not predict changes in Facebook use, $B = .04$, $\chi^2 = 2.37$, $p = .12$, but loneliness did, $B = .07$, $\chi^2 = 8.54$, $p < .01$. The more lonely people felt at one time point, the more people used Facebook over time. Given this significant relationship, we next examined whether controlling for loneliness renders the relationship between Facebook use and changes in affective and cognitive well-being non-significant—what one would predict if Facebook use is a proxy for loneliness. This was not the case. Facebook use continued to predict declines in affective well-being, $B = .08$, $\chi^2 = 27.87$, $p < .0001$, and cognitive well-being, $B = -.012$, $\beta = -.126$, $t(72) = 2.34$, $p = .02$, when loneliness was controlled for in each analysis. Neither worry nor loneliness interacted significantly with Facebook use to predict changes in affective or cognitive well-being ($ps > .44$).

MODERATION

Next, we examined whether a number of theoretically relevant individual-difference variables[13] including participants' number of Facebook Friends, their perceptions of their Facebook network support, depressive symptoms, loneliness, gender, self-esteem, time of study participation, and motivation for using Facebook (e.g., to find new friends, to share good or bad things, to obtain new information) interacted with Facebook use to predict changes in affective or cognitive well-being. [See Supporting Information 6 at the end of the article.] In no case did we observe any significant interactions ($ps > .16$).

20

___

13 *individual-difference variables* Variables indicating characteristics that individual participants already possess, which may affect study results but are not controlled by the study.

EXPLORATORY ANALYSES

Although we did not have *a priori* predictions[14] about whether Facebook use and direct social contact would interact to predict changes in affective and cognitive well-being, we nevertheless explored this issue in our final set of analyses. The results of these analyses indicated that Facebook use and direct social contact interacted significantly to predict changes in affective well-being, $B = .002$, $\chi^2 = 19.55$, $p < .0001$, but not changes in cognitive well-being, $B = .000$, $\beta = .129$, $t(71)=.39$, $p = .70$. To understand the meaning of the former interaction, we performed simple slope analyses.[15] These analyses indicated that the relationship between Facebook use and declines in affective well-being increased linearly with direct social contact. Specifically, whereas Facebook use did not predict significant declines in affective well-being when participants experienced low levels of direct social contact (i.e., 1 standard deviation below the sample mean for direct social contact; $B = .00$, $\chi^2 = .04$, $p = .84$), it did predict significant declines in well-being when participants experienced moderate levels of direct social contact (i.e., at the sample mean for direct social contact; $B = .05$, $\chi^2 = 11.21$, $p<.001$) and high levels of direct social contact (i.e., 1 standard deviation above the sample mean for direct social contact; $B = .10$, $\chi^2 = 28.82$, $p<.0001$).

DISCUSSION

Within a relatively short timespan, Facebook has revolutionized the way people interact. Yet, whether using Facebook predicts changes in subjective well-being over time is unknown. We addressed this issue by performing lagged analyses on experience sampled data, an approach that allowed us to take advantage of the relative timing of participants' naturally occurring behaviors and psychological states to draw inferences about their likely causal sequence.[17,18] These analyses indicated that Facebook use predicts declines in the two components of subjective well-being: how people feel moment to moment and how satisfied they are with their lives.

Critically, we found no evidence to support two plausible alternative interpretations of these results. First, interacting with other people "directly" did not predict declines in well-being. In fact, direct social network interactions led people to feel *better* over time. This suggests that Facebook use may constitute a unique form of social network interaction that predicts impoverished well-being. Second, multiple types of evidence indicated that it was not the case that Facebook use led to declines in well-being because people are more likely to

---

14 *a priori predictions* Predictions made before research began.

15 *slope analyses* Analyses showing the incline of the line that would be formed if a set of data were depicted in a graph.

use Facebook when they feel bad—neither affect nor worry predicted Facebook use and Facebook use continued to predict significant declines in well-being when controlling for loneliness (which did predict increases in Facebook use and reductions in emotional well-being).

Would engaging in any solitary activity similarly predict declines in well-being? We suspect that they would not because people often derive pleasure from engaging in some solitary activities (e.g., exercising, reading). Supporting this view, a number of recent studies indicate that people's *perceptions* of social isolation (i.e., how lonely they feel)—a variable that we assessed in this study, which did not influence our results—are a more powerful determinant of well-being than *objective* social isolation.[25] A related question concerns whether engaging in any Internet activity (e.g., email, web surfing) would likewise predict well-being declines. Here too prior research suggests that it would not. A number of studies indicate that whether interacting with the Internet predicts changes in well-being depends on how you use it (i.e., what sites you visit) and who you interact with.[26]

Future research

Although these findings raise numerous future research questions, four stand out as most pressing. First, do these findings generalize? We concentrated on young adults in this study because they represent a core Facebook user demographic. However, examining whether these findings generalize to additional age groups is important. Future research should also examine whether these findings generalize to other online social networks. As a recent review of the Facebook literature indicated[2] "[different online social networks] have varied histories and are associated with different patterns of use, user characteristics, and social functions" (p. 205). Therefore, it is possible that the current findings may not neatly generalize to other online social networks.

Second, what mechanisms underlie the deleterious effects of Facebook usage on well-being? Some researchers have speculated that online social networking may interfere with physical activity, which has cognitive and emotional replenishing effects[27] or trigger damaging social comparisons.[8,28] The latter idea is particularly interesting in light of the significant interaction we observed between direct social contact and Facebook use in this study—i.e., the more people interacted with other people directly, the more strongly Facebook use predicted declines in their affective well-being. If harmful social comparisons explain how Facebook use predicts declines in affective well-being, it is possible that interacting with other people directly either enhances the frequency of such comparisons or magnifies their emotional impact. Examining whether

25

these or other mechanisms explain the relationship between Facebook usage and well-being is important both from a basic science and practical perspective.

Finally, although the analytic approach we used in this study is useful for drawing inferences about the likely causal ordering of associations between naturally occurring variables, experiments that manipulate Facebook use in daily life are needed to corroborate these findings and establish definitive causal relations. Though potentially challenging to perform—Facebook use prevalence, its centrality to young adult daily social interactions, and addictive properties may make it a difficult intervention target—such studies are important for extending this work and informing future interventions.*

Caveats

Two caveats* are in order before concluding. First, although we observed statistically significant associations between Facebook usage and well-being, the sizes of these effects were relatively "small." This should not, however, undermine their practical significance.[29] Subjective well-being is a multiply determined outcome—it is unrealistic to expect any single factor to powerfully influence it. Moreover, in addition to being consequential in its own right, subjective well-being predicts an array of mental and physical health consequences. Therefore, identifying any factor that systematically influences it is important, especially when that factor is likely to accumulate over time among large numbers of people. Facebook usage would seem to fit both of these criteria.

Second, some research suggests that asking people to indicate how good or bad they feel using a single bipolar scale,* as we did in this study, can obscure interesting differences regarding whether a variable leads people to feel less positive, more negative or both less positive and more negative. Future research should administer two unipolar affect questions to assess positive and negative affect separately to address this issue.

CONCLUDING COMMENT

30 The human need for social connection is well established, as are the benefits that people derive from such connections.[30-34] On the surface, Facebook provides an invaluable resource for fulfilling such needs by allowing people to instantly connect. Rather than enhancing well-being, as frequent interactions with supportive "offline" social networks powerfully do, the current findings demonstrate that interacting with Facebook may predict the opposite result for young adults—it may undermine it.

(2013)

ACKNOWLEDGMENTS: We thank Emily Kean for her assistance running the study and Ozlem Ayduk and Phoebe Ellsworth for their feedback.

AUTHOR CONTRIBUTIONS: Conceived and designed the experiments: EK ED JP DSL NL JJ OY. Performed the experiments: HS NL. Analyzed the data: PV ED. Wrote the paper: EK ED PV JJ OY. Discussed the results and commented on the manuscript: EK PV ED JP DSL NL HS JJ OY.

SUPPORTING INFORMATION

1: We do not imply that no longitudinal research on Facebook has been performed. Rather, no published work that we are aware of has examined how Facebook influences subjective well-being over time (i.e., how people feel and their life satisfaction).

2: Additional measures were administered during Phases 1 and 2 for other purposes. The measures reported in the MS are those that were theoretically motivated.

3: Raw data are available upon request for replication purposes.

4: We also examined whether T_{0-1} (rather than T_{1-2}) Facebook use influences T_2 affect, controlling for T_1 affect. Nested time-lagged analyses indicated that this was also true, $B = .03$, $\chi^2 = 4.67$, $p = .03$.

5: Some research suggests that affect fluctuates throughout the day. Replicating this work, time of day was related to affective well-being such that people reported feeling better as the day progressed ($B = -1.06$, $\chi^2 = 21.49$, $p < .0001$). Controlling for time of day did not, however, substantively influence any of the results.

6: 98% of participants reported using Facebook to "keep in touch with friends." Therefore, we did not test for moderation with this variable.

REFERENCES

1. FacebookInformation (2012) Facebook Newsroom Website. Available: http://newsroom.fb.com/content/default.aspx?NewsAreaId=22. Accessed 2012 April 23.
2. Wilson RE, Gosling SD, Graham LT (2012) A Review of Facebook Research in the Social Sciences. Perspect Psychol Sci 7: 203–220.
3. Steptoe A, Wardle J (2011) Positive affect measured using ecological momentary assessment and survival in older men and women. Proc Natl Acad Sci USA 108: 18244–18248. doi: 10.1073/pnas.1110892108.
4. Boehm JK, Peterson C, Kivimaki M, Kubzansky L (2011) A prospective study of positive psychological well-being and coronary heart disease. Health Psychol 30: 259–267. doi: 10.1037/a0023124.
5. Diener E (2011) Happy people live longer: Subjective well-being contributes to health and longevity. Appl Psychol Health Well Being 3: 1–43. doi: 10.1111/j.1758-0854.2010.01045.x.
6. Valenzuela S, Park N, Kee KF (2009) Is There Social Capital in a Social Network Site?: Facebook Use and College Students' Life Satisfaction, Trust, and Participation. J Comput Mediat Commun 14: 875–901. doi: 10.1111/j.1083-6101.2009.01474.x.
7. Huang C (2010) Internet use and psychological well-being: A meta-analysis. Cyberpsychol Behav Soc Netw 13: 241–248.

8. Chou H, Edge N (2012) 'They are happier and having better lives than I am': The impact of using Facebook on perceptions of others' lives. Cyberpsychol Behav Soc Netw 15: 117–120. doi: 10.1089/cyber.2011.0324.

9. Forest AL, Wood JV (2012) When Social Networking Is Not Working: Individuals With Low Self-Esteem Recognize but Do Not Reap the Benefits of Self-Disclosure on Facebook. Psychol Sci 23: 295–302. doi: 10.1177/0956797611429709.

10. Manago AM, Taylor T, Greenfield PM (2012) Me and my 400 friends: The anatomy of college students' Facebook networks, their communication patterns, and well-being. Dev Psychol 48: 369–380. doi: 10.1037/a0026338.

11. Kim J, LaRose R, Peng W (2009) Loneliness as the cause and the effect of problematic Internet use: the relationship between Internet use and psychological well-being. Cyberpsychology & behavior: the impact of the Internet, multimedia and virtual reality on behavior and society 12: 451–455. doi: 10.1089/cpb.2008.0327.

12. Kahneman D, Krueger AB, Schkade DA, Schwarz N, Stone AA (2004) A survey method for characterizing daily life experience: The day reconstruction method. Science 306: 1776–1780. doi: 10.1126/science.1103572.

13. Diener E, Emmons RA, Larsen RJ, Griffin S (1985) The Satisfaction with Life Scale. J Pers Assess 49: 71–74. doi: 10.1207/s15327752jpa4901_13.

14. Kahneman D, Deaton A (2010) High income improves evaluation of life but not emotional well-being. Proc Natl Acad Sci USA 107: 16489–16493. doi: 10.1073/pnas.1011492107.

15. Diener E (1984) Subjective Well-Being. Psychol Bull 95: 542–575. doi: 10.1037/0033-2909.95.3.542.

16. Hofmann W, Vohs KD, Baumeister RF (2012) What people desire, feel conflicted about, and try to resist in everyday life. Psychol Sci doi: 10.1177/0956797612437426.

17. Bolger N, Davis A, Rafaeli E (2003) Diary methods: Capturing life as it is lived. Annu Rev Psychol 54: 579–616. doi: 10.1146/annurev.psych.54.101601.145030.

18. Adam EK, Hawkley LC, Kudielka BM, Cacioppo JT (2006) Day-to-day dynamics of experience—cortisol associations in a population-based sample of older adults. Proc Natl Acad Sci USA 103: 17058–17063. doi: 10.1073/pnas.0605053103.

19. Killingsworth MA, Gilbert DT (2010) A Wandering Mind Is an Unhappy Mind. Science 330: 932–932. doi: 10.1126/science.1192439.

20. Beck AT, Steer RA, Brown GK (1996) BDI-II Manual San Antonio: Harcourt Brace & Company.

21. Rosenberg M (1965) Society and the adolescent self-image. Princeton: Princeton University Press.

22. Cutrona CE (1989) Ratings of social support by adolescents and adult informants: Degree of correspondence and prediction of depressive symptoms. Journal of Personality and Social Psychology 57: 723–730. doi: 10.1037//0022-3514.57.4.723.

23. Russell D, Peplau LA, Cutrona CE (1980) The revised UCLA Loneliness Scale: Concurrent and discriminant validity evidence. J Pers Soc Psychol 39: 472–480. doi: 10.1037//0022-3514.39.3.472.

24. Moberly NJ, Watkins ER (2008) Ruminative self-focus, negative life events, and negative affect. Behav Res Ther 46: 1034–1039. doi: 10.1016/j.brat.2008.06.004.

25. Cacioppo JT, Hawkley LC, Norman GJ, Berntson GG (2011) Social isolation. Ann N Y Acad Sci 1231: 17–22. doi: 10.1111/j.1749-6632.2011.06028.x.

26. Bessiére K, Kiesler S, Kraut R, Boneva BS (2008) Effects of Internet use and social resources on changes in depression. Information, Communication, and Society 11: 47–70.

27. Kaplan S, Berman MG (2010) Directed Attention as a Common Resource for Executive Functioning and Self-Regulation. Perspect Psychol Sci 5: 43–57. doi: 10.1177/1745691609356784.

28. Haferkamp N, Kramer NC (2011) Social Comparison 2.0: Examining the Effects of Online Profiles on Social-Networking Sites. Cyberpsychol Behav Soc Netw 14: 309–314. doi: 10.1089/cyber.2010.0120.

29. Prentice DA, Miller DT (1992) When small effects are impressive. Psychological Bulletin 112: 160–164. doi: 10.1037/0033-2909.112.1.160.

30. Baumeister RF, Leary MR (1995) The need to belong: desire for interpersonal attachments as a fundamental human motivation. Psychol Bull 117: 497–529. doi: 10.1037/0033-2909.117.3.497.

31. Kross E, Berman MG, Mischel W, Smith EE, Wager TD (2011) Social rejection shares somatosensory representations with physical pain. Proc Natl Acad Sci USA 108: 6270–6275. doi: .10.1073/pnas.1102693108.

32. Eisenberger NI, Cole SW (2012) Social neuroscience and health: neurophysiological mechanisms linking social ties with physical health. Nat Neurosci 15: 669–674. doi: 10.1038/nn.3086.

33. House JS, Landis KR, Umberson D (1988) Social relationships and health. Science 241: 540–545. doi: 10.1126/science.3399889.

34. Ybarra O, Burnstein E, Winkielman P, Keller MC, Chan E, et al. (2008) Mental exercising through simple socializing: Social interaction promotes general cognitive functioning. Pers Soc Psychol Bull 34: 248–259. doi: 10.1177/0146167207310454.

Questions

1. How would you choose to present the data recorded in Phase 2 of the experiment? Explain your answer.

2. The article suggests that Facebook "undermines" well-being. What does this mean? What criteria were used to measure well-being?

3. How important do you think it is to study the effects of social media? Why?

4. Look up one of the questionnaires participants responded to in Phase 1 of the experiment. What do the results of the questionnaires tell you about the group of participants as a whole? Write a paragraph explaining what the questionnaire reveals about the group using data from Phase 1 of the experiment.

5. Read the article "Facebook Is Bad for You: Get a Life!," also included in this anthology. That article presents the results of this study; how accurately does it present them?

6. Choose a social media platform other than Facebook that is commonly used today. How is it different from Facebook? (Consider its structure as well as the ways users tend to engage with it.) In your view, do these differences make this platform any more or less likely than Facebook to negatively impact its users' well-being?

FACEBOOK IS BAD FOR YOU: GET A LIFE!

The following article, originally published in The Economist *in 2013, reports on the social psychology study "Facebook Use Predicts Declines in Subjective Well-Being in Young Adults." Like all* Economist *articles, it was published without any attribution of authorship.*

The study in question, by Ethan Kross and colleagues, is also included in this anthology.

❧

Those who have resisted the urge to join Facebook will surely feel vindicated when they read the latest research. A study just published by the *Public Library of Science*, conducted by Ethan Kross of the University of Michigan and Philippe Verduyn of Leuven University in Belgium, has shown that the more someone uses Facebook, the less satisfied he is with life.

Past investigations have found that using Facebook is associated with jealousy, social tension, isolation and depression. But these studies have all been "cross-sectional"—in other words, snapshots in time. As such, they risk confusing correlation with causation: perhaps those who spend more time on social media are more prone to negative emotions in the first place. The study conducted by Dr Kross and Dr Verduyn is the first to follow Facebook users for an extended period, to track how their emotions change.

The researchers recruited 82 Facebookers for their study. These volunteers, in their late teens or early 20s, agreed to have their Facebook activity observed for two weeks and to report, five times a day, on their state of mind and their direct social contacts (phone calls and meetings in person with other people). These reports were prompted by text messages, sent between 10am and midnight, asking them to complete a short questionnaire.

When the researchers analysed the results, they found that the more a volunteer used Facebook in the period between two questionnaires, the worse he reported feeling the next time he filled in a questionnaire. Volunteers were also asked to rate their satisfaction with life at the start and the end of the study. Those who used Facebook a lot were more likely to report a decline in satisfaction than those who visited the site infrequently. In contrast, there was a positive association between the amount of direct social contact a volunteer had and how positive he felt. In other words, the more volunteers socialised in the real world, the more positive they reported feeling the next time they filled in the questionnaire.

5   A volunteer's sex had no influence on these findings; nor did the size of his (or her) social network, his stated motivation for using Facebook, his level of loneliness or depression or his self-esteem. Dr Kross and Dr Verduyn therefore conclude that, rather than enhancing well-being, Facebook undermines it.

Their study does not tease out why socialising on Facebook has a different effect from socialising in person. But an earlier investigation, conducted by social scientists at Humboldt University and Darmstadt's Technical University, both in Germany, may have found the root cause. These researchers, who presented their findings at a conference in Leipzig in February, surveyed 584 users of Facebook aged mostly in their 20s. They found that the most common emotion aroused by using Facebook is envy. Endlessly comparing themselves with peers who have doctored their photographs, amplified their achievements and plagiarised their *bons mots*[1] can leave Facebook's users more than a little green-eyed.* Real-life encounters, by contrast, are more WYSIWYG (what you see is what you get).

What neither study proves is whether all this is true only for younger users of Facebook. Older ones may be more mellow, and thus less begrudging of their friends' successes, counterfeit or real. Maybe.

(2013)

Questions

1. This article refers to previous "cross-sectional" investigations into Facebook use. What, according to the article, is the problem with this type of study? In your view, how well does the approach taken in the new study by Kross and Verduyn address this concern?

2. Read the article "Facebook Use Predicts Declines in Subjective Well-Being in Young Adults," also included in this anthology. Discuss the tone of the writing in each piece. How does it reflect the intended audience for each?

3. What, if any, social media platforms do you use? How do you feel the use of social media impacts your life?

----

1   *bons mots*   Clever sayings or witticisms.

NATHAN HELLER

THE FAILURE OF FACEBOOK
DEMOCRACY

As an increasing number of people access news online, particularly via social media sites such as Facebook, questions have arisen about the effects of the Internet on the types of news we encounter. Algorithms on sites such as Google and Facebook tailor the information we receive to match our interests. These so-called "filter bubbles" are particularly prevalent on social media sites, where, it is argued, communities of friends or followers tend to share similar views and filter out opposing ones. A related concern is that the news people access through Facebook is often not fact-checked, so that "fake news" has begun to exert a significant influence on public discourse. The following article discusses the effects of filter bubbles and fake news on the democratic process; it first appeared in The New Yorker *on 18 November 2016, shortly after Donald Trump was elected President of the United States.*

☙

In December of 2007, the legal theorist Cass R. Sunstein wrote in *The Chronicle of Higher Education* about the filtering effects that frequently attend the spread of information on the Web. "As a result of the Internet, we live increasingly in an era of enclaves and niches—much of it voluntary, much of it produced by those who think they know, and often do know, what we're likely to like," Sunstein noted. In the piece, "The Polarization of Extremes," Sunstein argued that the trend promised ill effects for the direction—or, more precisely, the misdirection—of public opinion. "If people are sorted into enclaves and niches, what will happen to their views?" he wondered. "What are the eventual effects on democracy?"

This month has provided a jarring answer. The unexpected election of Donald Trump is said to owe debts to both niche extremism and rampant misinformation. Facebook, the most pervasive of the social networks, has received much scrutiny and blame. During the final weeks of the campaigns, it grew apparent that the site's "news" algorithm—a mechanism that trawls posts from one's online friends and rank-displays those deemed of interest—was not distinguishing between real news and false information: the sort of tall tales, groundless conspiracy theories, and oppositional propaganda that, in the Cenozoic era,[1] circulated mainly via forwarded e-mails. (In the run-up to the election, widely shared false stories included reports that Pope Francis has endorsed Donald Trump and that Hillary Clinton had commissioned murders.) On Thursday, the *Washington Post* published an interview with what it called an "impresario[2] of a Facebook fake-news empire." He took responsibility. "I think Trump is in the White House because of me," he said. "His followers don't fact-check anything—they'll post everything, believe anything."

Facebook is not the only network to have trafficked phony news, but its numbers have been striking. A much-cited Pew survey, released in May, suggested that forty-four per cent of the general population used Facebook as a news source, a figure unrivalled by other social networks. An analysis this week by Craig Silverman, of *BuzzFeed*, found that the twenty top-performing fake news stories on the network outperformed the twenty top real-news stories during the final three months before the election—and that seventeen of those fakes favored the Trump campaign. Trump's exponents, including the candidate himself, routinely cited fake information on camera. In the eyes of critics, Facebook's news feed has become a distribution channel for propagandistic misinformation. "As long as it's on Facebook and people can see it ... people start believing it," President Obama said right before the election. "It creates this dust cloud of nonsense."

The criticism has been hard to shake. Mark Zuckerberg, Facebook's founder and C.E.O., dismissed complaints at a conference late last week and again in a lengthy post over the weekend. "The hoaxes that do exist are not limited to one partisan view, or even to politics. Over all, this makes it extremely unlikely hoaxes changed the outcome of this election in one direction or the other," he wrote. "I believe we must proceed very carefully though. Identifying the 'truth' is complicated." Few members of the public were appeased (not least because Facebook's advertising strategy is premised on the idea that it can move the needle of public opinion), and even some Facebook employees were uneasy. On Monday, *BuzzFeed*'s Sheera Frenkel reported on an anonymous cabal of "renegade Facebook employees" who found Zuckerberg's claims

---

1   *Cenozoic era* Current geologic era spanning the past 66 million years; it followed the Mesozoic era. Heller is using the term playfully to refer to a recent "era" of technology (when we received news from friends via forwarded emails).

2   *impresario* Italian: person who organizes a show or entertainment (concert, circus, opera).

dishonest. They were working to develop formal recommendations for change. "You don't have to believe Facebook got Trump elected to be a little chilled by its current estrangement from fact," Brian Phillips observed in a cutting piece on MTV.com. "One of the conditions of democratic resistance is having an accurate picture of what to resist."

The democratic effects of widespread misinformation were Sunstein's preoccupation when he wrote about "self-sorting" in 2007. He cited an experiment previously run in Colorado. The study used liberal subjects from Boulder and conservative subjects from Colorado Springs. Participants had been divided into groups and instructed to discuss controversial issues: same-sex unions, global warming, affirmative action.* Researchers recorded individual opinions before and after fifteen minutes of discussion. Trends emerged. When participants spoke with politically like-minded people, their opinions usually became more extreme. Liberals grew more liberal in their thinking on a given issue; conservatives, more conservative. The range of opinion narrowed, too. Like-minded participants drifted toward consensus.

Sunstein projected that a similar drift would occur online, where information in support of preëxisting views was readily available (and even hard to avoid, due to the way Internet browsing works). He called the polarization that it produced "enclave extremism." One contributing factor, he contended, was the social flow of information: people who hung out with people of a similar view were apt to encounter a disproportionate amount of information in support of that view, intensifying their support. He thought more purely social effects were involved, too: "People want to be perceived favorably by other group members." Most citizens, on most issues, don't know precisely what they think, and are susceptible to minor suasion.[3] Enclave opinion, which builds confidence in one's views, allows general thoughts to sharpen and intensify. The risk was that bad ideas could gain wide adherence if the self-sorting worked out right.

Sunstein did not account for Facebook algorithms or the spread of demonstrably false information. The first factor amplifies the enclave effect he described; the second nurtures confident extremism. Even when information is accurate, enclave extremism helps explain how those who trade in fact, such as journalists, could manage to get the big-picture stuff, such as the electoral mood of the country, completely wrong.[4] In the days after Trump's election, many bemused coastal pundits lamented what the writer Eli Pariser

5

---

3   *suasion*   Influence; persuasion.

4   *fact ... wrong*   In the weeks leading up to the November 2016 election, most mainstream media outlets in the US expressed confidence that Hillary Clinton was on track to win the presidency.

has called a "filter bubble": an echo chamber of information and opinion which, in this case, led those writing the news to be disproportionately exposed to information in line with their existing theories. The more we rely on the digital sphere as our window onto the world, the more vulnerable to its weaknesses we are.

A couple of years ago, reporting from San Francisco, I noted an erosion of public meaning which seemed to be getting in the way of civic progress. A key cause, I suggested at the time, was technology's filtering effects—the way that, as we lived more of our lives in a personal bespoke,[5] we lost touch with the common ground, and the common language, that made meaningful public work possible. Perhaps filtering effects are at play, but nothing I've seen since has changed my mind. The most dangerous intellectual spectre today seems not to be lack of information but the absence of a common information sphere in which to share it across boundaries of belief.

Pauline Kael, a *New Yorker* film critic for many years, once famously quipped, in a speech, "I live in a rather special world. I only know one person who voted for Nixon."* Enclave extremism isn't new, in other words. What may be fresher is our oblivion of the moments when we're living in its thrall. If a majority of Americans are getting their news from Facebook, then Facebook surely has a civic obligation to insure the information it disseminates is sound. The long-term effects of enclave extremism, Sunstein observed, can be bad news for democracy: "Those who flock together, on the Internet or elsewhere, will end up both confident and wrong, simply because they have not been sufficiently exposed to counterarguments. They may even think of their fellow citizens as opponents or adversaries in some kind of 'war.'" A Presidential Administration with that outlook is dangerous. But a confident, misinformed public is much worse.

(2016)

Questions

1. If you are a member of any social networks (Facebook, Twitter, Instagram, Snapchat, etc.), do you think your membership in those networks has sorted you into a "niche" of friends with like-minded views? What effect (if any) does discourse with your social media friends have on your political and ethical opinions?

---

5   *bespoke*   Made to order, tailor-made.

2. Facebook has made changes to its algorithm since this article was published.

   a. Through your own research, identify the most significant of these changes.

   b. To what extent (if at all) do these changes address the problems of filter bubbles and fake news?

   c. What—if anything—more should Facebook do to address the problems of filter bubbles and/or fake news?

3. Heller argues that the more we rely on the Internet as our sphere of public discourse, the more "vulnerable we are to its weaknesses." What are these weaknesses? Does the Internet have strengths as a sphere of public discourse that counteract these weaknesses?

4. Heller argues that "enclave extremism" leads people in different groups to be both "confident and wrong," increasing the intensity of animosity between people with different values. To what extent do you see this phenomenon reflected in the present-day political landscape?

5. In what ways could politicians and corporations profit from a culture that is distancing itself from caring about fact and truth?

6. Do you see evidence of "enclave extremism" in your online communities? If so, how do you think it is created and perpetuated? If not, how do you think it is avoided?

7. In a democratic society, journalists, scholars, and newspapers traditionally have a responsibility to fact-check their articles and to correct any errors that are printed, allowing for a public discourse of varied opinions based on shared facts. Has the Internet altered this foundation of democracy? If so, how? What are the possible ramifications?

8. Heller points out that enclave extremism isn't new. Does the medium of the Internet make it a more dangerous phenomenon? Why or why not?

CAROLINE LESTER

A STUDY ON DRIVERLESS-CAR ETHICS OFFERS A TROUBLING LOOK INTO OUR VALUES

In 2016, a group of scientists and other scholars launched the Moral Machine, a platform that invites participants to judge what should happen in a series of scenarios in which a self-driving car can't avoid a fatal accident but has some control over who dies. With the Moral Machine, its founders hoped to create "a crowd-sourced picture of human opinion on how machines should make decisions when faced with moral dilemmas." This 2019 piece from The New Yorker *contemplates "The Moral Machine Experiment," a paper on the project published in the journal* Nature *in October 2018; some of the findings published in* Nature *are reprinted elsewhere in this anthology.*

❧

The first time Azim Shariff met Iyad Rahwan—the first real time, after communicating with him by phone and e-mail—was in a driverless car. It was November, 2012, and Rahwan, a thirty-four-year-old professor of computing and information science, was researching artificial intelligence at the Masdar Institute of Science and Technology, a university in Abu Dhabi. He was eager to explore how concepts within psychology—including social networks and collective reasoning—might inform machine learning, but there were few psychologists working in the U.A.E.[1] Shariff, a thirty-one-year-old with wild hair and expressive eyebrows, was teaching psychology at New York University's campus in Abu Dhabi; he guesses that he was one of four research psychologists in the region at the time, an estimate that Rahwan told me "doesn't sound like an exaggeration." Rahwan cold-e-mailed Shariff and invited him to visit his research group.

The lab was situated in Masdar City, an experimental planned community in the heart of Abu Dhabi. The city runs entirely on renewable energy and

---

1   *U.A.E.*   United Arab Emirates.

prohibits the use of gas-powered vehicles. Instead, residents travel by "personal rapid transit"—a system of small, driverless cars that snake around the streets on magnetized paths. Rahwan waited for Shariff in a parking lot near the city limits, where commuters transfer from gas-powered cars to the self-driving pods. The cars function more like trains than like true autonomous vehicles, or A.V.s; they don't deviate from set paths and make almost no decisions on their own. But, in 2012, when A.V.s were almost entirely theoretical, whirring around in a car with no steering wheel and no brakes felt electrifying for Shariff. As he traveled through the city with Rahwan, he held his phone out in front of him, filming the entire ride.

Today, cars with semi-autonomous features are already on the road. Automatic parallel parking has been commercially available since 2003. Cadillac allows drivers to go hands-free on pre-approved routes. Some B.M.W. S.U.V.s can be equipped with, for an additional seventeen-hundred dollars, a system that takes over during "monotonous traffic situations"—more colloquially known as traffic jams. But a mass-produced driverless car remains elusive. In 2013, the U.S. Department of Transportation's National Highway Traffic Safety Administration published a sliding scale that ranked cars on their level of autonomy. The vast majority of vehicles are still at level zero. A car at level four would be highly autonomous in basic situations, like highways, but would need a human operator. Cars at level five would drive as well as or better than humans, smoothly adapting to rapid changes in their environments, like swerving cars or stray pedestrians. This would require the vehicles to make value judgments, including in versions of a classic philosophy thought experiment called the trolley problem: if a car detects a sudden obstacle—say, a jackknifed truck—should it hit the truck and kill its own driver, or should it swerve onto a crowded sidewalk and kill pedestrians? A human driver might react randomly (if she has time to react at all), but the response of an autonomous vehicle would have to be programmed ahead of time. What should we tell the car to do?

Shariff moved to the U.S. at the end of 2012, and then to Canada. Rahwan eventually got a job at the M.I.T. Media Lab, in Cambridge, but the pair kept in touch. They reached out to a third collaborator with whom they previously worked, a French professor of cognitive science named Jean-François Bonnefon, and the scientists had periodic phone calls. "The three of us just jelled really well together," Shariff said. "We would kind of geek out." One of their most frequent topics of conversation was the ethics of self-driving cars. In 2015, Rahwan invited Shariff and Bonnefon to visit him in Boston. In the course of a week, they met regularly, either in the Media Lab, which, with its grid of steel and glass, looks like it's made of graph paper, or in one of the cafés on Kendall Square. On a drizzly day in November, they came up with an idea. Before determining the ethical decisions that A.V.s should make, they had to understand what decisions human drivers would make if they had the time to react. By crowdsourcing this question, they could figure out what people's values were. Rahwan still has his notes from that day, which include scribbled phrases like "# of people on the road," "# of people in the car," and "odds of dying."

5   In June of 2016, the Media Lab launched a Web site that invited people from all over the world to play a game called Moral Machine. In the game, players are presented with a version of the trolley problem: a driverless car can either stay its course and hit what is in its path, or swerve and hit something else. Each round features a new version of the problem, with different obstacles and different groups of people to be killed or spared. In the next two years, more than two million people—from some two hundred countries and territories—participated in the study, logging more than forty million decisions. It is the largest study on moral preferences for machine intelligence ever conducted.

The paper on the project was published in *Nature*, in October, 2018, and the results offer an unlikely window into people's values around the globe. On the whole, players showed little preference between action and inaction, which the scientists found surprising. "From the philosophical ... and legal perspective ... this question is very important," Shariff explained. But the players showed strong preferences for what kinds of people they hit. Those preferences were determined, in part, by where the players were from. Edmond Awad, a research fellow, and Sohan Dsouza, a graduate student working with Rahwan, noticed that the responses could be grouped into three large geographic "clusters": the Western cluster, including North America and Western Europe; the Eastern cluster, which was a mix of East Asian and Islamic countries; and the Southern cluster, which was composed of Latin-American countries and a smattering of Francophone countries.

We should be wary of drawing broad conclusions from the geographical differences, particularly because about seventy per cent of the respondents were male college graduates. Still, the cultural differences were stark. Players in Eastern-cluster countries were more likely than those in the Western and Southern countries to kill a young person and spare an old person (represented, in the game, by a stooped figure holding a cane). Players in Southern countries were more likely to kill a fat person (a figure with a large stomach) and spare an athletic person (a figure that appeared mid-jog, wearing shorts and a sweatband). Players in countries with high economic inequality (for example, in Venezuela and Colombia) were more likely to spare a business executive (a figure walking briskly, holding a briefcase) than a homeless person (a hunched figure with a hat, a beard, and patches on his clothes). In countries where the rule of law is particularly strong—like Japan or Germany—people were more likely to kill jaywalkers than lawful pedestrians. But, even with these differences, universal patterns revealed themselves. Most players sacrificed individuals to save larger groups. Most players spared women over men. Dog-lovers will be happy to learn that dogs were more likely to be spared than cats. Human-lovers will be disturbed to learn that dogs were more likely to be spared than criminals.

In its discussion, the paper skims over the uglier aspects of the study to identify "three strong preferences" that might provide a starting point for developing a standardized machine-ethics framework: sparing human lives, sparing more lives, and sparing young lives. The paper concludes with a soaring look into the future, and recasts machine ethics as a "unique opportunity to decide, as a community, what we believe to be right or wrong; and to make sure that machines, unlike humans, unerringly follow these moral preferences." But, when I asked Shariff what he thought of the human prejudice shown in the data, he laughed and said, "That suggests to us that we shouldn't leave decisions completely in the hands of the demos."

The U.S. government has clear guidelines for autonomous weapons—they can't be programmed to make "kill decisions" on their own—but no formal opinion on the ethics of driverless cars. Germany is the only country that has devised such a framework; in 2017, a German government commission—headed by Udo Di Fabio, a former judge on the country's highest constitutional court—released a report that suggested a number of guidelines for driverless vehicles. Among the report's twenty propositions, one stands out: "In the event of unavoidable accident situations, any distinction based on personal features (age, gender, physical or mental constitution) is strictly prohibited." When I sent Di Fabio the Moral Machine data, he was unsurprised by the respondents' prejudices. Philosophers and lawyers, he noted, often have very different understandings of ethical dilemmas than ordinary people do. This difference may irritate the specialists, he said, but "it should always make them think." Still, Di Fabio believes that we shouldn't capitulate to human biases when it comes to life-and-death decisions. "In Germany, people are very sensitive to such discussions," he told me, by e-mail. "This has to do with a dark past that has divided people up and sorted them out."

The decisions made by Germany will reverberate beyond its borders. 10 Volkswagen sells more automobiles than any other company in the world. But that manufacturing power comes with a complicated moral responsibility. What should a company do if another country wants its vehicles to reflect different moral calculations? Should a Western car de-prioritize the young in an Eastern country? Shariff leans toward adjusting each model for the country where it's meant to operate. Car manufacturers, he thinks, "should be sensitive to the cultural differences in the places they're instituting these ethical decisions."

Otherwise, the algorithms they export might start looking like a form of moral colonialism. But Di Fabio worries about letting autocratic governments tinker with the code. He imagines a future in which China wants the cars to favor people who rank higher in its new social-credit system, which scores citizens based on their civic behavior.

Both Di Fabio and Shariff agree that the advent of autonomous vehicles will force us to make our underlying moral calculations explicit. In twenty to fifty years, the majority of cars on the road will likely be driverless. If billions of machines are all programmed to make the same judgement call, it may be a lot more dangerous to cross the street as, say, an overweight man than as a fit woman. And, if companies decide to tweak the software to prioritize their customers over pedestrians, it may be more dangerous to be beside the road than on it. In a future dominated by driverless cars, moral texture will erode away in favor of a rigid ethical framework. Let's hope we're on the right side of the algorithm.

(2019)

Questions

1. Analyzing the data from the Moral Machine, researchers Awad and Dsouza "noticed that the responses could be grouped into three large geographic 'clusters'" (paragraph 6). What geographical differences did they find? What might account for them?

2. Lester notes that "about seventy per cent" of the participants in the study were "male college graduates" (paragraph 7). Why is this important? How might it have affected the results?

3. Did any of the moral preferences described in the article surprise you? Did you find any disturbing? Explain why or why not.

4. How, in your view, should self-driving cars be programmed to behave in situations like those presented in the Moral Machine game? Defend your view.

5. To what extent (if at all) should the majority view be taken into account by governments legislating on the guidelines for self-driving cars' moral behavior?

6. Read Edmond Awad et al.'s study "The Moral Machine Experiment" (*Nature*, 2018), available online. How does the tone of Lester's writing differ from Awad's? How effectively does Lester's article capture the salient points of the study?

Edmond Awad, Sohan Dsouza, Richard Kim,
Jonathan Schulz, Joseph Henrich, Azim Shariff,
Jean-François Bonnefon, & Iyad Rahwan

from The Moral Machine Experiment

The following graphs, from an article that first appeared in the prominent journal Nature, *present some of the results of a study conducted to measure "societal expectations about the ethical principles that should guide machine behavior." The scholars involved created the Moral Machine, an "experimental platform" in which participants were shown a series of scenarios in which a self-driving car had to make a choice to kill one individual or group of living beings over another (the experiment focused primarily on people, but cats and dogs were also included). An article from* The New Yorker *discussing the experiment's origins and findings is also included in this anthology.*

☯

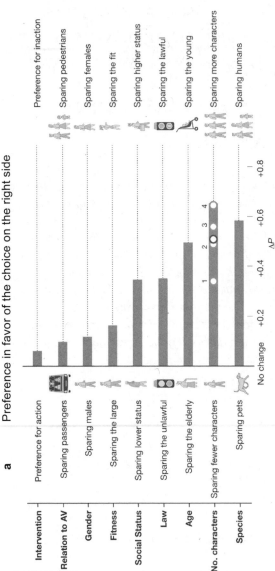

a, AMCE[1] for each preference. In each row, ΔP is the difference between the probability of sparing characters possessing the attribute on the right, and the probability of sparing characters possessing the attribute on the left, aggregated over all other attributes. For example, for the attribute age, the probability of sparing young characters is 0.49 (s.e.[2] = 0.0008) greater than the probability of sparing older characters. The 95% confidence intervals of the means are omitted owing to their insignificant width, given the sample size (n = 35.2 million). For the number of characters (No. characters), effect sizes are shown for each number of additional characters (1 to 4; n1 = 1.52 million, n2 = 1.52 million, n3 = 1.52 million, n4 = 1.53 million); the effect size for two additional characters overlaps with the mean effect of the attribute. AV, autonomous vehicle.

1   *AMCE*   Average marginal component effect, a number indicating the impact of a single attribute on the probability of an outcome. Here, the number indicates how much a particular characteristic made participants more likely to save an individual's life in the experiment.

2   *s.e.*   Standard error, an indicator of how well a sample group represents the population being analyzed.

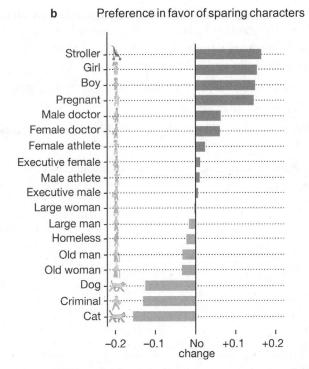

b, Relative advantage or penalty for each character, compared to an adult man or woman. For each character, ΔP is the difference the between the probability of sparing this character (when presented alone) and the probability of sparing one adult man or woman (n = 1 million). For example, the probability of sparing a girl is 0.15 (s.e. = 0.003) higher than the probability of sparing an adult man or woman.

(2018)

Questions

1. What kinds of people were participants more likely to save, and what kinds of people were they less likely to save? What values do you think underlie these patterns? To what extent do you think the choices participants made reflect sound ethical judgment, and to what extent do you think they reflect prejudice?

2. Participants were more likely to save women than men, but they were more likely to save male doctors than female doctors. How would you explain this discrepancy?

3. These findings suggest that, broadly speaking, people consciously or unconsciously prioritize certain lives over others. How (if at all) do you see this tendency reflected in government policy where you live? In other aspects of your community?

4. Participate in the Moral Machine experiment, available online.

   a. What was it like to participate?

   b. Which decisions did you find most difficult or uncomfortable, and why?

   c. Does your experience give you any insight into Awad and Dsouza's findings?

REPRESENTATION
AND IDENTITY

BINYAVANGA WAINAINA

HOW TO WRITE ABOUT AFRICA

*In this biting piece, a leading Kenyan writer provides a series of
instructions to foreigners aspiring to write about his home continent.
The essay first appeared in a special issue of the British literary
periodical* Granta *in 2005; the volume was entitled* The View from
Africa.

❧

Always use the word "Africa" or "Darkness" or "Safari" in your title. Sub-
titles may include the words "Zanzibar," "Masai," "Zulu," "Zambezi,"
"Congo," "Nile," "Big," "Sky," "Shadow," "Drum," "Sun" or "Bygone." Also
useful are words such as "Guerrillas," "Timeless," "Primordial" and "Tribal."
Note that "People" means Africans who are not black, while "The People"
means black Africans.

Never have a picture of a well-adjusted African on the cover of your book,
or in it, unless that African has won the Nobel Prize. An AK-47, prominent
ribs, naked breasts: use these. If you must include an African, make sure you
get one in Masai or Zulu or Dogon dress.

In your text, treat Africa as if it were one country. It is hot and dusty with
rolling grasslands and huge herds of animals and tall, thin people who are
starving. Or it is hot and steamy with very short people who eat primates. Don't
get bogged down with precise descriptions. Africa is big: fifty-four countries,
900 million people who are too busy starving and dying and warring and emigrating to read your book. The continent is full of deserts, jungles, highlands,
savannahs and many other things, but your reader doesn't care about all that, so
keep your descriptions romantic and evocative and unparticular.

Make sure you show how Africans have music and rhythm deep in their
souls, and eat things no other humans eat. Do not mention rice and beef and
wheat; monkey-brain is an African's cuisine of choice, along with goat, snake,
worms and grubs and all manner of game meat. Make sure you show that you
are able to eat such food without flinching, and describe how you learn to enjoy
it—because you care.

Taboo subjects: ordinary domestic scenes, love between Africans (unless
a death is involved), references to African writers or intellectuals, mention

of school-going children who are not suffering from yaws or Ebola fever or female genital mutilation.

Throughout the book, adopt a *sotto** voice, in conspiracy with the reader, and a sad *I-expected-so-much* tone. Establish early on that your liberalism is impeccable, and mention near the beginning how much you love Africa, how you fell in love with the place and can't live without her. Africa is the only continent you can love—take advantage of this. If you are a man, thrust yourself into her warm virgin forests. If you are a woman, treat Africa as a man who wears a bush jacket and disappears off into the sunset. Africa is to be pitied, worshipped or dominated. Whichever angle you take, be sure to leave the strong impression that without your intervention and your important book, Africa is doomed.

Your African characters may include naked warriors, loyal servants, diviners and seers, ancient wise men living in hermitic splendor. Or corrupt politicians, inept polygamous travel-guides, and prostitutes you have slept with. The Loyal Servant always behaves like a seven-year-old and needs a firm hand; he is scared of snakes, good with children, and always involving you in his complex domestic dramas. The Ancient Wise Man always comes from a noble tribe (not the money-grubbing tribes like the Gikuyu, the Igbo or the Shona). He has rheumy eyes and is close to the Earth. The Modern African is a fat man who steals and works in the visa office, refusing to give work permits to qualified Westerners who really care about Africa. He is an enemy of development, always using his government job to make it difficult for pragmatic and good-hearted expats to set up NGOs* or Legal Conservation Areas. Or he is an Oxford-educated intellectual turned serial-killing politician in a Savile Row suit. He is a cannibal who likes Cristal champagne, and his mother is a rich witch-doctor who really runs the country.

Among your characters you must always include The Starving African, who wanders the refugee camp nearly naked, and waits for the benevolence of the West. Her children have flies on their eyelids and pot bellies, and her breasts are flat and empty. She must look utterly helpless. She can have no past, no history; such diversions ruin the dramatic moment. Moans are good. She must never say anything about herself in the dialogue except to speak of her (unspeakable) suffering. Also be sure to include a warm and motherly woman who has a rolling laugh and who is concerned for your well-being. Just call her Mama. Her children are all delinquent. These characters should buzz around your main hero, making him look good. Your hero can teach them, bathe them, feed them; he carries lots of babies and has seen Death. Your hero is you (if reportage), or a beautiful, tragic international celebrity/aristocrat who now cares for animals (if fiction).

Bad Western characters may include children of Tory* cabinet ministers, Afrikaners, employees of the World Bank.* When talking about exploitation by foreigners mention the Chinese and Indian traders. Blame the West for Africa's situation. But do not be too specific.

Broad brushstrokes throughout are good. Avoid having the African characters laugh, or struggle to educate their kids, or just make do in mundane circumstances. Have them illuminate something about Europe or America in Africa. African characters should be colorful, exotic, larger than life—but empty inside, with no dialogue, no conflicts or resolutions in their stories, no depth or quirks to confuse the cause.

Describe, in detail, naked breasts (young, old, conservative, recently raped, big, small) or mutilated genitals, or enhanced genitals. Or any kind of genitals. And dead bodies. Or, better, naked dead bodies. And especially rotting naked dead bodies. Remember, any work you submit in which people look filthy and miserable will be referred to as the "real Africa," and you want that on your dust jacket. Do not feel queasy about this: you are trying to help them to get aid from the West. The biggest taboo in writing about Africa is to describe or show dead or suffering white people.

Animals, on the other hand, must be treated as well rounded, complex characters. They speak (or grunt while tossing their manes proudly) and have names, ambitions and desires. They also have family values: *see how lions teach their children?* Elephants are caring, and are good feminists or dignified patriarchs. So are gorillas. Never, ever say anything negative about an elephant or a gorilla. Elephants may attack people's property, destroy their crops, and even kill them. Always take the side of the elephant. Big cats have public-school[1] accents. Hyenas are fair game and have vaguely Middle Eastern accents. Any short Africans who live in the jungle or desert may be portrayed with good humor (unless they are in conflict with an elephant or chimpanzee or gorilla, in which case they are pure evil).

After celebrity activists and aid workers, conservationists are Africa's most important people. Do not offend them. You need them to invite you to their 30,000-acre game ranch or "conservation area," and this is the only way you will get to interview the celebrity activist. Often a book cover with a heroic-looking conservationist on it works magic for sales. Anybody white, tanned and wearing khaki who once had a pet antelope or a farm is a conservationist, one who is preserving Africa's rich heritage. When interviewing him or her, do not ask how much funding they have; do not ask how much money they make off their game. Never ask how much they pay their employees.

10

---

1   *public-school*   In many places outside North America, what North Americans call private schools are referred to as "public schools."

Readers will be put off if you don't mention the light in Africa. And sunsets, the African sunset is a must. It is always big and red. There is always a big sky. Wide empty spaces and game are critical—Africa is the Land of Wide Empty Spaces. When writing about the plight of flora and fauna, make sure you mention that Africa is overpopulated. When your main character is in a desert or jungle living with indigenous peoples (anybody short) it is okay to mention that Africa has been severely depopulated by Aids and War (use caps).

15   You'll also need a nightclub called Tropicana, where mercenaries, evil nouveau riche Africans and prostitutes and guerrillas and expats hang out.

Always end your book with Nelson Mandela* saying something about rainbows or renaissances. Because you care.

(2005)

Questions

1. What parts of this article, if any, do you find funny? What parts, if any, do you find disturbing? Explain.

2. Find a recent example of advertising, fiction, or nonfiction that depicts Africa or a place in Africa. To what extent does the example you chose display the characteristics Wainaina lampoons in this article?

3. What are the ethical responsibilities of white Western writers who want to depict African places and/or people in their work? What can white Western writers do to fulfill these responsibilities?

4. Find and read a short story by Wainaina or another contemporary African writer that depicts African places and/or people. To what extent does the story you chose challenge the sterotypes Wainaina draws attention to in "How to Write about Africa"?

KATY WALDMAN

from THERE ONCE WAS A GIRL
AGAINST THE FALSE NARRATIVES OF ANOREXIA

This personal essay was published 7 December 2015 in the online magazine Slate; *Waldman is a columnist for the magazine.*

℮

My parents have a small framed photograph of E and me in their upstairs hall. We must be 6 or 7. We are smiling in someone's backyard, our heads damp from running through a sprinkler, and we wear matching checkered bathing suits—mine pink, hers blue. My sister is lissome. To my eye, critical even now, I'm a little chubby. We look nice together, like two parts of a whole, both grinning. We look like we know all each other's secrets.

A neighbor has painted a Princess Jasmine[1] diadem on my forehead—a brilliant band of turquoise with a fat yellow jewel in the center. I think I remember how excited I was, feeling the tickle of the brush and the colors spreading over my skin. E isn't wearing face paint in the picture. I think I remember that, too—my sister turning the offer down, on some level aware that she needed no embellishment.

As I grew up with that photograph, I started to see it differently. At first I loved my Jasmine crown, but eventually the bewitching strap of blue began to strike me as tacky. It had something in common with the gaudy excess of my stomach curving out beneath my swimsuit. I came to understand my nature. I was the girl who used every art supply in the box instead of picking the best few; I told circular, giddy stories; I flailed around the pool, the slowest swimmer on the team. I realized how elegant E had always been, how she eschewed splashy statements even in kindergarten. She had a native understanding of an aesthetic principle that I couldn't grasp. *Less is more.*

If you were to ask me when the spores of anorexia first crept into my heart, that's the moment I might point to, me standing in front of the picture in the hall and seeing it with fresh eyes. *There. Start there.*

---

1   *Princess Jasmine*   Character in the Walt Disney animated feature film *Aladdin* (1992).

5   Here is a story for you. My parents, D and J, are lovely and kind and interest-ing people. My twin sister (we're fraternal) is beautiful and accomplished. When we were 14, my sister developed anorexia, impelled by perfectionism, genes, whatever spectral lever it is that tilts the cosmic pinball board and then everything changes. When we were 17, *I* developed anorexia, impelled by some unpoetic cacophony of motivations: wanting to be close to her, wanting to compete with her, wanting to rescue her, wanting to cancel her out. E has a routine that's more or less stayed the same since eighth grade—it allows her to eat (not much) and exercise (a lot) without really asking why. My parents raged for a few years against the routine but at this point regard it as normal-ish. (Their habit of ignoring it and at times facilitating it indicates something between denial and acceptance.) Are they wrong? Who knows. As I write these words, my sister is an exceedingly thin, charismatic, disciplined woman who does brilliant work in her Ivy League Ph.D. program, and is unhappy.

    I, meanwhile, tried for years to undo what I'd done to myself. I saw nutritionists (and refused to follow the menus they gave me). I tried medica-tion (taken sporadically). After college, I moved back to my parents' house in Washington, found a spectacular therapist, and achieved a measure of clarity. It helped, strange as it may sound, that I was a miserable anorexic, convinced that the disease was deeply *wrong for me* yet unable to shake its influence. Until I did. The sunlight of the real world began to disinfect my brain. I had friends, books, a job I loved. I moved out of my parents' home. I got better.

    Even now I worry I'm telling the story wrong. *Is* E unhappy? Did my parents enable us in our sickness, or were they just powerless to reverse the tide? I can hardly conjure those years of my life in memory without thinking I've committed some grave narrative sin.

    I'm not the most reliable narrator. (To be fair, you probably aren't, either.) I spin stories about people in order to understand them better, or to soothe or entertain myself. I sometimes balance my sanity on unstable materials—love objects that don't stay put where I've left them. It can be hard to accept that your "characters"—Mom, Dad, sister—don't belong to you, the tale-teller.

    The narrative impulse is one entwined with anorexia itself. Being sick means constructing an alternate reality, strapping it in place with sturdy mantras, surrendering to the beguiling logic of an old fairy tale: *There once was a girl who ate very little. There once lived a witch in a deep, dark wood.* Anorexics are convinced that they are hideous, bad, and unlovable. At the same time, they are constantly soliloquizing about their sacrifice, their nobility, their ethereal powers.

10   "[A]norexia emerges less palpably as a humiliating physical and psycho-logical affliction than as an elevated state of mind, an intellectualized halluci-nation," wrote Ginia Bellafante in a review of *Going Hungry*, a collection of

essays on eating disorders. "To read *Going Hungry* is to suspect an effort has been made to convince us there is no such thing as a superficial anorexic, no creature whose radical self-regulation comes unaccompanied by an impressive imagination or intelligence." Was this—an overestimation of sensitivities, a beatification—my particular problem? I'm not sure. In the depths of my disorder, I didn't regard myself as a fragile poet-fairy or believe I could paint with all the colors of the wind.* But perhaps the myths of beauty girdling anorexia fed into how I idealized my *sister*, how I assumed that she presided over aesthetic secrets I'd never understand. And I certainly permitted the voice of the disease to mingle confusingly with my parents', so that I ended up ascribing to them the hate I sometimes felt for myself. A kind of self-protective/self-destructive logic drove me to pin my family and me on a storyboard.

The anorexic impulse to lyricize one's illness is a prescription for estrangement, for controlling and muffling the messy truths about who we are. Despite its promise of expressiveness, it is the enemy of writing. It is certainly the enemy of living. We need to tackle the false narratives clustered around eating disorders in our culture—clichés that vex and complicate treatment, contributing to low recovery rates and a frightening death toll. By looking harder at both the literature and the science of anorexia, we can expose where the plotlines conflict, where the self-deception and self-sabotage sneak in.

The most specific thing I can contribute is my story. I want to tell it as honestly and accurately as I can.

Anorexia is one of nature's bleaker illustrations of "monkey see, monkey do."* I learned how to torture my portion of dinner—to endlessly deconstruct and rebuild and microwave it—from my sister. I also learned from her how to sit up straight, even in front of the television, clenching my abs and jiggling my legs. Most of all, I learned to say no, over and over, regardless of rhyme or reason or incentive or penalty. *No*, I will not eat starch. *No*, I will not have another bite of chicken. *No*, I do not want dessert or breakfast or lunch; I am not hungry; I will not use my common sense; *no, no, no*. I am sure E picked up equally delightful tics from me. Her methods were openly antagonistic, mine more deceitful. I used to throw away food, hiding it in napkins or slipping it to the dog. ("K is Ziggy's *favorite*," Mom would tease as our flop-eared pit-bull mix trailed me around the kitchen. "I love you too, buddy!" I'd trill, while fixing him with a lethal stare: *Not. One. Fucking. Word.*)

The contagion also spreads through language. The charge that anorexia memoirs are "how-to manuals in disguise" is well-established by now: Writers from Emma Woolf (Virginia's* great-niece) to teens on eating disorder-related Internet forums have faced criticism for wreathing their anorexia stories in beckoning particulars: minutes on the treadmill, target weights attained, calories consumed. Thanks to the disease's competitive nature, these tidbits, ostensibly offered as warnings, can read as inspiring benchmarks or even veiled instructions. Recalling her student-sensei relationship with Marya Hornbacher's *Wasted*, "a cornerstone, a beloved, poetic contemporary classic" of eating disorder literature, the writer Kelsey Osgood reports that she "incorporated some of Hornbacher's tricks into my own weight loss repertoire."

15

More fundamentally, though, anorexia is an inveterate liar whose grand theme is your identity. Because the channels through which it flows and acts are so often linguistic, the disorder has inspired a perverse literary tradition, replete with patron saints (Catherine of Siena,[2] herself a twin, who recorded the details of her miraculous asceticism in letters she sent to aspiring female mystics), glamorous elders (Emily Dickinson, Anne Sexton, Sylvia Plath),[3] tropes (fairies, snow), and devices (paradox, irony, the unreliable narrator). "Anorexic literature" commits the inherently literary, self-mythologizing qualities of anorexia to paper. From the novels of Charles Dickens[4] to the poetry of Louise Glück,[5] it contains and reproduces something more amoebic, perhaps more dangerous, than dieting tips: a specific persona and sensibility.

Who is this gauntly bewitching character? Ask Persephone, the goddess undone by six pomegranate seeds,[6] or one of opera's frail, tubercular heroines. Ask Sia[7] singing scratchy-voiced about hurt and smallness, or even Tinker Bell,* wasp-waisted, gossamer-winged, sacrificing her body for love and literally a goner if we don't clap for her. I don't mean to be snide: The eating-disordered quest for an audience speaks more to profound self-alienation than to any diva tendencies. Anorexia is the mental health equivalent of the red shoes that make you dance until you die.[8] It is a performance—of femininity, of damage, of power—that turns into a prison. The choreography becomes so

---

2   *Catherine of Siena*   Catholic saint (1347–80) who engaged in intense fasting as a spiritual practice.

3   *Emily Dickinson ... Sylvia Plath*   All three of these poets are thought by some scholars to have experienced eating disorders.

4   *Charles Dickens*   Several Dickens novels feature self-effacing, slender young women, some of whom waste away and die.

5   *Louise Glück*   Acclaimed poet (b. 1943) who was diagnosed with anorexia as a young woman.

6   *Persephone ... seeds*   In Greek mythology, Persephone was abducted to the underworld, where she was tricked into eating pomegranate seeds before being allowed to leave. Because she had eaten food in the underworld, she was obliged to return there every year; her absence from the world of the living causes winter.

7   *Sia*   Australian singer-songwriter (b. 1975).

8   *red shoes ... you die*   Element in the Hans Christian Andersen fairy tale "The Red Shoes."

absorbing that you can no longer access your own will or desires. You may require an external party to confirm for you that you exist.

We've long linked pathological thinness to profundity or poetic sensitivity. The roots of the romance go back to Catherine, who felt closer to God when she stopped eating and later, unable to consume food in spite of herself, considered her affliction holy. If excess flesh on a woman implied gluttony (a sin) or pregnancy (a shame), emaciation helped demonstrate the soul's dominion over the body. Anorexia mirabilis—the saintly loss of appetite—signaled an embrace of Christ-like abnegation[9] and suffering, or else a spirituality too pure to incline toward earthly pleasures.

And guess what? The archetype of the fasting mystic had a daughter. Equally lovely, equally slender—in her the delicacy of spirit won out once more over the coarseness of tissue. She rebelled against her mother by applying her native rigor not to prayer, but to an artistic sort of femininity. Think Jane Eyre, "delicate and aerial," or Elizabeth Gaskell's Ruth, "little" and "beautiful lithe." Consider Dorothea Brooke from *Middlemarch*,[10] her "hand and wrist ... so finely formed that she could wear sleeves not less bare of style than those in which the Blessed Virgin appeared to Italian painters." That Mary* reference is not coincidental—like her mom, the new anorexic was pure and asexual. Yet she was also a creator, driven and intense. As Florence Nightingale wrote in 1852: "If [a woman] has a knife and fork in her hands during three hours of the day, she cannot have a pencil or brush." The new anorexic's hands overflowed with pencils and brushes. When she suffered, her suffering became oil paintings, poetry....

In *Going Hungry*, young adult author Francesca Lia Block equates anorexia with "that perfect blend of angelic and demonic—the faerie. Ethereal, delicate, able to fly." She recalls her time under the sprite's spell in an outrageously irresponsible bout of lyricism: "I stared out the windows at the twisting, starving trees, the silvery, sorrowful sky. I wrote strange, surreal poetry. My father stopped at a Dairy Queen, and I ate a vanilla cone. It tasted fearsome and frightening. Like mortality."

It makes me wish there were a Bad Sex in Fiction award, but for thinspo.[11]   20
And yet—who was one of my favorite authors as a preteen? I remember 1999, when I was 11 years old, my whole being magnetized to Block's waifish

---

9   *abnegation*   Self-sacrifice.

10   *Jane Eyre ... Middlemarch*   Jane Eyre, Ruth, and Dorothea Brooke are all characters in nineteenth-century novels.

11   *thinspo*   Thinspiration, a source of motivation for someone with very low body weight goals.

bohemians, her purple-haired witch babies and genie changelings. I remember the spicy explosions of jacaranda, the porch scents of tangerine and cinnamon, all the deferred deliciousness of imaginary pleasure. Block recounts "a kiss about apple pie a la mode with the vanilla creaminess melting in the pie heat. A kiss about chocolate, when you haven't eaten chocolate for a year." Why didn't it strike me as weird that she always used food metaphors to describe nonfoods? That her protagonists were unfailingly languid and small-boned and lean? Most of all, I remember the moment in *The Hanged Man* when the heroine declares: "I will be thin and pure like a glass cup." A glass cup! It seemed impossibly poetic. This was years before Alice Gregory poked fun at Block in the *New Yorker* for composing "laughably elliptical passages that read like demented ads for diamonds or bottled water."

Though their effect is hard to quantify, "a lot of war stories and memoirs out there ... glorify the specialness and suffering of anorexia," says Dr. Angela Guarda, director of the Johns Hopkins Eating Disorders Program. "Anecdotally, patients often acknowledge that these writings romanticize the disorder," and that "reading them can be triggering and worsen their ED."[12] While the actual disease is not glamorous at all, Guarda reiterates (do you remember the boring calorie records from Lena Dunham's *Not That Kind of Girl*? Imagine them as the script for your entire life), "the idea of anorexia often is." Doctors at Johns Hopkins generally discourage patients from reading most autobiographical accounts of eating disorders, including the not-inconsiderable portion written by authors who "describe themselves as recovered and appear to still be ill."

But what happened with me and Block felt like a slightly different thing. I wasn't anorexic (yet), she wasn't writing an anorexia memoir (explicitly), and I'm not sure how anyone could have known to intervene.

Sadness is "interesting," notes Leslie Jamison in her magisterial essay on female pain, "and sickness [is] its handmaiden, providing not only cause but also symptoms and metaphors: a wracking cough, a wan pallor, an emaciated body." Children want desperately to be interesting. Block's slender, graceful wraiths with their dark secrets appealed to my ambition and sense of drama, not to mention my kiddie narcissism. Here's one Blockian character indulging in a Petrarchan inventory[13] of her own gaunt figure: "My shoulders, my collar-bone, my rib cage, my hip bones like part of an animal skull, my small thighs. In the mirror my face is pale and my eyes look bruised. My hair is pale and thin and the light comes through." *Bones, small, mirror, hair, pale, eyes, thin, light.*

---

12 *ED* Eating disorder.

13 *Petrarchan inventory* The Italian writer Francesco Petrarca (1304–74) is best known for his sonnets, some of which describe the attributes of Laura, the object of his unrequited love.

The single syllables stream by like stars, all of them smooth, bright, reflective, or feminine. The hair's thinness allows the light in. Projecting myself into that body, I think I loved the implication that someone might pay close enough attention to me to worry about my collarbone.

Was my collarbone interesting, though? Did it "unfurl like a bird's wing"? ...

Maybe Louise Glück could teach me how to be beautiful.   25

That's what I thought in college, when I signed up for my first poetry class. The conscious hope was probably closer to *Maybe Louise Glück can teach me how to write beautifully,* but, in practice, they amounted to the same thing.

If Block embodies the anorexic sensibility at its most childish and theatrical, then the poetry of Glück (another *Going Hungry* contributor) gives it a mature shape. Excising and refusing her way into loveliness, Glück distills in her first few books something of the anorexic mindset. She distrusts flourish, noise, and glitter. She sends critics scrambling for stern phrases like "lean intensity" and "exacting precision." Just as an anorexic returns again and again to the same menu ingredients, the same routines, Glück shuffles and reshuffles her ascetic hand of nouns: *pond, ice, hill, moon, stars.* These early poems read as meticulous renunciations, careful puncturings undertaken in order to pare back the many false things from the few true ones.

Depressed and isolated in my post-college eating disorder, I dwelt obsessively on a trio of lines from "Persephone the Wanderer": "Unlike the rest of us, she doesn't know/ what winter is, only that/ she is what causes it." For me, it gave anorexia the status of a season, dignifying it with myth.

During my eating disorder years, I dreaded the chaos I might unleash at any moment, my secret flaws irrupting in plain sight. Anorexia told me I was gross but promised me safety as soon as I attained some enchanted state of skinniness. My perfect body would be my charm against interior disaster, sheltering me from the storms of the Underworld, enfolding me in eternal summer.

I starved, in other words, to acquire that old classical capability: metamorphosis. We tell stories for the same reason—to transform, elevate, and save.   30

A fantasy of anorexia: total expressivity. See the anorexic's sadness, legible on her anatomy, her inner life and emotions immediately present to anyone who looks at her. In a reverse transubstantiation, flesh becomes word, becomes character. Only the most authentic artist could possibly live her art like that.

By definition, a sign *means* something. What does a body mean? Tell me in words free of romance. *Free of blossom and subterfuge.* Tell me what winter is.

Anorexic literature, Jamison says, is "nostalgic for the belief that starving could render angst articulate." Its valorizing metaphors—"bone as hieroglyph, clavicle as cry"—ascribe "eloquence to the starving body, a kind of lyric grace."

I have nothing pretty to say about my body when I get too thin. My skin dulls and develops scaly patches; my oversized noggin bobs on my pencil-neck like an idiot balloon. Eating disorder memoirists love to fetishize hipbones, but I am here to tell you that mine made zero aesthetic contributions to my stomach area. My hair! Stringy, limp, bad for the Jews.[14]

35   But unloveliness aside, instrumentalizing my body—presenting it for others to read like a character in a text—proved a highly effective way of losing myself. I don't mean that simply in the theoretical sense. I mean that the act of starving yourself is one of the most alienating experiences you can possibly have. Have you ever tried to do *anything* on a profoundly empty stomach? Despite myths about increased concentration, intensity, or imagination, you feel like a trace of grime on a countertop. Sure, hunger energizes you at first— experts disagree over whether hyperactivity in anorexics is primarily the result of hormonal cues or the conscious desire to burn calories. But then the fatigue sets in. You feel like a torn net through which the thoughts pass, hazily. You cannot speak or write or do. Starving doesn't transform your life into one glorious act of self-expression. Starving silences who you really are.

A more scientific explanation for this is that anorexia eats your brain. As Arielle Pardes writes in *Vice*, "When your body is in a period of starvation, it uses the fattiest tissue first—which, in the absence of body fat, is the brain. The brain is literally broken down, piece by piece, causing mental fogginess, lack of concentration, and an inability to focus." (Luckily, such volume loss is usually reversible with weight restoration.) Starvation also reduces cortical blood flow, further slowing the cognitive machinery and allowing anorexia's distortions to take root....

In 1873, the French doctor Charles Lasègue and the English physician Sir William Gull (who personally practiced on Queen Victoria) independently published papers defining *anorexia nervosa*, the nervous loss of appetite. For Lasègue, the anorexic was "a young girl, between fifteen and twenty years of age," who "suffers from some emotion which she avows or conceals." "Generally," he continued, the symptoms relate "to some real or imaginary marriage project, to a violence done to some sympathy, or to some more or

---

14 *bad for the Jews* Phrase used (often tongue-in-cheek) by Jewish people, with reference to those Jews who, through their behavior or appearance, are considered to embarrass Jews as a group.

less conscient[15] desire." In a cosmically apt coincidence, Lasègue also fathered the Waldman-friendly concept of folie à deux—"a delusion or mental illness shared by two people in close association."

Gull, for his part, prescribed "various remedies ... the preparation of cinchona, the bichloride of mercury, syrup of the phosphate of iron, citrate of quinine and iron." Alas, "no perceptible effect followed their administration."

So dawned a long history of people getting anorexia wrong. We still don't know exactly what causes it. In part this is because the type of controlled longitudinal study that would shed light on etiology is too vast and expensive for most researchers to undertake. (Anorexia afflicts only 1 percent of the population, so any experiment tracking a randomized group of people to see who falls ill would need thousands of participants to get significant results.) It's also because the U.S. underfunds eating disorder research: The National Institutes of Health allots only $1.20 in research dollars per affected ED patient, compared with, for instance, $159 per patient with schizophrenia (which also affects about 1 percent of the population). Mostly, though, it's because eating disorders are savagely complicated, the consummation of multiple interwoven genetic, environmental, and cultural factors. The history of anorexia is a history of simplistic explanations—of false narratives—that derive their staying power from the tiny grain of truth each one contains.

A SELECTION OF ANOREXIA NARRATIVES THROUGH HISTORY

Hysterical Women
As Julie Hepworth points out in her book *The Social Construction of Anorexia Nervosa*, the terms *anorexia* and *hysteria* were used interchangeably throughout the late 19th century. Lasègue proposed that hysteria disrupted the "gastric centre," prompting food aversion. Gull originally referred to anorexia as *hysteria apepsia*, on the theory that neurasthenic[16] women suffered from a pepsin imbalance that dulled their appetites. In his 1884 lecture series *On Visceral Neuroses*, physician T. Clifford Allbutt suggested that, like hysterics, fasting girls were responding histrionically—aka *over-reacting*—to the day's gender imperatives. The "invincible distaste for food," he said, reflected a normal desire to tame "animal propensities" gone awry in "high-spirited" patients.

40

15　*conscient*　Conscious.

16　*neurasthenic*　Suffering from neurasthenia, a condition whose symptoms include lethargy, headache, and anxiety.

An Endocrine Disorder

In the early 1900s, doctors performed an autopsy on an anorexic woman and discovered a shrunken pituitary gland. Hypothesizing that the disease arose from low levels of pituitary hormone, they proposed a treatment in which eating-disordered patients were injected with pituitary extract. When that didn't work, the sufferers had their bloodstreams flooded with thyroid juices, insulin, and estrogen. It took until 1940 or so for lackluster results—apparently hormone shots *can* help treat an eating disorder, but only when they are accompanied by high-calorie foods—to discredit the notion of anorexia as a purely endocrinological illness.

Fear of Pregnancy

In 1939, George H. Alexander, a Freudian analyst from Rhode Island, published a paper describing an anorexic teenager who started dieting after two of her classmates got pregnant and left school. Alexander theorized that his patient was in thrall to a paranoid fantasy in which "fat" equaled "expecting" and food symbolized an "impregnating agent." The suspicion that anorexic individuals starved themselves to quell an irrational terror of pregnancy took two decades to shake.

Controlling Moms, Indifferent Dads

With the rise of family systems therapy in the '60s and '70s, doctors tried to divine answers to the anorexia question in the entrails of household dynamics. Eating disorders were (and occasionally are still) viewed as veiled power struggles between compliant kids and pressuring mothers. [Anna Krugovoy] Silver, the author of *Victorian Literature and the Anorexic Body*, writes that anorexia "is, at least in part, a power stratagem in which a girl refuses to eat in order to gain influence and attention in her family." The typical family in this scenario is "controlling and non-confrontational," the girl "a goal-oriented perfectionist" who "often has a problematic, conflicted relationship with her mother."

The Patriarchy

In the '80s, feminism transformed our understanding of anorexia once more. Books like Susie Orbach's *Fat Is a Feminist Issue* and Naomi Wolf's *The Beauty Myth* raised awareness about the unrealistic representations of female bodies in media. Eating disorders became potent symbols of the way society expected women to turn themselves into broken ornaments, shrinking their identities and ambitions. "By the '90s," wrote *Going Hungry* editor Kate Taylor in *Slate* in 2005, "health-class presentations on eating disorders often involved rifling through magazines and discussing how unreasonably skinny the models were." If we could only change societal beauty standards and diet culture, we could defeat anorexia for good.

None of these narratives are entirely without merit. Hormones probably   45
do play a role in eating disorders. Many women get sick on the threshold of
puberty, which has led doctors to isolate estrogen as a possible precipitating
factor. Both leptin (a satiety hormone synthesized in fat tissue) and ghrelin
(a hunger hormone produced in the stomach and pancreas) are processed by
the insula, an area of the brain that tends to malfunction in eating-disordered
patients. Individuals with anorexia also demonstrate elevated cortisol levels,
though their heightened stress could as easily be a corollary of starvation as a
cause.

And it is true that some anorexia patients have overbearing mothers. It is
equally true that watching your daughter starve and exercise herself to death
tends to activate your inner control freak. One study found similarly chaotic
and unhelpful parental behavior at family dinners involving anorexic children
and those involving children with cystic fibrosis, a condition in which the
patient is often too sick to eat.

And it's true that a desire to forestall growing up and all the adult milestones
that entails—sex, marriage, pregnancy—might inspire a girl to start dieting. So
could saturation in our thin-is-in culture. Any impetus that gets a teenage girl
to begin restricting calories can trip the biological wire that detonates an eating
disorder.

That's what these explanations leave out: *There is a biological wire.*
Otherwise, why wouldn't we all have anorexia, inundated as we are in
Photoshop, thigh gaps,* and ambient pressure to look like Cara Delevingne?[17]
(As Guarda, of the Johns Hopkins Eating Disorders Program, told me: "The
same rain falls on everyone, which points to some degree of individual
vulnerability.")

Conversely, why would anorexia erupt in Ghana and among the Amish,
where super-skinny frames aren't in vogue? And if eating disorders were
truly "about" control and remastering the self—especially in the face of a
domineering parent—then how should we parse all the girls with perfectly
happy, healthy childhoods who nevertheless fall under anorexia's spell? I don't
remember feeling lost or powerless when I started dieting at 17. I was simply
terrified of gaining weight.

The facts are: You are seven to 11 times more likely to become anorexic if   50
you have a first-degree relative with the disease, and identical twins run a 50 to
80 percent larger risk of developing anorexia than fraternal twins. Individuals
who go on to develop anorexia also exhibit common personality traits, such as
introversion, perfectionism, sensitivity to criticism, vigilance, competitiveness,
obsessiveness, and risk-aversion.

---

17 *Cara Delevingne* English actor and fashion model (b. 1992).

Biology is the piece of the puzzle that most directly contradicts societal myths about anorexia, and it's the one that has the hardest time finding traction. Drawing instead on family systems theory, doctors with young anorexic patients often recommend what National Institute of Mental Health Director Tom Insel calls a "parentectomy": "exclusion of the parents or caregivers from ... the treatment plan." But studies in both the U.S. and the U.K. show that "outcomes appear much better if parents are empowered and included." Likewise, many therapists treat eating disorders by attempting to crack some psychological code—to unearth the mysterious psychic forces driving the illness. They should be prioritizing nutrition and weight restoration: Regardless of what precipitated the initial dieting behavior, a lion's share of anorexic symptoms—from erratic hunger cues to obsessive thinking—result from physical changes to the starving brain. In other words, much of what propels anorexia is simply anorexia....

Sometimes I start eating, and I can't stop.

This part is hard to write, but it is also part of the narrative. As I dipped in and out of recovery after college, my disorder started to morph, losing any illusory claim it could have made on wan, heroic reserve or glamorous pallor or what have you. I stored up my denials. Then I binged on whole boxes of cereal, cartons of cookie dough ice cream, vats of raisins stirred into Nutella or hot fudge. The beginnings of these episodes were glorious—radiant increments of permission in a fascistically regulated life, Bosch gardens[18] in which all the naked people were made of marzipan. But the middles and ends were crushing. The conviction, post binge, that you are the most disgusting, worthless, execrable creature on Earth is total, as consuming a psychic pain as I have ever experienced. I'd walk to work wondering why people weren't throwing things at me. If a colleague was kind, I'd feel so ashamed and undeserving my eyes would tear up. Time after time, the emotional fallout from bingeing proved so excruciating I would vow to never, *never*, do it again. And then—surprise!—I would.

This twist in the anorexia story often goes untold, because it doesn't harmonize with the martyr-romance of the eating disorder. But overeating is a common response to the physiological and psychological stresses of starvation: More than one-half of anorexics will flirt with bulimia or binge-eating disorder on their path to recovery. "Restricting makes food more rewarding," says Carrie Arnold, author of *Decoding Anorexia: How Breakthroughs in Science Offer Hope for Eating Disorders*. "After billions of years of evolution, our

---

18 *Bosch gardens* Refers to the Hieronymus Bosch painting *The Garden of Earthly Delights*, which depicts fantastical landscapes occupied by nude people and bizarre creatures.

brains and bodies *really* don't want to starve." The chronically hungry contend with a primal drive not only to ease their immediate pangs but to counteract profound nutritional deficits. As Arnold explains, "a flashing neon sign in the eating disordered brain is saying gorge nonstop." For the most part, people with anorexia prove adept at ignoring it—until they don't....

I used to flinch at that photograph of my sister and me in our bathing suits. Now 55
I come back to it with questions in my hands. E was always perfectionistic and risk-averse—the anorexic profile. I spent so much time resenting her for "choosing" to act out her eating disorder. But looking at the image with more than a decade of hindsight, I feel like she never even had a chance.

I was the daughter who wasn't allowed to touch the coloring books because I just scribbled all over them. And yet I had done this—I had seen what E's anorexia had wrought, and I had decided: *me too*. I had skipped meals and counted calories and performed crunches until the illness reached through the mirror and grabbed me and it was too late. Were my parents right that (if I'm keeping score) I was the truly sick one? The girl without as potent a genetic predisposition who nevertheless called down the demon, mustered it through sheer force of will?

Then I look at the picture for a third time, and something else jumps out at me. E and I are both smiling hugely. We're *happy*. She's rigid, and I'm sloppy, but neither of us is sick.

Though it makes me sad, I love to imagine the alternate world in which the W twins never got anorexia, in which no circumstance held a match to our biological kindling and convulsed the lives we should have led. I love to imagine all the things we would have accomplished already, the relationships we would have nourished. I love to envision my mom and dad without the lines of worry on their faces from years of beseeching their daughters to eat, the relaxed holiday visits, the quirky interests we've all cultivated in so much time *not* spent squalling about food. I picture E and me standing next to each other, as adults, our bond unbroken, looking like two parts of a whole, two people who know each other's secrets.

Memory, though, has furnished me with the artifacts I have, and I can't help seeing them through the gauze of the old story. I kneel on the floorboards of this attic and look into a box, one containing knickknacks from a gentler past: my dad's sweaty, post-tennis bear hugs; the sound of my mom puttering around the kitchen in the morning as she brews coffee. Gingerly I take out and examine the delicate things. Each is light as an insect, its surface worn and luminous with use. I stare at the box, sadness opening in me like a flower. I am frozen, and on the stair I hear the footsteps of my life.

(2015)

Questions

1. Have you ever come across an instance of an eating disorder (or another mental illness) being romanticized in a piece of writing or other media? Discuss.

2. At any point, do you think Waldman's own writing falls into any of the problematic tropes that she discusses? If you think it does, provide specific examples; if you think it doesn't, explain how she avoids these tropes.

3. Consider any one of the "Anorexia Narratives through History" Waldman summarizes in paragraphs 40–44. How close or how far from the truth do you think the narrative you chose was? What cultural factors might have been at play when this narrative arose?

4. Why do you think eating-disorder research receives relatively little funding? Do you think this should change?

5. Many of the texts Waldman discusses are frequently taught in university and college English departments. What—if anything—should professors do to prevent or mitigate the potential harm she argues literary representations of anorexia can cause?

BRYAN THAO WORRA

HOW CAN WRITERS OF COLOR RECONCILE H.P. LOVECRAFT'S INFLUENCE WITH HIS RACIST LEGACY?

With his dreadful monsters and his vision of a bleak, incomprehensible universe, writer H.P. Lovecraft has exerted an enormous influence on twentieth- and twenty-first-century horror and science fiction. He was also venomously racist, sympathizing with Hitler and the Ku Klux Klan. Lovecraft expressed these views openly; in one editorial, for example, he wrote that "The negro is fundamentally the biological inferior of all White and even Mongolian races, and the Northern people must occasionally be reminded of the danger which they incur in admitting him too freely to the privileges of society and government." His racism has not prevented his work from attracting an ever-increasing readership, and his imaginative worlds have generated a spin-off culture of video games, films, and literature.

In this 2018 article from the online magazine Twin Cities Geek, *Laotian-American author Bryan Thao Worra considers his relationship to Lovecraft's work and the capacity of horror and science fiction to resonate with the experiences of Laotian-Americans.*

❧

August 20, 2018, marks the 128th birthday of the polarizing American writer H.P. Lovecraft. A resident of Providence, Rhode Island, he is best known in fandom for his interconnected stories collectively referred to as the Cthulhu mythos[1]—or Yog-Sothothery, as he is said to have preferred. A consistent joke is that the list of things he wasn't afraid of was shorter than the list of things he was, and that is clearly reflected in his writing. He's one of the

---

1   *Cthulhu mythos*   Named for the divinely powerful monster featured in "The Call of Cthulhu," this name is often given to the fictional universe in which Lovecraft's works are set.

most surprising figures of the early 20th century to survive into modern times, with much of his writing initially dismissed for any number of flaws by readers both of his time and of the present. Highlights include an often archaic and florid vocabulary, vagaries of description, and any number of plot holes and formulaic techniques that either thrill you or appall you. "God, that hand! The window! The window!" indeed.

Since Lovecraft's death, we've seen numerous artists and writers cite his work as influences, including George R.R. Martin, Stephen King, Jorge Luis Borges, Neil Gaiman, Douglas Adams, and more. Some have drawn inspiration with great reverence; others, considerably less so. In full disclosure, I'm one of those so influenced—I hold a lifetime membership in the H.P. Lovecraft Historical Society, and I've written multiple books strongly featuring Lovecraftian poetry through a Lao American refugee lens. My award-winning poetry collection *DEMONSTRA*, which turns five this year, was released by Canada's Innsmouth[2] Free Press and responded significantly to many of the themes, ideas, and creations of Lovecraft and his fellow writers. My poem "The Pearl in the Shadows" opened the Martian Migraine anthology *Cthulhusattva*. And later this fall, my Lao Lovecraftian short story "A Model Apartment" is being reprinted in the Afrofuturist anthology *Sunspot Jungle* from Rosarium Publishing.

However, I certainly appreciate the opinion Dr. Nnedi Okorafor and others have that it's impossible to separate Lovecraft's racism from his legacy, and I absolutely think all writers should read some of the blistering critiques of his relationship to white supremacy and consider for themselves where they might stand on these issues. For a few strange eons, I was of the opinion that if someone was teaching themselves how to be racist by reading the work of Lovecraft, there was something pitiable about the matter, although it doesn't always seem so outlandish a premise as it once was.

One of the interesting challenges for writers of color is how to reconcile with these elements of Lovecraft's work. How do we turn a blind eye to it? Everyone will find their own level of water, certainly, and in my own experience I found it to be a continuum. Some days you just walk away entirely. Others you could feel compelled by some of the larger ideas he was aiming at and focus on those. Or perhaps you might try to draw inspiration for your work from the influences Lovecraft cited, like Lord Dunsany.[3]

5 For me, Kurodahan Press's 2002 release of the Lairs of the Hidden Gods series, collections of Cthulhu stories by weird writers of Japan, was significantly liberating for me. To see nonwhite writers besides myself taking on the

2   *Innsmouth*   Fictional town used as a setting by Lovecraft and his imitators.

3   *Lord Dunsany*   Pen name of Anglo-Irish fantasy writer Edward Plunkett, 18th Baron of Dunsany (1878–1957).

material suggested that there could be ways to work within the Cthulhu mythos after all. I later came to work frequently with Silvia Moreno-Garcia as she and her fellow writers at Innsmouth Free Press wrestled with these and other challenges of what Lovecraftian fiction means to women and people of color. There were many interesting successes in working with the themes and the tropes without descending into the racist or the misogynist. Some critics may disagree, but for the five years it ran, I think they made a good go at Innsmouth Free Press to find a middle ground and to push the possibilities of the better ideas that could be salvaged. History will see who prevails, over time.

Today you can go into any number of geek spaces and find them festooned with Lovecraftian objects. The author's most notable creation, the Great Old One Cthulhu, largely descended into parody as an unusually buff squid god slumbering deep beneath the oceans in the alien city of R'lyeh. Acclaimed game designer Sandy Petersen has spent the better part of the 2010s completing his work of bringing to life *Cthulhu Wars*, a massive board game inspired by the monsters of the Cthulhu mythos, and he's consistently received support to immortalize these terrors in plastic. And of course, Minnesota's Fantasy Flight Games has a whole collection of Lovecraft-inspired titles. So although the World Fantasy Award that Okorafor wrote about replaced its Lovecraft bust with a different statuette starting in 2016, there's little sign of interest in Lovecraft's work waning any time soon, elder or otherwise.

But the question remains: how do writers like me work with the controversial nature of Lovecraft? I often ask myself this as I reflect on the imaginative needs I had as a young Southeast Asian refugee finding his way through the cosmos—or at least, the American Midwest in the 1980s. Earlier this year, the Cambodian writer Bunkong Tuong wrote about how the Cure[4] helped him as a refugee when he first arrived in the US, and that resonates with me as I think about my odd relationship to the Cthulhu mythos, which began in the pre-Internet era.

In the 1980s, my first encounters with Lovecraft's work were the very crude advertisements for Chaosium's pen-and-paper *Call of Cthulhu* role-playing game, even as no one around me could remotely tell me how to pronounce "Cthulhu." I initially gave it very little thought. For some reason I ran into Lovecraft's work years later when it was being passed around on the bus by several older high-school kids properly regarded as unpleasant, antisocial bullies. Now, 30 years later, I can't really tell you why they let me borrow their copy of *The Lurking Fear*, or why I'd be interested at all in what scuzzy kids like those were reading. But to my surprise, I enjoyed the variety of quick, short reads in an eerie horror I'd never run into in school before. I still hated the

---

4   *the Cure*   Gothic rock/new wave band that became popular in the 1980s.

bullies, but at least I had something new to read, and it gave us something to talk about, even as it was clear how contemptuous we were of each other. Life was weird back then.

While I do not condone their behavior with or without their reading of Lovecraft, I suppose there was a particular kind of mental gymnastics that made me hopeful that maybe terrible people having an interesting taste in art meant there was some humanizing form of hope for almost anyone. I'll put together an essay on youthful naïveté another time. In the end, more of Lovecraft's work slithered its way onto my bookshelves over the decades, from the art of Gahan Wilson to role-playing games and at least one Cthulhu Christmas card for some reason. Chaosium even issued a Miskatonic University[5] student kit complete with a bumper sticker for the Fighting Cephalopods,[6] which I have kept longer than the bumper stickers for my own real-life college. Go 'Pods!

10   As for the larger picture?

Over the years, as I've tried to do my part to rebuild a postwar Lao literary tradition among my fellow refugees, I argued for years, somewhat heretically, that the work of Lovecraft might be a better influence on our literature than many examples of contemporary writing, whether from the Asian American community or mainstream literature. Is it possible that *The Shadow over Innsmouth* might capture our experience better than toxic themes of affluence in *Crazy Rich Asians*?[7] I still think there's a conversation to be held on this. In my experience over the decades, most Lao much preferred an old ghost story to *The World According to Garp*[8] or the angst of *Dawson's Creek*.[9] Films like *Blade Runner*[10] and its diverse Los Angeles of 2019, a world complete with Cambodian street geneticists, seemed more daring than *American Beauty*[11] or *The Great Gatsby*.[12]

---

5   *Miskatonic University*   Fictional university appearing in stories and role-playing games based on the Cthulhu Mythos.

6   *Fighting Cephalopods*   Football team at the fictional Miskatonic University.

7   *Crazy Rich Asians*   2013 novel by Kevin Kwan that formed the basis for a 2018 romantic comedy film of the same title. The film, which featured a predominantly Asian cast, was praised by most critics, but some argued that the film reinforced racial stereotypes and glorified extreme wealth.

8   *The World According to Garp*   1978 novel by John Irving that formed the basis for a 1982 film starring Robin Williams.

9   *Dawson's Creek*   Popular teen drama TV series (1998–2003).

10   *Blade Runner*   Influential 1982 science fiction film set in the year 2019.

11   *American Beauty*   1999 film about an upper-middle-class man who becomes infatuated with a teenage girl.

12   *The Great Gatsby*   1925 novel by F. Scott Fitzgerald about a millionaire in Long Island; it has been adapted into film several times, including by Baz Luhrmann in 2013.

In *DEMONSTRA*, I wanted to test whether the language and tropes of Lovecraft might be effective for probing sensitive inner experiences of the Lao in diaspora. A central question I had been asking was, "What's honestly scary to a 600-year-old culture that was secretly carpet-bombed and Agent Oranged during our bloody 20-year civil war?"[13] When we see so many stories of the postapocalypse in American media, it's a strange question, since Laos already had its apocalypse in the 1960s and '70s. One Lao nonprofit organization, Legacies of War, points out: "From 1964 to 1973, the U.S. dropped more than two million tons of ordnance on Laos during 580,000 bombing missions— equal to a planeload of bombs every 8 minutes, 24-hours a day, for 9 years" of our conflict. Over 30 percent failed to explode immediately and still contaminate the Lao countryside 40 years after the end of that bombing. Through such experiences, a society emerges with a drastically different view of the cosmos, true horror, and the rationality of the world after this sort of thing.

When I would read a story like *The Shadow over Innsmouth*, it felt more relevant to our journey than most of the refugee narratives on the market. Someone arrives in town to discover peculiar folks are nice at first, then turn into monstrous horrors who have bizarre traditions they want the protagonist to partake in? That's an oversimplification, certainly, but the seeds are there to be sown. It can be sensitive to have a conversation on the real politics that ignited the Laotian Secret War,[14] but a conversation on an alien war between Great Old Ones and Elder Things, with poor humanity caught between mindless horrors duking it out? There's a tale that could be told, although not without its complications. Are the Great Old Ones NATO or the Warsaw Pact[15] to Lovecraft's Elder Things and Elder Gods? Lovecraft's Fungi from Yuggoth appear in *The Whisperer in Darkness*; there, the reader learns these creatures take the brains of their victims to their distant planet in shiny metal cylinders. Simple science-fiction horror or an interesting metaphor for the cultural brain drain of a country as refugees board the metal cylinders of American planes to escape to safety?

---

13 *Agent Oranged ... civil war* Agent Orange is an extremely toxic chemical weapon most infamously used by the American military during the Vietnam War (1954–75) and in related wars such as the Laotian Civil War (1959–75). The Civil War in Laos was linked to the global Cold War (1947–91) that pitted a coalition of nations led by the United States against a coalition led by Russia. American and Russian involvement made the Civil War incredibly destructive to Laos.

14 *Laotian Secret War* The Civil War is sometimes referred to by this name because the United States did not declare its involvement despite significant participation in the conflict.

15 *NATO or the Warsaw Pact* NATO (the North Atlantic Treaty Organization) and the Warsaw Pact represented military alliances on opposite sides of the Cold War.

To be absolutely clear, one should not look *only* to Lovecraft for interesting ideas, especially refugee communities. There are times I find elements of his writing stomach churning. But frankly, I also find no shortage of other writers to read, genre and nongenre, who have held dismissive, contemptuous, racist, misogynistic, ableist, nationalistic, and paternalistic views of my people and especially my students. It's practically the entire body of world literature, despite the march of progress. But if I could find something to salvage from that body to help us speak to the human experience in even the lesser writers of the world, I felt there's some worthy measure of hope for all of us. Considering the alternative of imitating mere stock colonial narrative, I felt we were obliged to try.

15   If I encouraged my community to read only safe, respectable literature touching on Laos, we'd find our people depicted typically as the faceless, coolies,[16] or the enemy. In the works of writers like H.P. Lovecraft, and others, I felt we could at least start to flip the script and assert our true authentic voice from an unexpected direction. When I began writing in earnest, I had a desire to avoid many of the colonial, imperialist, and feudal trappings that disempower us. I saw science fiction, fantasy, and horror as a way to discuss our journeys and to empower ourselves, even as there can be no doubt these genres are filled with any number of paranoid and small-minded figures who may know how to put a sentence together but not necessarily an inclusive core. But like any zone of literature, one works at it.

Laos needed art that engaged our experience without reinforcing clichés that painted us simply as Vietnam Lite or an iteration of *Apocalypse Now*, *Full Metal Jacket*,[17] or the forgettable *Air America*, a Mel Gibson and Robert Downey Jr. vehicle that remains one the biggest Hollywood movies to date about our war. If Lao American art merely looks and sounds like *The Joy Luck Club*[18] run through a suburban blender, we're not pushing ourselves when this is the precise moment to push.

Now that we have at last a more diverse body of works to respond to and grow from, the time may come very soon for Lovecraft's place among the immortals of science fiction and fantasy to sink beneath the cold waves, and the stars might never be right again for his return. But I do thank him for opening up the doors to the many possibilities within his vast, uncaring, indifferent universe, for all of its forbidden horrors and unspeakable knowledge. That it

---

16   *coolies*   Derogatory term for unskilled Chinese and South Asian laborers.

17   *Apocalypse Now, Full Metal Jacket*   Classic American films about the Vietnam War.

18   *The Joy Luck Club*   Amy Tan's 1989 novel was adapted into a film in 1993. Both explore the relationships and cultural clash between four Chinese American women and their mothers.

could be glimpsed, expressed, and faced? For a Lao youth in a quiet corner of America, that acknowledgment was a strange and reassuring comfort—one that made all of the difference when it came to picking up his own pen.

(2018)

Questions

1. Worra writes that he "saw science fiction, fantasy, and horror as a way" for refugee writers "to discuss our journeys and to empower ourselves" (paragraph 15).

   a. What does Worra suggest these genres offer that other, more realistic genres don't?

   b. In your own view, what are the relative merits of realism and of fantasy/sci-fi/horror as ways of exploring political and philosophical questions in fiction?

2. Worra notes that, while several major American films attempt to depict the Vietnam War, only a few lesser-known films depict the war in Laos (paragraph 16). Why do you think the Laotian Civil War is not as frequently addressed in American popular culture as its counterpart in Vietnam?

3. Worra writes: "Now that we have at last a more diverse body of works to respond to and grow from, the time may come very soon for Lovecraft's place among the immortals of science fiction and fantasy to sink beneath the cold waves" (paragraph 17). Think of an artist who has been accused of racism or sexual misconduct. How do the allegations impact your understanding of and appreciation for their work?

4. Find a film, story, visual work, game, or other piece of art that is linked to the Cthulhu mythos and analyze it in light of Worra's argument. To what extent (if at all) would you describe the work you chose as racist, misogynist, ableist, or otherwise prejudiced? To what extent (if at all) would you describe the work as countering such prejudices?

5. Worra alludes to H.P. Lovecraft's reputation as a racist, an anti-Semite, and a white supremacist. Do your own research on this topic. What other information could the author have provided to support this assertion?

6. Read the selection from Katy Waldman's "There Once Was a Girl" reprinted in this anthology. Compare and contrast Waldman and Worra's treatments of prejudice in classic literature.

KRISTEN GILCHRIST

from "NEWSWORTHY" VICTIMS?

In December 2015, the federal government of Canada launched a National Inquiry into Missing and Murdered Indigenous Women. Aboriginal activists had for years been pressuring the government to respond to the disproportionate frequency of violent crime experienced by Aboriginal women: Aboriginal women constitute 2% of Canada's female population but 10% of the country's female homicide victims. Activists have questioned the roles of the government, police, and media in creating a situation in which the murders and disappearances of Aboriginal women have long gone underreported, and in which there has been a lack of public outcry outside Aboriginal communities. In the following article, Kristen Gilchrist analyzes trends in media coverage of the murders of white women and Aboriginal women. The article was first published in the journal Feminist Media Studies *in 2010.*

❦

ABSTRACT

More than 500 Aboriginal women have gone missing or been murdered in Canada since the 1980s yet press attention to this violence is relatively minimal. This paper compares local press coverage of matched cases: three missing/murdered Aboriginal women from Saskatchewan and three missing/murdered White women from Ontario. Quantitative and qualitative content analyses indicate stark disparities in the amount and content of coverage between groups. The Aboriginal women received three and a half times less coverage; their articles were shorter and less likely to appear on the front page. Depictions of the Aboriginal women were also more detached in tone and scant in detail in contrast to the more intimate portraits of the White women. Drawing on feminist media studies and theories of intersectionality, this paper argues that the simultaneous devaluation of Aboriginal womanhood and idealization of middle-class White womanhood contributes to broader systemic inequalities which re/produce racism, sexism, classism, and colonialism. This paper raises concerns about the broader implications of the relative invisibility of missing/

murdered Aboriginal women in the press, and their symbolic annihilation from the Canadian social landscape.

INTRODUCTION

Accounting for 2 percent of Canada's population, Aboriginal women are overrepresented as victims of sexual and physical violence and homicide.[1] Aboriginal women aged 25–44 are five times more likely to experience a violent death than any other Canadian woman (Department Of Indian & Northern Affairs 1996). Emerging research has shown that more than five hundred Aboriginal women from all walks of life have gone missing and/or been murdered in Canada since the 1980s—and this number continues to grow (Jacobs & Williams 2008; Native Women's Association of Canada [NWAC] 2008).[2] In the majority of cases the missing women were later found murdered, many in sexual homicides. Nearly half of murder cases remain unsolved (NWAC 2009).

This paper adopts a feminist intersectional approach emphasizing the multiple and connecting dimensions of inequality (Collins [1990] 2000). The intersectional/interlocking nature of racism, sexism, classism, and colonialism compound the vulnerabilities faced by Aboriginal women in Canada (Gilchrist 2008; Larocque 2007; McIvor 2007; Smith 2005). The racialization of Aboriginal women—the process by which they are racially marked and subjected to institutional and everyday racism (Jiwani & Young 2006)—is inextricably linked with and mutually constituted by these other oppressions (Monture-Angus 1995). The material effects of these interconnected disadvantages have led an advocacy group to proclaim Aboriginal women "the most victimized group in Canadian society" (The Elizabeth Fry Society of Saskatchewan, cited in Henry & Tator [2000] 2006, p. 121).

First, I draw on literature outlining the features of a newsworthy crime and victim, with particular emphasis on studies highlighting racial biases in news reporting of violent crimes against women. Next, I present research findings revealing significant disparities in press coverage of Aboriginal and White missing/murdered women. While the press demonstrated a continued, committed, and compassionate response to the White women, depicting them as "the girl next door," the Aboriginal women were largely ignored and thus relegated to the status of invisible "Others" (Jiwani & Young 2006). Links are made

---

1 [Gilchrist's note]   The terms Aboriginal, Native, First Nations, and Indigenous are used interchangeably. These are umbrella terms used to describe various First Nations, Inuit, and Métis communities and Nations in Canada.

2 [Gilchrist's note]   Missing refers to cases where women have disappeared under suspicious circumstances, with a strong likelihood that they may have been killed. Murdered refers to cases where missing women are found to be/identified as victims of homicide.

between the intersecting disadvantages experienced by Aboriginal women and the value judgments made by news organizations about what constitutes a crime or victim worthy of attention, or, who and what is *newsworthy*. Lastly, I explore how press disparities promote the symbolic annihilation, or systematic exclusion, trivialization, and marginalization of Aboriginal women's experiences (Sonwalkar 2005; Tuchman 1978).

NEWSMAKING AND NEWSWORTHINESS

5 Tuchman (1976, p. 97) referred to the news as "a constructed reality," while Cohen and Young (1973, p. 97) suggested that the news is "manufactured by journalists," and Schudson (1989, p. 265) pointed out that "news items are not simply selected but constructed." Rather than objectively reporting events and facts, newsmakers engage in a highly subjective and selective process of news production based on socially and culturally constructed criteria (Fowler 1991; Jewkes 2004; Zelizer 2005). Notably, decisions about who/what is newsworthy are filtered through a predominantly Western, White, heteronormative, middle-class, male lens (Henry & Tator [2000] 2006)....

GENDER, RACE, AND VIOLENCE IN THE NEWS

Hall (1973) argued that, of the millions of events that occur daily across the world, only a very tiny fraction will actually become part of the daily news landscape. Along the same lines, Meyers (1997) identified a hierarchy of crime operating in the news media, meaning that not all crimes are seen as equally newsworthy (see also Jewkes 2004). Severe violence, especially murder, is seen as most newsworthy, and young and elderly White females in particular receive considerable attention (Dowler 2004a, pp. 575–576). Sexually motivated homicides perpetrated by someone unknown to the victim will "invariably receive substantial, often sensational attention" (Jewkes 2004, p. 48). Previous literature has indicated that news stories exaggerate the risks of violent crimes faced by high-status White women (Reiner [1995] 2003, p. 386).

Carter (1998) and Jewkes (2004) have drawn attention to how particular forms of violence against women are deemed too routine or ordinary by newsmakers to be considered newsworthy. For instance, physical and sexual violence committed in the home, by acquaintances, and/or that is non-fatal, tends to fall at the bottom of the hierarchy of crime and is left off the news agenda. It is also useful to consider that the news media perpetuate a hierarchy of female victims, meaning that not all women who have experienced violence are treated equally. Media representations of violence against women often emphasize binary categories which differentiate "good" from "bad" women. "Good" women are seen as innocent and worth saving or avenging, whereas "bad" women are positioned as unworthy victims and beyond redemption

(Jiwani 2008). Like social relations in general, this binary is deeply tied to race and class. Traditionally, it has been middle-class White women who have been constructed as "innocent" and "good" (Collins [1990] 2000). The idealization, or placing of certain bodies in higher regard, subordinates and relegates bodies—in particular "raced" or racialized female bodies—to the status of "Others" (Crenshaw 1991; Mclaughlin 1991).

What must be underscored is that binaries of good/bad, worthy/unworthy, pure/impure, and the like, are relational and mutually dependent on one another. In other words, these binaries develop in the context of each other and each is inextricably bound to the other (Collins 1998). In order for there to be a "bad," "unworthy," "impure," "disreputable" woman/victim there must simultaneously be a "good," "worthy," "pure," and "respectable" woman/victim against whom she is judged. Simplistic binaries produce/reproduce hegemonic assumptions about acceptable and deviant expressions of femininity (Madriz 1997). Idealized depictions of heterosexual, able-bodied, middle-class, attractive White women have become the metaphor for "innocence" both in news discourse and in society more generally (Jewkes 2004; Wilcox 2005). The ideologies of human superiority and inferiority underlying these binaries encourage the valuing of some lives over others and act as powerful justifications for continued racial, gender, and class-based oppression (Collins [1990] 2000)....

Meyers (1997) argued that compared with high-status White women, poor and/or racialized crime victims are often depicted in the news as more blameworthy for their victimization. To illustrate, in sexual assault and sexual homicide cases, if a victim is judged to have deviated from patriarchal notions of appropriate feminine behavior by drinking/using drugs, dressing provocatively (or not conservatively), and especially if she engages in sex for money, she is likely to be constructed as, at least partially, responsible for violence against her (Ardovi-Brooker & Caringella-Macdonald 2002; Jiwani & Young 2006; Madriz 1997). Likewise, Mclaughlin (1991) found that television representations of prostitution tended to align the dangers of sex work with the sex worker herself, and accordingly assigned victims rather than offenders blame for violence. As pointed out by Wilcox (2005, p. 529), the presumption in the news media is that male offenders are guilty only to the extent that their female victims are innocent.

In her analysis of Canadian news discourses of the more than sixty missing/murdered women from a poverty-stricken area in Vancouver's Downtown Eastside, Jiwani (2008) argued that because many of the victims were poor sex workers and/or Aboriginal, the women were labeled as "high-risk," implying that violence occurred because women put themselves at risk because of their bad choices. This discourse blames women and obscures the unequal

10

social conditions which governed and shaped "choices" made under these circumstances. Aboriginal scholar Martin-Hill (2003) maintained that the disappearances/murders of the Downtown Eastside women and the high number of missing/murdered Aboriginal women in Canada, signals that Aboriginal women are viewed as disposable and so brutal victimization against them is justified because victims are stigmatized as prostitutes, street people, and addicts—even if they are not. The invocation of such stereotypes mitigates the seriousness of their victimization; signaling to the public that crimes against them do not matter. Degrading stereotypes also render racialized women's experiences of violence invisible, especially in relation to high-status White victims (Ardovi-Brooker & Caringella-Macdonald 2002)....

The racial and social status of female victims also influences whether crimes against them are reported at all (Chermak 1995; Dowler, Fleming & Muzzatti 2006). In a study of local crime newscasts in Canada and the United States, Dowler (2004b) established that minority crime victims received not just a less sympathetic tone of news reporting but also less media attention than White victims (cited in Dowler, Fleming & Muzzatti 2006; see also Meyers 1997). In the United States, Black and Hispanic male and female crime victims face a higher likelihood than Whites of receiving no coverage at all (Buckler & Travis 2005). Likewise, in his study of press coverage of crime in Toronto, Ontario, Canada, Wortley (2002) found that Black female crime victims rarely made it on the front page of the newspaper, were relegated to the back pages, or not mentioned at all. Entman and Rojecki's (2001) study of broadcast news in Chicago ascertained that the ratio of time spent on White (male and female) victims compared to Black victims exceeded three to one. Blacks while underrepresented as victims were overrepresented as perpetrators....

Much of the Canadian literature about missing/murdered women focuses on the Downtown Eastside women and how their criminalized statuses as poor, drug-using, sex workers falling outside of societal expectations of the "good"/"worthy" victims influenced news reaction to the cases (Gilchrist 2008; Jiwani 2008; Jiwani & Young 2006; Martin-Hill 2003). My research diverges considerably from previous analyses in that it contrasts press coverage of Aboriginal and White missing/murdered women who are matched in other ways. The Aboriginal women in the study have been selected because they are those who by all accounts "fit in." Such a research design allowed me to build on the previous studies above by determining what difference it made to media coverage simply that women were Aboriginal or White, when they were very similar in other respects.

CASES

The focus of my analyses was on six cases. The disappearances/murders of three Aboriginal women from Saskatchewan: Daleen Bosse (age 26) who disappeared in Saskatoon, and Melanie Geddes (age 24) and Amber Redman (age 19) who disappeared in the Regina area. The coverage of these cases was contrasted with that of three White women from Ontario: Ardeth Wood (age 27) who went missing in Ottawa, Alicia Ross (age 25) who vanished in the Toronto area, and Jennifer Teague (age 18) who disappeared in the Ottawa area. All six women disappeared during the spring and summer months between 2003 and 2005. Four of the women, Amber Redman, Melanie Geddes, Alicia Ross, and Jennifer Teague disappeared within a seven week period in the summer of 2005. All six young women attended school or were working and maintained close connections with friends and family. None had known connections with the sex industry nor were they believed by their families to be runaways.[3]

METHODS AND FINDINGS

My objective was to explore whether there were identifiable differences in local press reporting of missing/murdered Aboriginal and White women. To gather data for comparison I utilized the *Canadian Newsstand* online newspaper database and searched for articles printed about each woman from the first day of coverage about her disappearance through November 30, 2006. Local newspapers were selected given Greer's (2003) emphasis on the importance of spatial and cultural proximity in determining the newsworthiness of an event. The most widely read local newspapers corresponding with the city where each woman disappeared/was murdered, were selected for quantitative and qualitative content analyses.[4] Quantitative content analysis is a methodological approach which codes print and visual text(s) into categories and then counts the frequencies and occurrences of each (Ahuvia 2001; Reason & Garcia 2007). The quantitative component of this research consisted of counting and comparing the number of times victims were mentioned in any capacity in their

3   [Gilchrist's note]   During the time period explored for this research, all of the White women were found to be victims of homicide and White male perpetrators were criminally charged. By contrast, only Melanie Geddes was identified as murdered during this time. At the time of this article's publication, her perpetrator(s) remain at large. It was not until 2008 that evidence led police to the discovery of both Amber Redman and Daleen Bosse's remains. In early 2009, an Aboriginal man pled guilty to the second-degree murder of Amber Redman. A White man awaits trial in the murder of Daleen Bosse.

4   [Gilchrist's note]   The *Saskatoon Star-Phoenix* was selected for Daleen Bosse and the *Regina Leader-Post* was selected for Amber Redman and Melanie Geddes. The *Toronto Star* was selected for Alicia Ross's case while the *Ottawa Citizen* was selected for its local coverage of Ardeth Wood and Jennifer Teague.

respective local newspapers, the number of articles addressing the victims and their cases specifically, the number of words printed about the victims in these articles, and the placement of articles within the newspaper.

15   Interpretive content analysis goes beyond simply quantifying explicit elements of the text and thus was used to supplement my quantitative findings. A qualitative or interpretive analysis seeks to understand the subtle meanings and implications of the text(s) and is considered a more holistic approach to understanding context as well as content (Ahuvia 2001; Reason & Garcia 2007). Headlines, articles, and accompanying photographs were analyzed and specific attention was paid to the language used to describe and memorialize the victims, the general tone and themes in the coverage, information that was present in some articles but missing in others, and the types of photographs presented. Sixty articles—ten for each woman—were selected for in-depth analysis. Articles longer than three hundred words which discussed the cases at several integral points were selected, including the initial disappearance, subsequent searches, police investigations, memorials, community rallies, and vigils.

Amount of Coverage

When the number of articles mentioning the White and Aboriginal women in any capacity were counted, it was found that the White women were mentioned in the local press a total of 511 times compared with only eighty-two times for the Aboriginal women; more than six times as often (see Table 1).

When this analysis was broken down to include only articles discussing the missing/murdered women's cases specifically, disparities remained. The Aboriginal women garnered just fifty-three articles compared with 187 articles for the White women; representing three and a half times less coverage overall for the Aboriginal women (see Table 2).

There were 135,249 words published in articles related to the White women's disappearances/murders and 28,493 words about the Aboriginal women; representing a word count of more than four to one for the White women (see Table 3).

Further, articles about the White women averaged 713 words whereas Aboriginal women's articles averaged 518 words; 1.4 times fewer words (see Table 4).

Placement

20   Thirty-seven percent of articles about the White women appeared on the front page versus 25 percent of articles about Aboriginal women. It was not uncommon in the White women's cases—especially in the *Ottawa Citizen*'s coverage—for text and photographs to take up several pages of news or city sections.

TABLE 1

Comparison of Number of Articles That Mention Victims in Any Capacity

White victims	Number of times mentioned in local press	Aboriginal victims	Number of times mentioned in local press
Ardeth Wood	253	Daleen Bosse	16
Alicia Ross	61	Amber Redman	37
Jennifer Teague	197	Melanie Geddes	29
Total	511	Total	82
Average	170	Average	27

TABLE 2

Comparison of Number of Articles Discussing Victims/Case

White victims	Number of articles written about case	Aboriginal victims	Number of articles written about case
Ardeth Wood	82	Daleen Bosse	14
Alicia Ross	33	Amber Redman	26
Jennifer Teague	72	Melanie Geddes	13
Total	187	Total	53
Average	62	Average	18

TABLE 3

Comparison of Number of Words Printed about Victims (using Table 2 data)

White victims	Number of words printed in articles	Aboriginal victims	Number of words printed in articles
Ardeth Wood	61,809	Daleen Bosse	6,559
Alicia Ross	22,616	Amber Redman	15,638
Jennifer Teague	50,824	Melanie Geddes	6,296
Total	135,249	Total	28,493
Average	45,083	Average	9,498

TABLE 4

Comparison of Average Number of Words Printed about Victims (using Table 2 data)

White victims	Average number of words per article	Aboriginal victims	Average number of words per article
Ardeth Wood	747	Daleen Bosse	469
Alicia Ross	685	Amber Redman	601
Jennifer Teague	706	Melanie Geddes	484
Total	2,138	Total	1,554
Average	713	Average	518

On the day that police/coroners identified the murdered body of Ardeth Wood there were nine articles printed about the case; two on the front page and seven in the "A"/news section.

Additional analysis of newspapers on microfiche obtained from the *National Archives of Canada* demonstrated that Aboriginal women's articles tended to be hidden amongst advertisements and soft news.[5]* In the majority of instances greater space and prominence was given to events of much lesser significance, for example, an article about an October snowfall entitled "Snowfalls in the southeast" (*Regina Leader-Post* 2005d, p. A1), a picture of two geese in the street with a caption that reads "A LITTLE OFF COURSE" (*Saskatoon Star-Phoenix* 2005a, p. A3), a photograph of classic cars accompanied by the headline, "CLASSICS: Summer is a great time for car lovers" (*Regina Leader-Post* 2005c, p. B1), and a photograph depicting flowers from "The Lily Society" (*Regina Leader-Post* 2005a, p. A12).

Articles discussing memorials to remember missing/murdered Aboriginal women were smaller in size than an advertisement offering a department store credit card (*Regina Leader-Post* 2005b, p. A12), and an ad for an automobile dealership offering customers an "Employee Discount" (*Saskatoon Star-Phoenix* 2005b, p. A5). Entman and Rojecki cautioned that poorly placed articles convey to readers that "events lack urgency and social importance," a condition which may "reduce the salience and emotional potency of stories whose content might otherwise be alarming or provoke hostility" (2001, p. 90). Articles about the (as yet) unsolved disappearances/murders of Aboriginal women were relegated to the periphery of the page and, by extension, of reader's consciousness.

HEADLINES

Having laid out the quantitative findings, I now move to outlining the qualitative dimensions of coverage, beginning with the headlines.[6] Headlines are

---

5 [Gilchrist's note]   This analysis draws on the sixty articles selected for qualitative/interpretive analysis.

6 [Gilchrist's note]   Critics might argue that these findings are problematic given that the White women were from Ontario while the Aboriginal women were from Saskatchewan. Granted, Ontario is the most populous Canadian province and closer to the major national media markets influencing the amount of national media coverage for the White women. However, in selecting the most widely read local newspaper corresponding with the cities where the women disappeared/were murdered this largely resolves the problems of potential geographic and market differences between the provinces. Even though both Saskatchewan newspapers are smaller than the Ontario newspapers, they also have correspondingly less local news to cover, and one could reasonably expect that such a case would receive at least as much coverage in a Saskatchewan newspaper as an Ontario

a crucial element of press reporting given the limited space journalists have to communicate to readers the relevance of what has taken place (Teo 2000). Headlines printed about the Aboriginal women, often referred to them impersonally and rarely by name. For example, "RCMP identifies *woman's* remains" (Pruden 2006, p. A3; emphasis mine), "*Teen's* family keeping vigil" (Pruden 2005a, p. B1; emphasis mine), "Fear growing for family of missing *mom*" (Pruden 2005b, p. A1; emphasis mine), and "Trek raises awareness for missing *aboriginal* women" (Haight 2005, p. A3; emphasis mine). Detached descriptions of the Aboriginal women were in opposition to headlines about the White women referring to them by first and last names, and nicknames. Headlines were often also written as heartfelt personal messages from the victims' friends and family to the women, as with "*Ardeth Wood* 'lives in the light of God'" (Harvey 2003, p. B1; emphasis mine), "*Jenny* we love you, we miss you" (Mick 2005b, p. A1; emphasis mine), and "'Waiting for *Alicia*'" (Diebel 2005, p. A6; emphasis mine).

ARTICLES

As noted by Wortley (2002), how the news media depict a crime victim is almost as important as whether the crime is reported at all. Representations of both groups routinely invoked purported "good victim" characteristics. However, this tendency was amplified in the White women's coverage. The White women were discussed in glowing ways, using potent adjectives and imagery. For instance, Ardeth was described as "devout," "so beautiful," "imaginative," "promising," and possessing an "indomitable spirit," while Alicia was referred to as "cherished," "a lily among the thorns," "blossoming," "vibrant," "strong," and as having a "luminous smile." Similarly, Jennifer was said to be "gifted," "optimistic," and "a miniature dynamo" that "lit the room in life." Such complimentary adjectives were commonplace and often a single article would include multiple adjectives of this nature. There was also considerable overlap in the words used to describe the White women, especially adjectives describing their beauty and/or blondness.

Although adjectives like "shy," "nice," "caring," "a good mom," "pretty," "educated," and "positive" were used to represent the three Aboriginal women, the impact of these words was in some ways neutralized because of their superficial and fleeting use. For instance, Melanie Geddes was described as a mother to three beautiful daughters and as the common-law wife of a very caring man, but this information was not bolstered with stories and memories

25

newspaper. In addition, the qualitative component of this research provides strong support that geographical differences do not account for/explain the stark disparities found along several other dimensions of coverage.

as was the case for the White women. The amount of personal information included in accounts of the White women far outweighed the amount and depth of information presented about the Aboriginal women. Articles about the White women included what amounted to full biographies of their lives, offering thoroughly detailed accounts of their hobbies, idiosyncrasies, personalities, families, goals, and other intimate personal information. For instance, listing Alicia Ross's music preferences as Led Zeppelin, Pink Floyd, and The Beatles is not particularly newsworthy nor does it assist police in generating leads about her disappearance/murder. However, it paints her as relatable to readers. Representations of Jennifer Teague and Alicia Ross portrayed them as the "girl next door" who shared the values, dreams, and experiences of an imagined [White] Canadian public. Ardeth Wood was typically represented as an angel whose chastity, grace, and godliness rendered her innocent but also vulnerable and fragile to her attacker (see Madriz 1997; Meyers 1997). Below is a passage taken from the *Ottawa Citizen*'s coverage of Jennifer Teague's murder:

> She shared her grandmother's stubborn spirit, her mother's gutsy determination, and according to those who loved her, a feisty spirit all her own. After 10 days of sleepless anxiety and hope, Jennifer Teague's family now knows the worst: that the teen who would sometimes make her brothers dinner before heading to work or soccer practice, is never coming home ... And that they have been robbed of their baby sister, only daughter, and bubbly friend—by a killer who walks free. (Hayley Mick 2005a, p. A1)

Given that articles about the Aboriginal women were considerably shorter, details of an intimate or personal nature were sporadic. Beyond superficial details, readers did not get the same sense of who the Aboriginal women were or what they meant to their loved ones or communities.

TONE AND THEMES

The tone of coverage for both groups was comparable, conveying a sense of desperation to locate the missing women and reunite them with their anguished loved ones. Faith and prayer were highlighted as ways for the families to cope with their tragic losses, and outpourings of compassion, grief, and support from their respective communities were displayed in coverage of both groups. Coverage of the White women, however, placed a heightened emphasis on the police and community doing "whatever it takes" to find the women and bring their killers to "justice" (Duffy & Mccooey 2005). Following the discovery of Ardeth Wood's remains, the *Ottawa Citizen* published some articles under the byline: "THE HUNT FOR ARDETH'S KILLER." Articles also communicated both a fear and outrage that violent predators are stalking our streets, fracturing our communities, and harming our daughters (Mick 2005a). Although articles about the Aboriginal women emphasized Native spirituality and communities as a place of solace for victims' families, this was depicted more as something *they* (Aboriginals) do to get through *their* grief over *their* missing daughters (Cowan 2005b; Polischuk 2005; see also Jiwani & Young 2006).

PHOTOGRAPHS

Visual images presented alongside text make the information presented more memorable, gives readers the feeling that they are experiencing or witnessing the events on a more personal level, and encourages them to identify with and become emotionally invested in the events (Graber 1996). Upon examination of the number and types of photographs found in the coverage of both groups, obvious qualitative differences were identified. Press coverage of the White women included photographs that were large, centrally placed, continued on in series for several pages, and often depicted the women as young children or alongside family members. Photographs also depicted police officers investigating the crimes alongside detailed maps and grids of search areas, images of community searchers, families in mourning, and sketches of suspects. By contrast, photographs of the Aboriginal women were considerably smaller, normally passport sized. If photographs were shown at all, they were less visible, not often centrally placed, and less intimate, as they rarely included images of victims' families and never included childhood photographs. The lack of visual imagery in these cases denied readers the same opportunity to identify with or become emotionally invested in the Aboriginal women's cases as they unfolded.

Overall, findings indicated identifiable quantitative and qualitative differences in local press coverage of the missing/murdered Aboriginal and White women. Disparities were found in the amount of coverage as well as in the wording, themes, tone, presentation, and placement of articles, headlines, and photographs. The Aboriginal women received three and a half times less coverage; their articles and photographs were smaller, less empathetic and provided minimal details. While violence against the White women was constructed as victimization done to or felt by all of us this was not replicated in the Aboriginal women's coverage....

CONCLUSION: CONSTITUTING AN INVISIBLE "OTHER"

Intersecting legacies of oppression have situated Aboriginal women on the margins of Canadian press and society (Gilchrist 2007; Jiwani & Young 2006). Jiwani and Young (2006, p. 912) argued bluntly that Aboriginal women are positioned "in the lowest rungs of the social order, thereby making them expendable and invisible, if not disposable." Jiwani (2008, p. 137) added that

30

missing/murdered Aboriginal women are seen by the media "less as victims deserving rescue than as bodies that simply do not matter."

In stark contrast to the compassionate and in-depth coverage of the White women, the Aboriginal women were not seen to be "eminently newsworthy" (Jewkes 2004, p. 51) and were mostly "filtered out" of the press (Chermak 1995, p. 73); reinforcing the belief that White lives are more valuable (Entman & Rojecki 2001). Carter (1998, p. 230) cautioned that when newsmakers cease to report certain types of crime it creates the impression that they are no longer a cause for concern. The lack of coverage to missing/murdered Aboriginal women appears to suggest that their stories are not dramatic or worthy enough to tell, that Aboriginal women's victimization is too routine or ordinary, and/or irrelevant to (White) readers. The common news adage "if it bleeds it leads"* is not an accurate one as "it really depends on who is bleeding" (Dowler, Fleming & Muzzatti 2006, p. 841).

(2010)

REFERENCES[7]

AHUVIA, AARON (2001) 'Traditional, interpretive, and reception based content analyses: improving the ability to address issues of pragmatic and theoretical concern', *Social Indicators Research*, vol. 54, pp. 139–172.

ARDOVI-BROOKER, JOANNE & CARINGELLA-MACDONALD, SUSAN (2002) 'Media attributions of blame and sympathy in ten rape cases', *The Justice Professional*, vol. 15, pp. 3–18.

BUCKLER, KEVIN & TRAVIS, LAWRENCE (2005) 'Assessing the newsworthiness of homicide events: an analysis of coverage in the *Houston Chronicle*', *Journal of Criminal Justice and Popular Culture*, vol. 12, no. 1, pp. 1–25.

CARTER, CYNTHIA (1998) 'When the "extraordinary" becomes the "ordinary": everyday news of sexual violence', in *News, Gender and Power*, eds Cynthia Carter, Gill Branston & Stuart Allan, Routledge, London, pp. 219–232.

CHERMAK, STEVEN M. (1995) *Victims and the News: Crime and the American News Media*, Westview Press, Boulder.

COHEN, STANLEY & YOUNG, JOCK (eds) (1973) *The Manufacture Of News: A Reader*, Sage, Beverley Hills.

COLLINS, PATRICIA HILL [1990] (2000) *Black Feminist Thought: Knowledge, Consciousness, and the Politics of Empowerment*, 2nd edn, Routledge, New York.

COWAN, PAMELA (2005b) 'Family still clings to hope', *Regina Leader-Post*, 8 Oct., p. A6.

CRENSHAW, KIMBERLE (1991) 'Mapping the margins: intersectionality, identity politics, and violence against women of colour', *Stanford Law Review*, vol. 43, no. 6, pp. 1241–1299.

DEPARTMENT OF INDIAN AND NORTHERN AFFAIRS. (1996) *Aboriginal Women: A Demographic, Social, and Economic Profile*, Information Quality and Research Directorate, Information Management Branch, Corporate Services, Ottawa.

---

7   *References*   References have been excerpted to show only those cited in the excerpts reprinted here.

DIEBEL, LINDA (2005) 'Waiting for Alicia', *Toronto Star*, 28 Aug., p. A6.

DOWLER, KENNETH (2004a) 'Comparing American and Canadian local television crime stories: a content analysis', *Canadian Journal of Criminology and Criminal Justice*, vol. 46, no. 5, pp. 573–597.

DOWLER, KENNETH (2004b) 'Dual realities? Criminality, victimization, and the presentation of race on local television news', *Journal of Crime and Justice*, vol. 27, pp. 79–99.

DOWLER, KENNETH, FLEMING, THOMAS & MUZZATTI, STEPHEN L. (2006) 'Constructing crime: media, crime, and popular culture', *Canadian Journal of Criminology and Criminal Justice*, vol. 48, no. 6, pp. 837–866.

DUFFY, ANDREW & MCCOOEY, PAULA (2005) 'Why this two-year-old act of evil is still unsolved', *Ottawa Citizen*, 6 Aug., p. A1.

ENTMAN, ROBERT M. & ROJECKI, ANDREW (2001) *The Black Image in the White Mind: Media and Race in America*, The University of Chicago Press, Chicago.

FOWLER, ROGER (1991) *Language in the News: Discourse and Ideology in the Press*, London, Routledge.

GILCHRIST, KRISTEN (2007) *Invisible Victims: Disparity in Print-Media Coverage of Missing and Murdered Aboriginal and White Women*, MA Thesis, The University of Ottawa.

GILCHRIST, KRISTEN (2008) 'Multiple disadvantages: the missing and murdered women of Vancouver', in *Gender Relations in Canada: Intersectionality and Beyond*, eds Andrea Doucet & Janet Siltanen, Oxford University Press, New York, pp. 174–175.

GRABER, DORIS A. (1996) 'Say it with pictures', *Annals of the American Academy of Political and Social Science*, vol. 546, no. 1, pp. 85–96.

GREER, CHRIS (2003) *Sex Crime and the Media: Sex Offending and the Press in a Divided Society*, Willan, Cullompton.

HAIGHT, LANA (2005) 'Trek raises awareness for missing Aboriginal women', *Regina Leader-Post*, 23 July, p. A3.

HALL, STUART (1973) 'The determination of news photographs', in *The Manufacture of News:A Reader*, eds Stanley Cohen & Jock Young, Sage, Beverly Hills, pp. 176–190.

HARVEY, BOB (2003) 'Ardeth Wood "lives in the light of God"', *Ottawa Citizen*, 19 Aug., p. B1.

HENRY, FRANCES & TATOR, CAROL [2000] (2006) *The Colour of Democracy: Racism in Canadian Society*, 3rd edn, Nelson, Toronto.

JACOBS, BEVERLY & WILLIAMS, ANDREA (2008) 'Legacy of residential schools: missing and murdered Aboriginal women', in *From Truth to Reconciliation: Transforming the Legacy of Residential Schools*, eds Marlene Brant Castellano, Linda Archibald & Mike DeGagne, Aboriginal Healing Foundation, Ottawa, pp. 119–142.

JEWKES, YVONNE (2004) *Media & Crime*, Sage, London.

JIWANI, YASMIN (2008) 'Mediations of domination: gendered violence within and across borders', in *Feminist Intervention in International Communication: Minding the Gap*, eds Katherine Sarikakis & Leslie Regan Shade, Rowman & Littlefield, Plymouth, pp. 129–145.

JIWANI, YASMIN & YOUNG, MARYLYNN (2006) 'Missing and murdered women: reproducing marginality in news discourse', *Canadian Journal of Communication*, vol. 31, pp. 895–917.

LAROCQUE, EMMA (2007) 'Metis and feminist: ethical reflections on feminism, human rights and decolonization', in *Making Space for Indigenous Feminism*, ed. Joyce Green, Fernwood, Halifax, pp. 53–70.

MADRIZ, ESTHER (1997) *Nothing Bad Happens to Good Girls: Fear of Crime in Women's Lives*, The University of California Press, Berkeley.

MARTIN-HILL, DAWN (2003) 'She no speaks and other colonial constructs of "the traditional woman"', in *Strong Women Stories: Native Vision and Community Survival*, eds Bonita Lawrence & Kim Anderson, Sumach Press, Toronto, pp. 106–120.

MCIVOR, SHARON WITH KUOKKANEN, RAUNA (2007) 'Sharon McIvor: woman of action', in *Making Space for Indigenous Feminism*, ed. Joyce Green, Fernwood, Halifax, pp. 241–254.

MCLAUGHLIN, LISA (1991) 'Discourses of prostitution/discourses of sexuality', *Critical Studies in Mass Communication*, vol. 8, pp. 249–272.

MEYERS, MARIAN (1997) *News Coverage of Violence Against Women: Engendering Blame*, Sage, Newbury Park.

MICK, HAYLEY (2005a) 'Feisty, gutsy, vibrant', *Ottawa Citizen*, 20 Sept., p. A1.

MICK, HAYLEY (2005b) 'Jenny we love you, we miss you', *Ottawa Citizen*, 2 Oct., p. A1.

MONTURE-ANGUS, PATRICIA (1995) *Thunder in My Soul: A Mohawk Woman Speaks*, Fernwood, Halifax.

NATIVE WOMEN'S ASSOCIATION OF CANADA (2008) *Voices of our Sisters in Spirit: A Research and Policy Report to Families and Communities*, Native Women's Association of Canada, Ottawa.

NATIVE WOMEN'S ASSOCIATION OF CANADA (2009) *Voices of our Sisters in Spirit: A Research and Policy Report to Families and Communities*, 2nd edn, Native Women's Association of Canada, Ottawa.

POLISCHUK, HEATHER (2005) 'Mother still searching', *Regina Leader-Post*, 15 April, p. A1.

PRUDEN, JANA (2005a) 'Teen's family keeping vigil', *Regina Leader-Post*, 9 Aug., p. B1.

PRUDEN, JANA (2005b) 'Fear growing for family of missing mom', *Regina Leader-Post*, 18 Aug., p. A1.

PRUDEN, JANA (2006) 'RCMP identifies woman's remains', *Saskatoon Star-Phoenix*, 2 Feb., p. A3.

REASON, MATTHEW & GARCIA, BEATRIZ (2007) 'Approaches to the newspaper archive: content analysis and press coverage of Glasgow's year of culture', Media, Culture & Society, vol. 29, no. 2, pp. 304–331.

REGINA LEADER-POST (2005a) 'The Lily society', 23 July, p. A12.

REGINA LEADER-POST (2005b) Advertisement offering a department store credit card, 23 July, p. A12.

REGINA LEADER-POST (2005c) 'Classics: summer is a great time for car lovers', 22 Aug, p. B1.

REGINA LEADER-POST (2005d) 'Snowfalls in the southeast', 6 Oct., p. A1.

REINER, ROBERT (2003) 'Media made criminality: the representation of crime in the mass media', in *Oxford Handbook of Criminology*, 8th edn, eds Mike Maguire, Rod Morgan & Robert Reiner, Oxford University Press, Oxford, pp. 376–417.

SASKATOON STAR-PHOENIX (2005a) 'A little off course', 12 May, p. A3.

SASKATOON STAR-PHOENIX (2005b) 'Employee discount', 22 Aug., p. A5.

SCHUDSON, MICHAEL (1989) 'The sociology of news production', Media, Culture & Society, vol. 11, no. 3, pp. 263–282.

SMITH, ANDREA (2005) *Conquest: Sexual Violence and American Indian Genocide*, South End Press, Boston.

SONWALKAR, PRASUN (2005) 'Banal journalism: the centrality of the "us-them" binary in news discourse', in *Journalism: Critical Issues*, ed. Stuart Allan, Open University Press, New York, pp. 261–273.

TEO, PETER (2000) 'Racism in the news: a critical discourse analysis of news reporting in two Australian newspapers', *Discourse & Society*, vol. 11, no. 1, pp. 7–49.

TUCHMAN, GAYE (1976) 'Telling stories', *Journal of Communication*, vol. 26, fall, pp. 93–97.

TUCHMAN, GAYE (1978) 'Introduction: the symbolic annihilation of women by the mass media', in *Hearth and Home: Images of Women in the Mass Media*, eds Gaye Tuchman, Arlene Kaplan Daniels & James Benet, Oxford University Press, New York, pp. 3–38.

WILCOX, PAULA (2005) 'Beauty and the beast: gendered and raced discourse in news', *Social & Legal Studies*, vol. 14, no. 4, pp. 515–532.

WORTLEY, SCOT (2002) 'Misrepresentation or reality? The depiction of race and crime in the Toronto print media', in *Marginality & Condemnation: An Introduction to Critical Criminology*, eds Bernard Schissel & Carolyn Brooks, Fernwood, Halifax, pp. 55–82.

ZELIZER, BARBIE (2005) 'Journalism through the camera's eye', in *Journalism: Critical Issues*, ed. Stuart Allan, Open University Press, New York, pp. 167–176.

Questions

1. What does Gilchrist find through her qualitative analysis of the news coverage of these murders? In your opinion, is this kind of analysis as important, less important, or more important than the quantitative analyses?

2. What "broader systemic inequalities" does Gilchrist's study reveal?

3. According to Gilchrist's research, what informs dominant ideas about what is "newsworthy"? What crimes are usually deemed newsworthy?

4. How do the presence and/or absence of victim photographs affect the rhetorical power of a newspaper or magazine article?

5. Find a recent news article, in a print or online newspaper, that reports a murder.

   a. Following Gilchrist's example, make a qualitative analysis determining the extent to which the murder is presented as important and emotionally impactful.

   b. What identity categories does the victim belong to (race, gender, age, etc.)? Is any information or speculation provided as to the identity of the perpetrator(s)?

   c. To what extent is bias regarding these identity categories reflected in the article?

LAILA LALAMI

MY LIFE AS A MUSLIM IN
THE WEST'S "GRAY ZONE"

This essay discussing the position of Muslims in Western societies since 2001 was first published in the 20 November 2015 issue of The New York Times Magazine.

❧

S ome months ago, I gave a reading from my most recent novel in Scottsdale, Ariz. During the discussion that followed, a woman asked me to talk about my upbringing in Morocco. It's natural for readers to be curious about a writer they've come to hear, I told myself. I continued to tell myself this even after the conversation drifted to Islam, and then to ISIS. Eventually, another woman raised her hand and said that the only Muslims she saw when she turned on the television were extremists. "Why aren't we hearing more from people like you?" she asked me.

"You are," I said with a nervous laugh. "Right now." I wanted to tell her that there were plenty of ordinary Muslims in this country. We come in all races and ethnicities. Some of us are more visible by virtue of beards or head scarves. Others are less conspicuous, unless they give book talks and it becomes clear that they, too, identify as Muslims.

To be fair, I'm not a very good Muslim. I don't perform daily prayers anymore. I have never been on a pilgrimage to Mecca.[1] I partake of the forbidden drink.[2] I do give to charity whenever I can, but I imagine that this would not be enough to save me were I to have the misfortune, through an accident of birth or migration, to live in a place like Raqqa, Syria, where in the last two years, the group variously known as Daesh, ISIL or ISIS has established a caliphate: a successor to past Islamic empires. Life in Raqqa reportedly follows rules that range from the horrifying to the absurd: The heads of people who have been executed are posted on spikes in the town's main square; women must wear a

---

1   *pilgrimage to Mecca*   The Hajj is an annual journey to Saudi Arabia to visit the most holy city in Islam; making this pilgrimage at least once in an adult's lifetime is a religious requirement within most branches of Islam.

2   *forbidden drink*   Alcohol, which is forbidden in the Qur'an.

niqab[3] and be accompanied by a male companion when they go out; smoking and swearing are not allowed; chemistry is no longer taught in schools and traffic police are not permitted to have whistles because ISIS considers them un-Islamic.

As part of its efforts to spread its message outside the territory it controls, ISIS puts out an English-language magazine, *Dabiq*, which can be found online. In February, *Dabiq* featured a 12-page article, complete with high-resolution photos and multiple footnotes, cheering the terrorist attacks of Sept. 11 and claiming that they made manifest for the world two camps: the camp of Islam under the caliphate and the camp of the West under the crusaders. The article ran under the title "The Extinction of the Grayzone." The gray zone is the space inhabited by any Muslim who has not joined the ranks of either ISIS or the crusaders. Throughout the article, these Muslims are called "the grayish," "the hypocrites" and, for variety, "the grayish hypocrites."

On Nov. 13, men who had sworn allegiance to ISIS struck the city of Paris, killing 130 people at different locations mostly in the 10th and 11th arrondissements, neighborhoods that are known for their multiculturalism. As soon as I heard about the attacks, I tried to reach a cousin of mine, who is studying in Paris. I couldn't. I spent the next two hours in a state of crushing fear until he posted on Facebook that he was safe. Relieved, I went back to scrolling through my feed, which is how I found out that my friend Najlae Benmbarek, a Moroccan journalist, lost her cousin. A recently married architect, Mohamed Amine Ibnolmobarak was eating dinner with his wife at the Carillon restaurant when an ISIS terrorist killed him.

It was probably not a coincidence that the Paris attacks were aimed at restaurants, a concert hall and a sports stadium, places of leisure and community, nor that the victims included Muslims. As *Dabiq* makes clear, ISIS wants to eliminate coexistence between religions and to create a response from the West that will force Muslims to choose sides: either they "apostatize and adopt" the infidel religion of the crusaders[4] or "they perform *hijrah*[5] to the Islamic State and thereby escape persecution from the crusader governments and citizens." For ISIS to win, the gray zone must be eliminated.

Whose lives are gray? Mine, certainly. I was born in one nation (Morocco) speaking Arabic, came to my love of literature through a second language (French) and now live in a third country (America), where I write books and teach classes in yet another language (English). I have made my home in

5

---

3 *niqab* Cloth to cover the face.

4 *apostatize and ... crusaders* I.e., relinquish Islam and adopt Christianity.

5 *hijrah* Migration for religious purposes; "the Hijrah" typically refers to Muhammad's migration from Mecca to Medina to escape assassination.

between all these cultures, all these languages, all these countries. And I have found it a glorious place to be. My friends are atheists and Muslims, Jews and Christians, believers and doubters. Each one makes my life richer.

This gray life of mine is not unique. I share it with millions of people around the world. My brother in Dallas is a practicing Muslim—he prays, he fasts, he attends mosque—but he, too, would be considered to be in the gray zone, because he despises ISIS and everything it stands for.

Most of the time, gray lives go unnoticed in America. Other times, especially when people are scared, gray lives become targets. Hate crimes against Muslims spike after every major terrorist attack. But rather than stigmatize this hate, politicians and pundits often stoke it with fiery rhetoric, further diminishing the gray zone. Every time the gray zone recedes, ISIS gains ground.

10 The language that ISIS uses may be new, but the message is not. When President George W. Bush spoke to a joint session of Congress after the terrorist attacks of Sept. 11, he declared, "Either you are with us or you are with the terrorists." It was a decisive threat, and it worked well for him in those early, confusing days, so he returned to it. "Either you are with us," he said in 2002, "or you are with the enemy. There's no in between." This polarized thinking led to the United States invasion of Iraq, which led to the destabilization of the Middle East, which in turn led to the creation of ISIS.

Terrorist attacks affect all of us in the same way: We experience sorrow and anger at the loss of life. For Muslims, however, there is an additional layer of grief as we become subjects of suspicion. Muslims are called upon to condemn terrorism, but no matter how often or how loud or how clear the condemnations, the calls remain. Imagine if, after every mass shooting in a school or a movie theater in the United States, young white men in this country were told that they must publicly denounce gun violence. The reason this is not the case is that we presume each young white man to be solely responsible for his actions, whereas Muslims are held collectively responsible. To be a Muslim in the West is to be constantly on trial.

The attacks in Paris have generated the same polarization as all previous attacks have. Even though most of the suspects were French and Belgian nationals who could have gained entry to the United States on their passports, Republican governors in 30 states say that they will refuse to take in any refugees from Syria without even more stringent screening. Barely two days after the attacks, Jeb Bush* told CNN's Jake Tapper that the United States should focus its efforts only on helping Syrian refugees who are Christian.

Ted Cruz* went a step further, offering to draft legislation that would ban Muslim Syrian refugees from the United States. When he was asked by Dana Bash of CNN what would have happened to him if his father, a Cuban refugee who was fleeing communism, had been refused entry, he implied that it was a different situation because of the special risks associated with ISIS.

As it happens, I am married to a son of Cuban refugees. Like Cruz's father, they came to this country because America was a safe haven. What would have been their fate if an American legislator said that they could not be allowed in because the Soviet Union was trying to infiltrate the United States?

The other day, my daughter said to me, "I want to be president." She has been saying this a lot lately, usually the morning after a presidential debate, when our breakfast-table conversation veers toward the elections. My daughter is 12. She plays the violin and the guitar; she loves math and history; she's quick-witted and sharp-tongued and above all she's very kind to others. "I'd vote for you," I told her. And then I looked away, because I didn't have the heart to tell her that half the people in this country—in her country—say they would not vote for a Muslim presidential candidate.

I worry about her growing up in a place where some of the people who are seeking the highest office in the land cannot make a simple distinction between Islam and ISIS, between Muslim and terrorist. Ben Carson* has said he "would not advocate that we put a Muslim in charge of this nation."

Right now, my daughter still has the innocence and ambition that are the natural attributes of the young. But what will happen when she comes of age and starts to realize that her life, like mine, is constantly under question? How do you explain to a child that she is not wanted in her own country? I have not yet had the courage to do that. My daughter has never heard of the gray zone, though she has lived in it her entire life. Perhaps this is my attempt at keeping the world around all of us as gray as possible. It is a form of resistance, the only form of resistance I know.

(2015)

Questions

1. According to Lalami, what is the gray zone, and who occupies it?

2. Lalami writes that whenever "the gray zone recedes, ISIS gains ground." What causes the gray zone to recede? Why is this good for ISIS and bad for the West?

3. Lalami contrasts the public response to mass killings conducted by Muslims with the public response to mass killings conducted by young white men. How and why, according to Lalami, do these events tend to be treated differently? To what extent (if at all) is this difference justified?

4. What prejudices are revealed by the questions asked at the book signing described in the opening paragraph?

5. Lalami writes that "rather than stigmatize [hatred of Muslims], politicians and pundits often stoke it with fiery rhetoric." Look online and find an example of such rhetoric quoted in a news article from this week.

6. Who is the intended audience for this piece? How is the piece crafted to be persuasive to this particular audience?

CLAIMING
BLACKNESS

ADILIFU NAMA

from SUPER BLACK: AMERICAN POP CULTURE AND BLACK SUPERHEROES

A scholar of African American studies with a focus on popular culture, Adilifu Nama has published books such as Black Space: Imagining Race in Science Fiction Film *(2008) and* Race on the QT: Blackness and the Films of Quentin Tarantino *(2015). The following selection is from the introduction to his book* Super Black: American Pop Culture and Black Superheroes *(2011). In the book, Nama examines characters from DC and Marvel, including Black Panther, Black Lightning, Storm, Luke Cage, Blade, the Falcon, and Nubia. He argues that "Black superheroes are not the disposable refuse of American pop culture, but serve as a source of potent racial meaning that has substance and resonance far beyond their function and anticipated shelf life."*

❧

My problem ... and I'll speak as a writer now ... with writing a black character in either the Marvel or DC universe is that he is not a man. He is a symbol.

—DWAYNE MCDUFFIE, *Comics Journal*

Circa 1975, when I was five or six, my father took me to a toy store. I went straight to the section where all the superhero action figures were on display, enclosed in window-boxed packaging. They were eight-inch toys made by the now defunct Mego Corporation. Prior to this moment, superheroes inhabited the television reruns of Filmation's *The Superman/Aquaman Hour of Adventure* (1967–1968) and the few comic books I had tucked in the corner of my room. Now I was poised to have a handful of superheroes of my very own and I would be able to dictate the terms, times, and types of superhero adventures I could enjoy. I mentally pleaded with my bladder to stop distracting me long enough to concentrate on prioritizing which superhero figure to choose. I wanted to grab them all right then and there. Since I could not, I examined them all and mentally separated various superhero figures into two groups: my must-haves and my want-to-haves. I made sure to point to the Falcon superhero first, and after he was firmly in my grasp I asked my pops* if I could get a few more. His "yes" gave me the go-ahead to scrutinize several other superhero figures and pick the ones I thought looked best. Aquaman, Captain America, and Spider-Man made the cut. Over time I would later acquire Batman, Hulk, Iron Man, Thor, and the Human Torch, but it was the Falcon that captured my imagination most and cemented my attachment to virtually all things super-hero. Why? He was a black man that could fly.

With the Falcon I was able to imagine myself as a superhero, rising above my socioeconomic environment, beating the neighborhood bullies, command-ing respect from my male peers, and enjoying approval from all of the pretty girls that made me feel so nervous. I later became captivated by another "fly-ing" black man, the legendary Dr. J (Julius Erving), a basketball player known for defying gravity and for dunking the basketball right in his opponents' faces. Although I dutifully tried to imitate the "moves" I had seen Dr. J perform and dedicated virtually all of my free time to watching, playing, and practicing basketball, I never forgot about the Falcon. The Falcon was my first and my favorite flying black superhero.

The image of a black man gliding through the air, compelling attention, awe, and respect, made a lasting impact on my imagination. The Falcon also operated on a broader social level. The image of the Falcon gliding across an urban skyline symbolized the unprecedented access and upward social mobil-ity many African Americans were experiencing in education and professional positions in the wake of hard-earned antidiscrimination laws and affirmative action. In this sense, black superheroes like the Falcon are not only fantastic representations of our dreams, desires, and idealized projections of ourselves, they are also a symbolic extension of America's shifting political ethos and racial landscape.$_1$

Even though I am, in the popular parlance of the black barbershop, a "grownass man," I still enjoy seeing superheroes save the day in comics, films, live-action television shows, cartoons, and video games. My enjoyment of superheroes as a mature adult, however, does not take place without some degree of trepidation. When parents see me gleefully poking around a local comic book store alongside their children, or catch me dragging my wife into the latest superhero film, I often detect their scornful glances that betray feel-ings ranging from mild annoyance to awkward disdain for what they probably perceive as an adult still stuck in adolescence. Nonetheless, I am not deterred

---

NB Explanatory footnotes are indicated by superscript numbers in this anthology; numbers that refer to the author's list of references are indicated by subscript numbers.

by their embarrassment for me because I know that the imaginative realms and representational schemes that black superheroes occupy in comics, cartoons, television, and film express powerful visuals, compelling narratives, and multiple meanings around a range of racial ideas and beliefs circulating in American culture.

Despite the symbolic significance of black superheroes in American 5
popular culture, the topic remains, for the most part, unexamined. Admittedly, there are a few scholarly studies concerning black superheroes, but they are topical or truncated glimpses of the fascinating racial complexity black superheroes articulate. For example, Fredrik Stromberg's *Black Images in the Comics: A Visual History* (2003) includes only a handful of black superheroes alongside a wide-ranging pictorial documentation of black comic figures. Richard Reynolds's *Super Heroes: A Modern Mythology* (1992) contains just a few paragraphs about black superheroes and even boasts that black superheroes have very little to offer in the way of ideological meaning.[2] In contrast, Bradford W. Wright's definitive text *Comic Book Nation: The Transformation of Youth Culture in America* (2003) addresses the importance of superhero comic books to American culture and aptly touches on race. Yet Wright's discussion of black superheroes and their cultural significance is subsumed under broader social themes. Consequently, his analysis flattens distinguishing features between black superheroes and has very little to say about what black superheroes articulate concerning the cultural politics of race and blackness in America.

Even the most definitive text to date on the topic, Jeffrey A. Brown's *Black Superheroes, Milestone Comics, and Their Fans* (2001), devotes scant attention and analysis to the cultural work, symbolism, and sociological significance of the mainstream black superheroes that populate DC and Marvel comics. Instead, Brown invests virtually all his analytic efforts in covering the significance of black comic-book company Milestone Comics, negotiating the fickle terrain of a predominantly white comic-book culture, and discussing how racialized notions of hypermasculinity are a signature feature of black superheroes. As a result, the broad scope and social significance of black superheroes across the Marvel and DC Comics universes and in their television and film incarnations is severely diminished. In addition, the full range of cultural work that black superheroes have performed across several decades is completely ignored. In short, the bulk of analysis concerning black superheroes has come to obvious conclusions, is embarrassingly reductive, and neglects to draw deeper connections across significant cultural dynamics, social trends, and historical events. Most often the topic of blackness in the superhero genre compels discussions over the difficulty white audiences might experience identifying with black superheroes or knee-jerk criticisms that frame the genre as racially biased.[3]

Certainly, comic books featuring heroes like Tarzan, the beneficent white jungle-savior, presented black characters as stereotypically subservient, primitive, or savage. Moreover, such examples make easy fodder for critique and open up a Pandora's box* of vexing sociopsychological questions about racial projection and reader identification with superhero characters that promote racially insensitive images and ideas. Yet by using these issues as a point of analytical departure, the dynamic and rich source of racial meaning presented in the superhero universes of DC Comics, Marvel Comics, television, and film becomes buried beneath a mound of superficial critiques. Either black superheroes are critiqued as updated racial stereotypes from America's comic-book past, or they are uncritically affixed to the blaxploitation film[1] craze as negative representations of blackness.[4] What emerges from such nearsighted analysis is an incomplete description of the fascinating and complex ideological give and take that black superheroes have with American culture. In stark contrast, *Super Black* calls attention to black superheroes as a fascinating racial phenomenon and a powerful source of racial meaning, narrative, and imagination in American society that expresses a myriad of racial assumptions, political perspectives, and fantastic (re)imaginings of black identity.

The superhero archetype is heavily steeped in affirming a division between right and wrong, thus superheroes operate within a moral framework. Moreover, virtually all superheroes are victorious, not because of superior strength or weaponry, but because of moral determination demonstrated by concern for others and notions of justice.[5] Accordingly, black superheroes are not merely figures that defeat costumed supervillains: they symbolize American racial morality and ethics. They overtly represent or implicitly signify social discourse and accepted wisdom concerning notions of racial reciprocity, racial equality, racial forgiveness, and, ultimately, racial justice. But black superheroes are not only representative of what is racially right. They are also ripe metaphors for race relations in America, and are often reflective of escalating and declining racial unrest. In this sense, black superheroes in American comic books and, to a lesser extent, in Hollywood films and television are cultural ciphers for accepted wisdom regarding racial justice and the shifting politics of black racial formation in America....

... My approach employs an eclectic synthesis of cultural criticism, historical and cultural contextualization, and a hearty dash of textual analysis intent on yielding information, insights, and connections between text, ideas, and important moments in the cultural history of black superheroes and black racial formation. Most importantly, this book [*Super Black*] adopts a self-conscious

---

1   *blaxploitation film*   Film genre whose primary characteristics were low budgets, violent action scenes, and predominantly Black casts with Black actors playing lead roles.

critically celebratory perspective for examining the various expressions of superhero blackness. In other words, the purpose of this book is to reclaim black superheroes from the easily perceived, easily argued, and clichéd assumptions used to examine them that diminish their sociocultural significance and view the cultural work they perform as tired tropes about blackness primarily written by white men. The point is not to uncritically embrace these figures. Rather the mission of my analysis is to steer the discussion away from theoretical dead ends or conversations that lead only in one direction to one conclusion: black superheroes are negative stereotypes....

(2011)

REFERENCES[2]

1. See Richard Reynolds, *Super Heroes: A Modern Mythology* (Jackson: University Press of Mississippi, 1994), and Danny Fingeroth, *Superman on the Couch: What Superheroes Really Tell Us about Ourselves and Our Society* (New York: Continuum, 2004).
2. Reynolds, *Super Heroes*, 77.
3. See Anna Beatrice Scott, "Superpower vs Supernatural: Black Superheroes and the Quest for a Mutant Reality," *Journal of Visual Culture* 5, no. 3 (December 2006): 295–314; Marc Singer, "'Black Skins' and White Masks: Comic Books and the Secret of Race," *African American Review* 36, no. 1 (Spring 2002): 107–119; Jeffery Brown, *Black Superheroes, Milestone Comics, and Their Fans* (Jackson: University Press of Mississippi, 2000).
4. See Christian Davenport, "Black Is the Color of My Comic Book Character: An Examination of Ethnic Stereotypes," *Inks: Cartoon and Comic Art Studies* 4, no. 1 (1997): 20–28; Trina Robbins, *The Great Women Superheroes* (New York: Kitchen Sink Press, 1996), 148; Ora C. McWilliams, "Not Just Another Racist Honkey: A History of Racial Representation in Captain America and Related Publications," in *Captain America and the Struggle of the Superhero: Critical Essays*, ed., Robert G. Weiner, 66–78 (Jefferson, NC: McFarland, 2009); Darius James's opening salvo, "Straight-up Real Nigga," in the graphic comic *Cage* (New York: Marvel Comics, 2003), by Brian Azzarello, Richard Corben, and Jose Villarubia.
5. Reynolds, *Super Heroes*, 41.

Questions

1. Consider the quotation from Dwayne McDuffie that opens this introduction. To what extent (if at all) does Nama endorse McDuffie's view? To what extent (if at all) does he contradict McDuffie?

---

2   *References*   References have been excerpted to reflect only those noted in the portion of Nama's text reprinted here.

2. What does Nama mean by a *"critically celebratory"* approach to examining comics? Does this strike you as a productive approach? Why or why not?

3. Nama suggests that, in most scholarly analysis, "the dynamic and rich source of racial meaning presented in the superhero universes of DC Comics, Marvel Comics, television, and film becomes buried beneath a mound of superficial critiques" (paragraph 7). Read Carvell Wallace's "Why *Black Panther* Is a Defining Moment for Black America," also reprinted in this anthology. To what extent (if at all) does Nama's critique apply to Wallace's essay? To what extent do Nama's and Wallace's pieces complement each other?

4. Examine a recent DC or Marvel work that features a Black hero (see, for example, the Marvel film *Black Panther* [2018]; an episode of the Marvel TV series *Luke Cage* [2016–18] or the DC TV series *Black Lightning* [2018–]; an issue of Ta-Nehisi Coates's *Black Panther* comic [2016–]; or the video game *Marvel: Future Fight* [2015; you may wish to focus on one playable character, such as Luke Cage, Storm, Falcon, Blade, or Black Panther]). Discuss the work you chose with Nama's argument in mind; what (if anything) does the work suggest about "American racial morality and ethics"?

CARVELL WALLACE

WHY *BLACK PANTHER* IS A DEFINING MOMENT FOR BLACK AMERICA

The Marvel Cinematic Universe—a franchise that includes numerous interconnected films and television shows based on characters and storylines from Marvel comic books—has been a popular culture phenomenon since the release of its first film, Iron Man, *in 2008.* Black Panther, *released almost ten years later, was the first film in the series to feature a Black protagonist: Black Panther, who had, in 1966, also made history as the first Black superhero to appear in a Marvel comic book. Eagerly anticipated, the film garnered broad critical acclaim and was a tremendous financial success, with one of the highest-earning opening weekends in history. In the following piece from the* New York Times Magazine, *African American writer and journalist Carvell Wallace argues for the film's importance.*

❧

The Grand Lake Theater—the kind of old-time movie house with cavernous ceilings and ornate crown moldings—is one place I take my kids to remind us that we belong to Oakland, Calif. Whenever there is a film or community event that has meaning for this town, the Grand Lake is where you go to see it. There are local film festivals, indie film festivals, erotic film festivals, congressional town halls, political fund-raisers. After Hurricane Katrina, the lobby served as a drop-off for donations. We run into friends and classmates there. On weekends we meet at the farmers' market across the street for coffee.

The last momentous community event I experienced at the Grand Lake was a weeknight viewing of *Fruitvale Station*, the 2013 film directed by the Bay Area native Ryan Coogler. It was about the real-life police shooting of Oscar Grant, 22, right here in Oakland, where Grant's killing landed less like a news story and more like the death of a friend or a child. He had worked at a popular grocery, gone to schools and summer camps with the children of acquaintances. His death—he was shot by the transit police while handcuffed, unarmed and face down on a train-station platform, early in the morning of New Year's Day 2009—sparked intense grief, outrage and sustained protest, years before Black Lives Matter took shape as a movement. Coogler's telling took us slowly through the minutiae of Grant's last day alive: We saw his family and child, his struggles at work, his relationship to a gentrifying city, his attempts to make sense of a young life that felt both aimless and daunting. But the moment I remember most took place after the movie was over: A group of us, friends and strangers alike and nearly all black, stood in the cool night under the marquee, crying and holding one another. It didn't matter that we didn't know one another. We knew enough.

On a misty morning this January, I found myself standing at that same spot, having gotten out of my car to take a picture of the Grand Lake's marquee. The words *Black Panther* were on it, placed dead center. They were not in normal-size letters; the theater was using the biggest ones it had. All the other titles huddled together in another corner of the marquee. A month away from its Feb. 16 opening, *Black Panther* was, already and by a wide margin, the most important thing happening at the Grand Lake.

Marvel Comics's Black Panther was originally conceived in 1966 by Stan Lee and Jack Kirby, two Jewish New Yorkers, as a bid to offer black readers a character to identify with. The titular hero, whose real name is T'Challa, is heir apparent to the throne of Wakanda, a fictional African nation. The tiny country has, for centuries, been in nearly sole possession of vibranium, an alien element acquired from a fallen meteor. (Vibranium is powerful and nearly indestructible; it's in the special alloy Captain America's shield is made of.) Wakanda's rulers have wisely kept their homeland and its elemental riches hidden from the world, and in its isolation the nation has grown wildly powerful and technologically advanced. Its secret, of course, is inevitably discovered, and as the world's evil powers plot to extract the resources of yet another African nation, T'Challa's father is cruelly assassinated, forcing the end of Wakanda's sequestration. The young king will be forced to don the virtually indestructible vibranium Black Panther suit and face a duplicitous world on behalf of his people.

5   This is the subject of Ryan Coogler's third feature film—after *Fruitvale Station* and *Creed* (2015)—and when glimpses of the work first appeared last June, the response was frenzied. The trailer *teaser*—not even the full trailer—racked up 89 million views in 24 hours. On Jan. 10, 2018, after tickets were made available for presale, Fandango's managing editor, Erik Davis, tweeted that the movie's first 24 hours of advance ticket sales exceeded those of any other movie from the Marvel Cinematic Universe.

The black internet was, to put it mildly, exploding. Twitter reported that *Black Panther* was one of the most tweeted-about films of 2017, despite not even opening that year. There were plans for viewing parties, a fund-raiser to arrange a private screening for the Boys & Girls Club of Harlem,* hashtags like

#BlackPantherSoLit and #WelcomeToWakanda. When the date of the premiere was announced, people began posting pictures of what might be called African-Americana, a kitsch version of an older generation's pride touchstones—kente cloth du-rags, candy-colored nine-button suits, King Jaffe Joffer from *Coming to America*[1] with his lion-hide sash—alongside captions like "This is how I'ma show up to the Black Panther premiere." Someone described how they'd feel approaching the box office by simply posting a video of the Compton rapper Buddy Crip-walking[2] in front of a Moroccan hotel.

None of this is because *Black Panther* is the first major black superhero movie. Far from it. In the mid-1990s, the Damon Wayans vehicle *Blankman* and Robert Townsend's *The Meteor Man* played black-superhero premises for campy laughs. Superheroes are powerful and beloved, held in high esteem by society at large; the idea that a normal black person could experience such a thing in America was so far-fetched as to effectively constitute gallows humor.[3] *Blade*, released in 1998, featured Wesley Snipes as a Marvel vampire hunter, and *Hancock* (2008) depicted Will Smith as a slacker antihero, but in each case the actor's blackness seemed somewhat incidental.

Black Panther, by contrast, is steeped very specifically and purposefully in its blackness. "It's the first time in a very long time that we're seeing a film with centered black people, where we have a lot of agency," says Jamie Broadnax, the founder of Black Girl Nerds, a pop-culture site focused on sci-fi and comic-book fandoms. These characters, she notes, "are rulers of a kingdom, inventors and creators of advanced technology. We're not dealing with black pain, and black suffering, and black poverty"—the usual topics of acclaimed movies about the black experience.

In a video posted to Twitter in December, which has since gone viral, three young men are seen fawning over the *Black Panther* poster at a movie theater. One jokingly embraces the poster while another asks, rhetorically: "This is what white people get to feel all the time?" There is laughter before someone says, as though delivering the punch line to the most painful joke ever told: "I would love this country, too."

Ryan Coogler saw his first Black Panther comic book as a child, at an Oakland shop called Dr. Comics & Mr. Games, about a mile from the Grand Lake

10

---

1   *kente cloth* Brightly colored woven cloth traditionally made in Ghana; *du-rags* Tight-fitting headwear; *King Jaffe ... America* 1988 romantic comedy film featuring Eddie Murphy as the colorfully attired Akeem Joffer, Prince of the fictional African country Zamunda.

2   *Crip-walking* Dance move originated by the Los Angeles Crip gang in the 1970s.

3   *gallows humor* Ironic comedy that exploits grim subject matter; also known as "dark comedy."

Theater. When I sat down with him in early February, at the Montage Hotel in Beverly Hills, I told him about the night I saw *Fruitvale Station*, and he listened with his head down, slowly nodding. When he looked up at me, he seemed to be blinking back tears of his own.

Coogler played football in high school, and between his fitness and his humble listening poses—leaning forward, elbows propped on knees—he reminds me of what might happen if a mild-mannered athlete accidentally discovered a radioactive movie camera and was gifted with remarkable artistic vision. He's interested in questions of identity: What does it mean to be a black person or an African person? "You know, you got to have the race conversation," he told me, describing how his parents prepared him for the world. "And you can't have that without having the slavery conversation. And with the slavery conversation comes a question of, O.K., so what about before that? And then when you ask that question, they got to tell you about a place that nine times out of 10 they've never been before. So you end up hearing about Africa, but it's a skewed version of it. It's not a tactile version."

Around the time he was wrapping up *Creed*, Coogler made his first journey to the continent, visiting Kenya, South Africa and the Kingdom of Lesotho, a tiny nation in the center of the South African landmass. Tucked high amid rough mountains, Lesotho was spared much of the colonization of its neighbors, and Coogler based much of his concept of Wakanda on it. While he was there, he told me, he was being shown around by an older woman who said she'd been a lover of the South African pop star Brenda Fassie. Riding along the hills with this woman, Coogler was told that they would need to visit an even older woman in order to drop off some watermelon. During their journey, they would stop occasionally to approach a shepherd and give him a piece of watermelon; each time the shepherd would gingerly take the piece, wrap it in cloth and tuck it away as though it were a religious totem. Time passed. Another bit of travel, another shepherd, another gift of watermelon. Eventually Coogler grew frustrated: "Why are we stopping so much?" he asked. "Watermelon is sacred," he was told. "It hydrates, it nourishes and its seeds are used for offerings." When they arrived at the old woman's home, it turned out that she was, in fact, a watermelon farmer, but her crop had not yet ripened—she needed a delivery to help her last the next few weeks.

When I was a kid, I refused to eat watermelon[4] in front of white people. To this day, the word itself makes me uncomfortable. Coogler told me that in high school he and his black football teammates used to have the same rule: Never eat watermelon in front of white teammates. Centuries of demonizing

---

4   *watermelon*   Watermelon has long been associated with demeaning racist stereotypes of Black Americans.

and ridiculing blackness have, in effect, forced black people to abandon what was once sacred. When we spoke of Africa and black Americans' attempts to reconnect with what we're told is our lost home, I admitted that I sometimes wondered if we could ever fully be part of what was left behind. He dipped his head, fell briefly quiet and then looked back at me with a solemn expression. "I think we can," he said. "It's no question. It's almost as if we've been brainwashed into thinking that we can't have that connection."

Black Panther is a Hollywood movie, and Wakanda is a fictional nation. But coming when they do, from a director like Coogler, they must also function as a place for multiple generations of black Americans to store some of our most deeply held aspirations. We have for centuries sought to either find or create a promised land where we would be untroubled by the criminal horrors of our American existence. From Paul Cuffee's attempts in 1811 to repatriate blacks to Sierra Leone and Marcus Garvey's back-to-Africa Black Star shipping line to the Afrocentric movements of the '60s and '70s,[5] black people have populated the Africa of our imagination with our most yearning attempts at self-realization. In my earliest memories, the Africa of my family was a warm fever dream, seen on the record covers I stared at alone, the sun setting over glowing, haloed Afros, the smell of incense and oils at the homes of my father's friends—a beauty so pure as to make the world outside, one of car commercials and blond sitcom families, feel empty and perverse in comparison. As I grew into adolescence, I began to see these romantic visions as just another irrelevant habit of the older folks, like a folk remedy or a warning to wear a jacket on a breezy day. But by then my generation was building its own African dreamscape, populated by KRS-One, Public Enemy and Poor Righteous Teachers;[6] we were indoctrinating ourselves into a prideful militancy about our worth. By the end of the century, "Black Star" was not just the name of Garvey's shipping line but also one of the greatest hip-hop albums[7] ever made.

---

5   *Paul Cuffee's ... Leone*   Son of a Black former slave and a Native American woman, Paul Cuffee (1759–1817) was a shipping magnate who worked to assist in the resettlement of former slaves;   *Marcus Garvey's ... line*   Jamaican Black nationalist Marcus Garvey (1887–1940) launched a shipping company, Black Star, to improve transatlantic economic connections between Blacks and to return African Americans to their ancestral homes in Africa;   *Afrocentric movements ... '70s*   Movements focused on the celebration and study of African history and culture as a means of empowering people of African ancestry.

6   *KRS-One ... Poor Righteous Teachers*   Black rap and Hip Hop artists known for politically engaged work.

7   *"Black Star" ... albums*   Hip Hop duo Black Star released *Mos Def & Telib Kweli Are Black Star* in 1998.

15   Never mind that most of us had never been to Africa. The point was not verisimilitude or a precise accounting of Africa's reality. It was the envisioning of a free self. Nina Simone[8] once described freedom as the absence of fear, and as with all humans, the attempt of black Americans to picture a homeland, whether real or mythical, was an attempt to picture a place where there was no fear. This is why it doesn't matter that Wakanda was an idea from a comic book, created by two Jewish artists. No one knows colonization better than the colonized, and black folks wasted no time in recolonizing Wakanda. No genocide or takeover of land was required. Wakanda is ours now. We do with it as we please.

Until recently, most popular speculation on what the future would be like had been provided by white writers and futurists, like Isaac Asimov and Gene Roddenberry.[9] Not coincidentally, these futures tended to carry the power dynamics of the present into perpetuity. Think of the original *Star Trek*, with its peaceful, international crew, still under the charge of a white man from Iowa. At the time, the character of Lieutenant Uhura, played by Nichelle Nichols, was so vital for African-Americans—the black woman of the future as an accomplished philologist—that, as Nichols told NPR, the Rev. Dr. Martin Luther King Jr. himself persuaded her not to quit the show after the first season. It was a symbol of great progress that she was conceived as something more than a maid. But so much still stood in the way of her being conceived as a captain.

The artistic movement called Afrofuturism, a decidedly black creation, is meant to go far beyond the limitations of the white imagination. It isn't just the idea that black people will exist in the future, will use technology and science, will travel deep into space. It is the idea that we will have won the future. There exists, somewhere within us, an image in which we are whole, in which we are home. Afrofuturism is, if nothing else, an attempt to imagine what that home would be. *Black Panther* cannot help being part of this. "Wakanda itself is a dream state," says the director Ava DuVernay, "a place that's been in the hearts and minds and spirits of black people since we were brought here in chains." She and Coogler have spent the past few months working across the hall from each other in the same editing facility, with him tending to *Black Panther* and her to her much-anticipated film of Madeleine L'Engle's *A Wrinkle in Time*. At

---

8   *Nina Simone* African American composer, pianist, performer, and civil rights activist (1933–2003).

9   *Isaac Asimov* Russian-American science fiction writer and scientist (1920–92); *Gene Roddenberry* Film and television writer and producer (1921–91) best known as the creator of *Star Trek*.

the heart of Wakanda, she suggests, lie some of our most excruciating existential questions: "What if they didn't come?" she asked me. "And what if they didn't take us? What would that have been?"

Afrofuturism, from its earliest iterations, has been an attempt to imagine an answer to these questions. The movement spans from free-jazz thinkers like Sun Ra, who wrote of an African past filled with alien technology and extraterrestrial beings, to the art of Krista Franklin and Ytasha Womack, to the writers Octavia Butler, Nnedi Okorafor and Derrick Bell, to the music of Jamila Woods and Janelle Monáe. Their work, says John I. Jennings—a media and cultural studies professor at the University of California, Riverside, and co-author of "Black Comix Returns"—is a way of upending the system, "because it jumps past the victory. Afrofuturism is like, 'We already won.'" Comic books are uniquely suited to handling this proposition. In them the laws of our familiar world are broken: Mild-mannered students become godlike creatures, mutants walk among us and untold power is, in an instant, granted to the most downtrodden. They offer an escape from reality, and who might need to escape reality more than a people kidnapped to a stolen land and treated as less-than-complete humans?

At the same time, it is notable that despite selling more than a million books and being the first science-fiction author to win a MacArthur fellowship, Octavia Butler, one of Afrofuturism's most important voices, never saw her work transferred to film, even as studios churned out adaptations of lesser works on a monthly basis. Butler's writing not only featured African-Americans as protagonists; it specifically highlighted African-American women. If projects by and about black men have a hard time getting made, projects by and about black women have a nearly impossible one. In March, Disney will release *A Wrinkle in Time*, featuring Storm Reid and Oprah Winfrey in lead roles; the excitement around this female-led film does not seem to compare, as of yet, with the explosion that came with *Black Panther*. But by focusing on a black female hero—one who indeed saves the universe—DuVernay is embodying the deepest and most powerful essence of Afrofuturism: to imagine ourselves in places where we had not been previously imagined.

Can films like these significantly change things for black people in America? The expectations around *Black Panther* remind me of the way I heard the elders in my family talking about the mini-series *Roots*, which aired on ABC in 1977. A multigenerational drama based on the best-selling book in which Alex Haley traced his own family history, *Roots* told the story of an African slave kidnapped and brought to America, and traced his progeny through over 100 years of American history. It was an attempt to claim for us a home, because to be black in America is to be both with and without one: You are told that you must honor this land, that to refuse this is tantamount

20

to hatred—but you are also told that you do not belong here, that you are a burden, an animal, a slave. Haley, through research and narrative and a fair bit of invention, was doing precisely what Afrofuturism does: imagining our blackness as a thing with meaning and with lineage, with value and place.

"The climate was very different in 1977," the actor LeVar Burton recalled to me recently. Burton was just 19 when he landed an audition, his first ever, for the lead role of young Kunta Kinte in the mini-series. "We had been through the civil rights movement, and there were visible changes as a result, like there was no more Jim Crow,"* he told me. "We felt that there were advancements that had been made, so the conversation had really sort of fallen off the table." The series, he said, was poised to reignite that conversation. "The story had never been told before from the point of view of the Africans. America, both black and white, was getting an emotional education about the costs of slavery to our common American psyche."

To say that *Roots* held the attention of a nation for its eight-consecutive-night run in January 1977 would be an understatement. Its final episode was viewed by 51.1 percent of all American homes with televisions, a kind of reach that seemed sure to bring about some change in opportunities, some new standing in American culture. "The expectation," Burton says, "was that this was going to lead to all kinds of positive portrayals of black people on the screen both big and small, and it just didn't happen. It didn't go down that way, and it's taken years."

Here in Oakland, I am doing what it seems every other black person in the country is doing: assembling my delegation to Wakanda. We bought tickets for the opening as soon as they were available—the first time in my life I've done that. Our contingent is made up of my 12-year-old daughter and her friend; my 14-year-old son and his friend; one of my oldest confidants, dating back to adolescence; and two of my closest current friends. Not everyone knows everyone else. But we all know enough. Our group will be eight black people strong.

Beyond the question of what the movie will bring to African-Americans sits what might be a more important question: What will black people bring to *Black Panther*? The film arrives as a corporate product, but we are using it for our own purposes, posting with unbridled ardor about what we're going to wear to the opening night, announcing the depths of the squads we'll be rolling with, declaring that Feb. 16, 2018, will be "the Blackest Day in History."

25   This is all part of a tradition of unrestrained celebration and joy that we have come to rely on for our spiritual survival. We know that there is no end to the reminders that our lives, our hearts, our personhoods are expendable. Yes, many nonblack people will say differently; they will declare their love for us,

they will post Martin Luther King Jr. and Nelson Mandela quotes one or two days a year. But the actions of our country and its collective society, and our experiences within it, speak unquestionably to the opposite. Love for black people isn't just *saying* Oscar Grant should not be dead. Love for black people is Oscar Grant not being dead in the first place.

This is why we love ourselves in the loud and public way we do—because we have to counter his death with the very same force with which such deaths attack our souls. The writer and academic Eve L. Ewing told me a story about her partner, a professor of economics at the University of Chicago: When it is time for graduation, he makes the walk from his office to the celebration site in his full regalia—the gown with velvet panels, full bell sleeves and golden piping, the velvet tam with gold-strand bullion tassel. And when he does it, every year, like clockwork, some older black woman or man he doesn't know will pull over, roll down their window, stop him and say, with a slow head shake and a deep, wide smile, something like: "I am just so *proud* of you!"

This is how we do with one another. We hold one another as a family because we must be a family in order to survive. Our individual successes and failures belong, in a perfectly real sense, to all of us. That can be for good or ill. But when it is good, it is very good. It is sunlight and gold on vast African mountains, it is the shining splendor of the Wakandan warriors poised and ready to fight, it is a collective soul as timeless and indestructible as vibranium. And with this love we seek to make the future ours, by making the present ours. We seek to make a place where we belong.

(2018)

Questions

1. What, according to Wallace, makes *Black Panther* different from previous movies with Black superhero protagonists?

2. What, if any, purpose(s) do works of Afrofuturism such as *Black Panther* serve that cannot be served by realist fiction?

3. Wallace notes that Black Panther was originally created by white Jewish writers. In your view, does this matter? Why or why not?

4. Wallace recounts a story Coogler tells about delivering watermelon in Lesotho (paragraph 12). What is the significance of this story in the context of Wallace's essay?

5. Wallace asks, "Can films like [*Black Panther* and *A Wrinkle in Time*] significantly change things for black people in America" (paragraph 20)? In your view, can they? If not, why not? If so, how?

6. Watch *Black Panther* and answer the following questions, supporting your answers with evidence from the film:

   a. Wallace claims that *Black Panther* "is steeped very specifically and purposefully in its blackness" (paragraph 8). What (if anything) makes the film "steeped ... in blackness," and how (if at all) can this engagement with blackness be read as "purposefu[l]"?

   b. How (if at all) does Wakanda "function as a place for multiple generations of black Americans to store some of our most deeply held aspirations" (paragraph 14)?

BRENT STAPLES

THE MOVIE *GET OUT* IS A STRONG ANTIDOTE TO THE MYTH OF "POSTRACIAL" AMERICA

This New York Times *editorial discusses the acclaimed horror film* Get Out *(2017), written and directed by Jordan Peele.*

ℭ

The touchstone scene in the new horror film *Get Out* depicts a 20-something white woman named Rose appraising the sculpted torsos of black athletes on a laptop as she sits in her bedroom sipping milk through a straw. In another context— say, in the popular HBO television series *Girls*[1]—this would be an unremarkable example of a millennial catching a glimpse of beefcake on the way to bed.

In this case, the director Jordan Peele wants the audience to see Rose as what she is: the 21st-century equivalent of the plantation owner who studies the teeth and muscles of the human beings he is about to buy at a slave market. Like her antebellum[2] predecessors, Rose—who has recently delivered her black boyfriend into the hands of her monstrous family—is on the hunt for the handsomest, buffest specimen she can find.

Get Out speaks in several voices on several themes. It subverts the horror genre itself—which has the well-documented habit of killing off black characters first. It comments on the re-emergence of white supremacy at the highest levels of American politics. It lampoons the easy listening racism that so often lies behind the liberal smile in the "postracial" United States. And it probes the systematic devaluation of black life that killed people like Trayvon Martin, Walter Scott, Tamir Rice and Eric Garner.[3]

---

1   *Girls*   Television show (2012–17) in which the four main characters are all white women in their twenties.

2   *antebellum*   I.e., before the Civil War.

3   *Trayvon Martin*   Seventeen-year-old Black teenager who was fatally shot without cause by a neighborhood watch coordinator in Florida in 2012; *Walter Scott*   Fifty-year-old Black man who was shot from behind and killed by police during an April 2015 traffic stop in South Carolina; *Tamir Rice*   Twelve-year-old Black child shot and killed by Cleveland police in 2014; *Eric Garner*   Forty-three-year old Black man [continued]

The film is a disquisition on the continuing impact of slavery in American life. Among other things, it argues that present-day race relations are heavily determined by the myths that were created to justify enslavement—particularly the notion that black people were never fully human.

5   The project of reconnecting this history to contemporary life is well underway. Historians have shown, for example, that slavery, once abolished under law, continued by other means, not least of all as disenfranchisement, mass incarceration and forced labor. Lynchings,* those carnivals of blood once attended by thousands of people, morphed into a sanitized, state-sanctioned death penalty that is still disproportionately used against people of color.

Novelists have followed the same line of inquiry, urged on by the desire to debunk the delusional rhetoric of "postracialism" that gained currency when the country elected its first African-American president.

This counternarrative pervades Paul Beatty's complex comic novel *The Sellout*—winner of the 2016 Man Booker Prize—whose African-American narrator attempts to resurrect slavery and segregation as a way of both deconstructing white supremacy and preventing the black community where he grew up from being erased.

Similarly, the Ben H. Winters thriller *Underground Airlines* unveils an eerily familiar America in which the Civil War never happened and the United States Marshals Service[4] cooperates with slave-holding states to track down people who have escaped to freedom.

The novelist Colson Whitehead deploys the counternarrative to great effect in *The Underground Railroad*—winner of the 2016 National Book Award—by subverting the shiny, optimistic escape-to-freedom story as it is so often told.

10   The underground railroad in this case is a real train that runs underground, not straight and true, but through dead ends and hellish catastrophes. This train travels across time as it takes the bondswoman from one destination to another, exposing her to unspeakable violence and the evolving versions of white supremacy that formed the actual journey from slavery to freedom.

Despite its comic elements, *Get Out* is cut from the same cloth. Indeed, the affluent white community into which Rose introduces her African-American

---

killed by New York police in 2014 when he was arrested under suspicion of illegally selling individual cigarettes.

4   *United States Marshals Service*   Under the Fugitive Slave Law of 1850 this branch of federal law enforcement was responsible for hunting down and arresting fugitives from slavery.

boyfriend, Chris, has the flavor of the Stepford[5] stop on Mr. Whitehead's dystopian railroad.

Rose's family plays to a familiar plantation trope with black retainers who are eerily not quite right but who are represented as being almost like family. The patriarch tries to set Chris at ease, assuring him that he likes black people and "would have voted for Obama a third time" were it possible.

The faux affability heightens the sense of the sinister. Chris learns that the white people around him are coveting his body and would like nothing more than to try it on as a kind of second skin.

It would be wrong to reduce this film to an attack on white liberals who mouth racial platitudes. Mr. Peele sets out to debunk the myth of "postracialism" generally—by showing that the country is still gripped by historically conditioned preconceptions of race and blackness.

(2017)

Questions

1. Watch *Get Out*. To what extent does Staples's review accurately characterize the film? Can you think of anything worthy of comment that is not mentioned in this review?

2. Staples argues that *Get Out* is a "disquisition on the continuing impact of slavery in American life" (paragraph 4). How did Staples come to that conclusion? What examples does he provide?

3. In the style of Staples's review, write your own review of a film or other artistic work that you feel advances a praiseworthy social critique.

4. What is "postracialism"? To what extent do you think "the delusional rhetoric of 'postracialism'" holds currency in American discourse today? Offer evidence in support of your view.

5. In this film review, Staples discusses several novels that address similar concepts to those explored in *Get Out*. Why do you think he might have chosen to do this?

---

5   *Stepford*   Reference to *The Stepford Wives* (novel 1974, films 1975 and 2004), a satirical thriller about a town in which all the women are blindly compliant and submissive homemakers.

ZADIE SMITH

GETTING IN AND OUT: WHO OWNS BLACK PAIN?

British writer Zadie Smith is best known for acclaimed novels such as White Teeth *(2000) and* NW *(2012). In this essay for* Harper's Magazine, *she discusses depictions of Black suffering in the arts, including writer-director Jordon Peele's acclaimed 2017 horror film* Get Out, *an examination of race in the United States.*

Smith links her reading of this film to the controversy surrounding Dana Schutz's painting Open Casket, *which appeared in the 2017 Whitney Biennial, an influential art show held at the Whitney Museum in New York. The painting is based upon a photograph of the body of Emmett Till, a 14-year-old Black child who in 1955 was murdered and mutilated by a white mob after a white woman falsely accused him of attempting to flirt with her. Till's mother famously held an open-casket funeral to draw attention to the brutality of racist violence in Mississippi, and he became an emblematic figure of the Civil Rights Movement. Schutz's painting was condemned by those who argued that it was unacceptably exploitative for her, as a white artist, to portray the subject.*

❧

You are white—
yet a part of me, as I am a part of you.
That's American.
Sometimes perhaps you don't want to be a part of me.
Nor do I often want to be a part of you.
But we are, that's true!
As I learn from you,
I guess you learn from me—
although you're older—and white—
and somewhat more free.
—Langston Hughes

Early on, as the opening credits roll, a woodland scene. We're upstate, viewing the forest from a passing car. Trees upon trees, lovely, dark and deep.[1] There are no people to be seen in this wood—but you get the feeling that somebody's in there somewhere. Now we switch to a different world. Still photographs, taken in the shadow of public housing: the basketball court, the abandoned lot, the street corner. Here black folk hang out on sun-warmed concrete, laughing, crying, living, surviving. The shots of the woods and those of the city both have their natural audience, people for whom such images are familiar and benign. There are those who think of Frostian[2] woods as the pastoral, as America the Beautiful,* and others who see summer in the city as, likewise, beautiful and American. One of the marvelous tricks of Jordan Peele's debut feature, *Get Out*, is to reverse these constituencies, revealing two separate planets of American fear—separate but not equal. One side can claim a long, distinguished cinematic history: Why should I fear the black man in the city? The second, though not entirely unknown (*Deliverance*, *The Wicker Man*[3]), is certainly more obscure: Why should I fear the white man in the woods?

A few years ago I interviewed Peele as he came to the end of a long run on the celebrated Comedy Central sketch show *Key and Peele*. On that occasion he spoke about comic reversals—"I think reversals end up being the real bread and butter of the show*"—and about finding the emotional root of a joke in order to intensify it: "What's the mythology that is funny just because people know it's not true?" *Get Out* is structured around such inversions and reversals, although here "funny" has been replaced, more often than not, with "scary," and a further question has been posed: Which mythology? Or, more precisely: Whose? Instead of the familiar, terrified white man, robbed at gunpoint by a black man on a city street, we meet a black man walking in the leafy white suburbs, stalked by a white man in a slow-moving vehicle from whose stereo issues perhaps the whitest song in the world: "Run, rabbit, run, rabbit, run run run…"

Get Out flips the script, offering a compendium of black fears about white folk. White women who date black men. Waspy* families. Waspy family garden parties. Ukuleles. Crazy younger brothers. Crazy younger brothers who

---

1   *lovely, dark and deep*   Reference to American poet Robert Frost's famous poem "Stopping by Woods on a Snowy Evening" (1923).

2   *Frostian*   In the vein of Robert Frost, whose poetry frequently addresses nature and country life.

3   *Deliverance*   1972 film in which a group of friends from the city venture into the wilderness, where they are attacked by local white people;   *The Wicker Man*   1973 film in which a police officer travels to a remote Scottish island, where he is sacrificed in a pagan ritual.

play ukuleles. Sexual psychopaths, hunting, guns, cannibalism, mind control, well-meaning conversations about Obama. The police. Well-meaning conversations about basketball. Spontaneous roughhousing, spontaneous touching of one's biceps or hair. Lifestyle cults, actual cults. Houses with no other houses anywhere near them. Fondness for woods. The game bingo. Servile household staff, sexual enslavement, nostalgia for slavery—slavery itself. Every one of these reversals "lands"—just like a good joke—simultaneously describing and interpreting the situation at hand, and this, I think, is what accounts for the homogeneity of reactions to *Get Out*: It is a film that contains its own commentary.

For black viewers there is the pleasure of vindication. It's not often they have both their real and their irrational fears so thoroughly indulged. For white liberals—whom the movie purports to have in its satirical sights—there is the cringe of recognition, that queer but illuminating feeling of being suddenly "othered." (Oh, that's how *we* look to *them*?) And, I suppose, the satisfaction of being in on the joke. For example, there is the moment when the white girl, Rose (Allison Williams), and her new black boyfriend, Chris (Daniel Kaluuya), hit a deer on the way to her parents' country house. She's driving, yet when the police stop them he's the one asked for his license. Rose is sufficiently "woke" to step in front of her man and give the cop a self-righteous earful—but oblivious to the fact that only a white girl would dare assume she could do so with impunity. The audience—on both sides of the divide—groans with recognition. Chris himself—surely mindful of what happened to Sandra Bland, and Walter Scott, and Terence Crutcher, and Samuel DuBose[4]—smiles wryly but remains polite and deferential throughout. He is a photographer, those were his photographs of black city life we saw behind the credits, and that white and black Americans view the same situations through very different lenses is something he already understands.

5   This point is made a second time, more fiercely, in one of the final scenes. Chris is standing in those dark woods again, covered in blood; on the ground before him lies Rose, far more badly wounded. A cop car is approaching. Chris eyes it with resigned dread. As it happens, he is the victim in this gruesome tableau, but neither he nor anyone else in the cinema expects that to count

---

4   *Sandra Bland*   Twenty-eight-year-old Black woman who in July 2015 was found hanged in a Texas jail cell after she was arrested during a mishandled traffic stop;   *Walter Scott*   Fifty-year-old Black man who was shot from behind and killed by police during an April 2015 traffic stop in South Carolina;   *Terence Crutcher*   Forty-year-old Black man who, in September 2016, was shot and killed by Oklahoma police as he was walking to his car;   *Samuel DuBose*   Forty-three-year-old Black man who in July 2015 was shot and killed during a traffic stop by a University of Cincinnati police officer as DuBose attempted to drive away.

for a goddamned thing. ("You're really in for it now, you poor motherfucker," someone in the row behind me said. These days, a cop is apparently a more frightening prospect than a lobotomy-performing cult.) But then the car door opens and something unexpected happens: It is not the dreaded white cop after all but a concerned friend, Rod Williams (Lil Rel Howery), the charming and paranoid brother who warned Chris, at the very start, not to go stay with a load of white folks in the woods. Rod—who works for the TSA—surveys the bloody scene and does not immediately assume that Chris is the perp. A collective gasp of delight bursts over the audience, but in this final reversal the joke's on us. How, in 2017, are we still in a world where presuming a black man innocent until proven guilty is the material of comic fantasy?

These are the type of self-contained, ironic, politically charged sketches at which Peele has long excelled. But there's a deeper seam in *Get Out*, which is mined through visual symbol rather than situational comedy. I will not easily forget the lengthy close-ups of suffering black faces; suffering, but trapped behind masks, like so many cinematic analogues of the arguments of Frantz Fanon.[5] Chris himself, and the white family's maid, and the white family's groundskeeper, and the young, lobotomized beau of an old white lady—all frozen in attitudes of trauma, shock, or bland servility, or wearing chillingly fixed grins. In each case, the eyes register an internal desperation. *Get me out!* The oppressed. The cannibalized. The living dead. When a single tear or a dribble of blood runs down these masks, we are to understand this as a sign that there is still somebody in there. Somebody human. Somebody who has the potential to be whole.

As the movie progresses we learn what's going on: Black people aren't being murdered or destroyed up here in the woods, they're being used. A white grandmother's brain is now in her black maid's body. A blind old white gallerist hopes to place his brain in Chris's cranium and thus see with the young black photographer's eyes, be in his young black skin. Remnants of the black "host" remain after these operations—but not enough to make a person.

Peele has found a concrete metaphor for the ultimate unspoken fear: that to be oppressed is not so much to be hated as obscenely loved. Disgust and passion are intertwined. Our antipathies are simultaneously a record of our desires, our sublimated wishes, our deepest envies. The capacity to give birth or to make food from one's body; perceived intellectual, physical, or sexual superiority; perceived intimacy with the natural world, animals, and plants; perceived self-sufficiency in a faith or in a community. There are few qualities

---

5   *Frantz Fanon*   In *Black Skin, White Masks* (1957), Martinican anti-colonial theorist Frantz Fanon argues that colonization imposes a sense of inferiority on Black individuals, prompting a desire to imitate the colonizing culture.

in others that we cannot transform into a form of fear and loathing in ourselves. In the documentary *I Am Not Your Negro* (2016), James Baldwin gets to the heart of it:

> What white people have to do is try to find out in their hearts why it was necessary for them to have a nigger in the first place. Because I am not a nigger. I'm a man.... If I'm not the nigger here, and if you invented him, you the white people invented him, then you have to find out why. And the future of the country depends on that.

But there is an important difference between the invented "nigger" of 1963 and the invented African American of 2017: The disgust has mostly fallen away. We were declared beautiful back in the Sixties, but it has only recently been discovered that we are so. In the liberal circles depicted in *Get Out*, everything that was once reviled—our eyes, our skin, our backsides, our noses, our arms, our legs, our breasts, and of course our hair—is now openly envied and celebrated and aestheticized and deployed in secondary images to sell stuff. As one character tells Chris, "black is in fashion now."

10   To be clear, the life of the black citizen in America is no more envied or desired today than it was back in 1963. Her schools are still avoided and her housing still substandard and her neighborhood still feared and her personal and professional outcomes disproportionately linked to her zip code.* But her physical self is no longer reviled. If she is a child and comes up for adoption, many a white family will be delighted to have her, and if she is in your social class and social circle, she is very welcome to come to the party; indeed, it's not really a party unless she does come. No one will call her the n-word on national television, least of all a black intellectual. (The Baldwin quote is from a television interview.) For liberals the word is interdicted and unsayable.

But in place of the old disgust comes a new kind of cannibalism. The white people in *Get Out* want to get inside the black experience: They want to wear it like a skin and walk around in it. The modern word for this is "appropriation." There is an argument that there are many things that are "ours" and must not be touched or even looked at sideways, including (but not limited to) our voices, our personal style, our hair, our cultural products, our history, and, perhaps more than anything else, our pain. A people from whom so much has been stolen are understandably protective of their possessions, especially the ineffable kind. In these debates my mind always turns to a line of Nabokov,[6] a writer for whom arrival in America meant the loss of pretty much everything, including

---

6   *Nabokov*   Vladimir Nabokov (1899–1977), a Russian-born novelist and poet, was forced by political circumstances to leave Russia. Around the time of his immigration to America in 1940, he began to write primarily in English.

a language: "Why not leave their private sorrows to people? Is sorrow not, one asks, the only thing in the world people really possess?"

Two weeks after watching *Get Out*, I stood with my children in front of *Open Casket*, Dana Schutz's painting of Emmett Till, the black teenager who, in 1955, was beaten and lynched after being accused of flirting with a white woman. My children did not know what they were looking at and were too young for me to explain. Before I came, I had read the widely circulated letter to the curators of the Whitney Biennial objecting to their inclusion of this painting:

> I am writing to ask you to remove Dana Schutz's painting *Open Casket* and with the urgent recommendation that the painting be destroyed and not entered into any market or museum ... because it is not acceptable for a white person to transmute Black suffering into profit and fun, though the practice has been normalized for a long time.

I knew, from reading about this debate, that in fact the painting had never been for sale, so I focused instead on the other prong of the argument—an artist's right to a particular subject. "The subject matter is not Schutz's; white free speech and white creative freedom have been founded on the constraint of others, and are not natural rights."

I want to follow the letter very precisely, along its own logic, in which natural rights are replaced with racial ones. I will apply it personally. If *I* were an artist, and if I could paint—could the subject matter be mine? I am biracial. I have Afro-hair, my skin is brown, I am identified, by others and by myself, as a black woman. And so, by the logic of the letter—if I understand it correctly—this question of subject matter, in my case, would not come up, as it would not come up for the author of the letter, Hannah Black, who also happens to be biracial, and brown. Neither of us is American, but the author appears to speak confidently in defense of the African-American experience, so I, like her, will assume a transnational unity. I will assume that Emmett Till, if I could paint, could be my subject too.

Now I want to inch a step further. I turn from the painting to my children.   15
Their beloved father is white, I am biracial, so, by the old racial classifications of America, they are "quadroons."[7] Could *they* take black suffering as a subject of their art, should they ever make any? Their grandmother is as black as the ace of spades, as the British used to say; their mother is what the French still call café au lait. They themselves are sort of yellowy. When exactly does black suffering cease to be their concern? Their grandmother—raised on a

---

7   *quadroons*   Racial classification applied to people who are one-quarter Black. Terms such as these were current during the era of slavery and remain associated with that time.

postcolonial island, in extreme poverty, descended from slaves—knew black suffering intimately. But her grandchildren look white. Are they? If they are, shouldn't white people like my children concern themselves with the suffering of Emmett Till? Is making art a form of concern? Does it matter which form the concern takes? Could they be painters of occasional black subjects? (Dana Schutz paints many subjects.) Or must their concern take a different form: civil rights law, public-school teaching? If they ignore the warnings of the letter and take black suffering as their subject in a work of art, what should be the consequence? If their painting turns out to be a not especially distinguished expression of or engagement with their supposed concern, must it be removed from wherever it hangs? Destroyed? To what purpose?

Often I look at my children and remember that quadroons—green-eyed, yellow-haired people like my children—must have been standing on those auction blocks with their café au lait mothers and dark-skinned grandmothers. And I think too of how they would have had many opportunities to "pass," to sneak out and be lost in the white majority, not visibly connected to black suffering and so able to walk through town, marry white, lighten up the race again. To be biracial in America at that time was almost always to be the issue[8] of rape. It was in a literal sense to live with the enemy within, to have your physical being exist as an embodiment of the oppression of your people. Perhaps this trace of shame and inner conflict has never entirely left the biracial experience.

To be biracial at any time is complex. Speaking for myself, I know that racially charged historical moments, like this one, can increase the ever-present torsion within my experience until it feels like something's got to give. You start to yearn for absolute clarity: personal, genetic, political. I stood in front of the painting and thought how cathartic it would be if this picture filled me with rage. But it never got that deep into me, as either representation or appropriation. I think of it as a questionably successful example of both, but the letter condemning it will not contend with its relative success or failure, the letter lives in a binary world in which the painting is either facilely celebrated as proof of the autonomy of art or condemned to the philistine art bonfire. The first option, as the letter rightly argues, is often just hoary old white privilege dressed up as aesthetic theory, but the second is—let's face it—the province of Nazis and censorious evangelicals. Art is a traffic in symbols and images, it has never been politically or historically neutral, and I do not find discussions on appropriation and representation to be in any way trivial. Each individual example has to be *thought through*, and we have every right to include such considerations in our evaluations of art (and also to point out the often dubious neutrality of supposedly pure aesthetic criteria). But when arguments of

---

8　*issue*　Offspring.

appropriation are linked to a racial essentialism no more sophisticated than antebellum miscegenation laws,[9] well, then we head quickly into absurdity. Is Hannah Black black enough to write this letter? Are my children too white to engage with black suffering? How black is black enough? Does an "octoroon"[10] still count?

When I looked at *Open Casket*, the truth is I didn't feel very much. I tried to transfer to the painting—or even to Dana Schutz—some of the cold fury that is sparked by looking at the historical photograph of Emmett Till, whose mother insisted he have an open casket, or by considering the crimes of Carolyn Bryant, the white woman who falsely accused him of harassing her, but nothing I saw in that canvas could provoke such an emotion. The painting is an abstraction without much intensity, and there's a clear caution in the brushstrokes around the eyes: Schutz has gone in only so far. Yet the anxious aporia in the upper face is countered by the area around the mouth, where the canvas roils, coming toward us three-dimensionally, like a swelling—the flesh garroted, twisted, striped—as if something is pushing from behind the death mask, trying to get out. That *did* move me.

What's harder to see is why this picture was singled out. A few floors up hung a painting by a white artist, Eric Fischl, *A Visit to?/?A Visit from?/?The Island*, in which rich white holidaymakers on a beach are juxtaposed with black boat people washed up on the sand, some dead, some half-naked, desperate, writhing, suffering. Painted in 1983, by an artist now in his late sixties, it is presumably for sale, yet it goes unmentioned in a letter whose main effect has been to divert attention from everything else in the show. Henry Taylor, Deana Lawson, Lyle Ashton Harris, and Cauleen Smith were just a few of the artists of color lighting up the Whitney in a thrilling biennial that delved deep into black experience, illuminating its joys and suffering both. Looking at their work, I found I resented the implication that black pain is so raw and unprocessed—and black art practice so vulnerable and invisible—that a single painting by a white woman can radically influence it one way or another. Nor did I need to convince myself of my own authenticity by drawing a line between somebody else's supposed fraudulence and the fears I have concerning my own (thus evincing an unfortunate tendency toward overcompensation that, it must be admitted, is not unknown among us biracial folks). No. The viewer is not a fraud. Neither is the painter. The truth is that this painting and I are simply not in profound communication.

---

9   *racial essentialism* Idea that there are fundamental, unchangeable differences between races; *antebellum miscegenation laws* Pre-Civil War regulations prohibiting interracial marriage and, in some cases, any sexual relations between races.

10   *octoroon* Racial classification applied to people who are one eighth Black; it is part of the same classification system as "quadroon."

20   This is always a risk in art. The solution remains as it has always been: Get out (of the gallery) or go deeper in (to the argument). Write a screed against it. Critique the hell out of it. Tear it to shreds in your review or paint another painting in response. But remove it? Destroy it? Instead I turned from the painting, not offended, not especially shocked or moved, not even terribly engaged by it, and walked with the children to the next room.

      We have been warned not to get under one another's skin, to keep our distance. But Jordan Peele's horror-fantasy—in which we are inside one another's skin and intimately involved in one another's suffering—is neither a horror nor a fantasy. It is a fact of our experience. The real fantasy is that we can get out of one another's way, make a clean cut between black and white, a final cathartic separation between us and them. For the many of us in loving, mixed families, this is the true impossibility. There are people online who seem astounded that *Get Out* was written and directed by a man with a white wife and a white mother, a man who may soon have—depending on how the unpredictable phenotype lottery goes—a white-appearing child. But this is the history of race in America. Families can become black, then white, then black again within a few generations. And even when Americans are not genetically mixed, they live in a mixed society at the national level if no other. There is no getting out of our intertwined history.

      But in this moment of resurgent black consciousness, God knows it feels good—therapeutic!—to mark a clear separation from white America, the better to speak in a collective voice. We will not be moved. We can't breathe.[11] We will not be executed for traffic violations or for the wearing of hoodies. We will no longer tolerate substandard schools, housing, health care. *Get Out*—as evidenced by its huge box office—is the right movie for this moment. It is the opposite of post-black or postracial. It reveals race as the fundamental American lens through which everything is seen. That part, to my mind, is right on the money. But the "us" and "them"? That's a cheaper gag. Whether they like it or not, Americans are one people. (And the binary of black and white is only one part of this nation's infinitely variegated racial composition.) Lobotomies are the cleanest cut; real life is messier. I can't wait for Peele— with his abundant gifts, black-nerd smarts, comprehensive cinematic fandom, and complex personal experience—to go deeper in, and out the other side.

(2017)

---

11 *We can't breathe* Reference to "I can't breathe," the last words of Eric Garner, a 43-year old Black man killed by New York police in 2014 when he was arrested under suspicion of illegally selling individual cigarettes. The phrase became a common protest chant at demonstrations against police brutality.

Questions

1. Consider the following passage:

   > Jordan Peele's horror-fantasy—in which we are inside one another's skin and intimately involved in one another's suffering—is neither a horror nor a fantasy. It is a fact of our experience. The real fantasy is that we can get out of one another's way, make a clean cut between black and white, a final cathartic separation between us and them. (paragraph 21)

   What does Smith mean by this passage? How does she relate these ideas to the controversy surrounding Schutz's painting?

2. Consider the following critique of this article, advanced by Candace McDuffie on the *Ploughshares* literary blog:

   > … [I]t is clear that [Smith] is more interested in being an ethnographer to black culture than a black woman. Although she states that she is identified by herself and others as black, she centers whiteness in an essay that was supposed to focus on black pain. She measures blackness only by its physical proximity to whiteness. While Smith acknowledges the complexities of being biracial, she doesn't probe her privilege of having light skin nor does she pay the same attention to what cultural appropriation actually is. Smith … views it as a particular population of people guarding their culture in a malicious manner and not factoring in our justification for being so protective of it. Since black people were brought to this country, our bodies have been commodified for labor, for sexual exploitation, and even for entertainment.

   To what extent do you agree with McDuffie's critique? Explain your view.

3. Consider the photographs of Emmett Till that are reprinted in this anthology's color insert. What qualities of these photographs and their historical context make it so controversial for Schutz to use Till's image? Do you agree with those who condemn her choice?

4. Find an image of Schutz's *Open Casket* online.

   a. In your view, how well does this painting address its subject? What does it mean to address well a subject such as Till's death—or is such a thing impossible?

   b. To what extent (if at all) is the painting's quality relevant to the question of whether or not it was wrong for Schutz to use Till's image?

5. Watch *Get Out* and read Brent Staples's article "The Movie *Get Out* Is a Strong Antidote to the Myth of 'Postracial' America" (the latter is also included in this anthology). Then, write an analysis of the film that draws on the commentary of both Staples and Smith.

6. Smith uses the terms "octoroon" and "quadroon" in this essay. What is the rhetorical impact of this choice?

7. Smith was born in England to a white father and a Black mother. How, if at all, is her personal experience of race and culture reflected in this essay?

LANGUAGE AND
CULTURE

GLORIA ANZALDÚA

from BORDERLANDS/LA FRONTERA: THE NEW MESTIZA

HOW TO TAME A WILD TONGUE

Poet, critical theorist, and editor Gloria Anzaldúa grounded much of her scholarly writing in her experiences as a lesbian and as a Chicana (a woman of Mexican ancestry living in America). The following piece is taken from Borderlands/La Frontera, *her pioneering work about living on the borders between genders, sexual orientations, cultures, races, and languages—and near the line between Texas and Mexico. As she phrases it in her preface, "The actual physical borderland that I'm dealing with in this book is the Texas-US Southwest/Mexican border. The psychological borderlands, the sexual borderlands and the spiritual borderlands are not particular to the Southwest. In fact, the Borderlands are physically present whenever two or more cultures edge each other, where people of different races occupy the same territory, where under, lower, middle and upper classes touch, where the space between two individuals shrinks with intimacy."*

&

"We're going to have to control your tongue," the dentist says, pulling out all the metal from my mouth. Silver bits plop and tinkle into the basin. My mouth is a motherlode.

The dentist is cleaning out my roots. I get a whiff of the stench when I gasp. "I can't cap that tooth yet, you're still draining," he says.

"We're going to have to do something about your tongue," I hear the anger rising in his voice. My tongue keeps pushing out the wads of cotton, pushing, back the drills, the long thin needles. "I've never seen anything as strong or as stubborn," he says. And I think, how do you tame a wild tongue, train it to be quiet, how do you bridle and saddle it? How do you make it lie down?

"Who is to say that robbing a people of its language is less violent than war?"
—Ray Gwyn Smith[1]

I remember being caught speaking Spanish at recess—that was good for three licks on the knuckles with a sharp ruler. I remember being sent to the corner of the classroom for "talking back" to the Anglo teacher when all I was trying to do was tell her how to pronounce my name. "If you want to be American, speak 'American.' If you don't like it, go back to Mexico where you belong."

5   "I want you to speak English. *Pa' hallar buen trabajo tienes que saber hablar el inglés bien. Qué vale toda tu educación si todavía hablas inglés con un* 'accent,'" my mother would say, mortified that I spoke English like a Mexican. At Pan American University, I, and all Chicano students, were required to take two speech classes. Their purpose: to get rid of our accents.

Attacks on one's form of expression with the intent to censor are a violation of the First Amendment.* *El Anglo con cara de inocente nos arrancó la lengua.* Wild tongues can't be tamed, they can only be cut out.

OVERCOMING THE TRADITION OF SILENCE

Ahogadas, escupimos el oscuro.
Peleando con nuestra propia sombra
el silencio nos sepulta.

En boca cerrada no entran moscas. "Flies don't enter a closed mouth" is a saying I kept hearing when I was a child. *Ser habladora* was to be a gossip and a liar, to talk too much. *Muchachitas bien criadas*, well-bred girls don't answer back. *Es una falta de respeto* to talk back to one's mother or father. I remember one of the sins I'd recite to the priest in the confession box the few times I went to confession: talking back to my mother, *hablar pa' 'trás, repelar. Hocicona, repelona, chismosa*, having a big mouth, questioning, carrying tales are all signs of being *mal criada*. In my culture they are all words that are derogatory if applied to women—I've never heard them applied to men.

The first time I heard two women, a Puerto Rican and a Cuban, say the word "*nosotras*,"[2] I was shocked. I had not known the word existed. Chicanas use *nosotros* whether we're male or female. We are robbed of our female being by the masculine plural. Language is a male discourse.

---

1   [Anzaldúa's note]   Ray Gwyn Smith, *Moorland Is Cold Country*, unpublished book.
2   *nosotras*   Spanish: us, we. *Nosotras* is a feminine form; *nosotros* is a masculine form.

And our tongues have become
dry   the wilderness has
dried out our tongues   and
we have forgotten speech.
—Irena Klepfisz[3]

Even our own people, other Spanish speakers *nos quieren poner candados en la boca*. They would hold us back with their bag of *reglas de academia*.

OYÉ COMO LADRA: EL LENGUAJE DE LA FRONTERA

Quien tiene boca se equivoca.
—Mexican saying

"*Pocho*, cultural traitor, you're speaking the oppressor's language by speaking   10
English, you're ruining the Spanish language," I have been accused by various
Latinos and Latinas. Chicano Spanish is considered by the purist and by most
Latinos deficient, a mutilation of Spanish.

But Chicano Spanish is a border tongue which developed naturally.
Change, *evolución, enriquecimiento de palabras nuevas por invención o adop-ción* have created variants of Chicano Spanish, *un nuevo lenguaje. Un lenguaje que corresponde a un modo de vivir*. Chicano Spanish is not incorrect, it is a
living language.

For a people who are neither Spanish nor live in a country in which Spanish
is the first language; for a people who live in a country in which English is
the reigning tongue but who are not Anglo; for a people who cannot entirely
identify with either standard (formal, Castillian) Spanish nor standard English,
what recourse is left to them but to create their own language? A language
which they can connect their identity to, one capable of communicating the
realities and values true to themselves—a language with terms that are neither
español ni inglés, but both. We speak a patois, a forked tongue, a variation of
two languages.

Chicano Spanish sprang out of the Chicanos' need to identify ourselves as a
distinct people. We needed a language with which we could communicate with
ourselves, a secret language. For some of us, language is a homeland closer
than the Southwest—for many Chicanos today live in the Midwest and the
East. And because we are a complex, heterogeneous people, we speak many
languages. Some of the languages we speak are:

---

3   [Anzaldúa's note]   Irena Klepfisz, "*Di rayze abeym*/The Journey Home," in *The Tribe of Dina: A Jewish Women's Anthology*, Melanie Kaye/Kantrowitz and Irena Klepfisz, eds. (Montpelier, VT: Sinister Wisdom Books, 1986), 49.

1. Standard English
2. Working class and slang English
3. Standard Spanish
4. Standard Mexican Spanish
5. North Mexican Spanish dialect
6. Chicano Spanish (Texas, New Mexico, Arizona and California have regional variations)
7. Tex-Mex
8. *Pachuco* (called *caló*)

My "home" tongues are the languages I speak with my sister and brothers, with my friends. They are the last five listed, with 6 and 7 being closest to my heart. From school, the media and job situations, I've picked up standard and working class English. From Mamagrande Locha and from reading Spanish and Mexican literature, I've picked up Standard Spanish and Standard Mexican Spanish. From *los recién llegados*, Mexican immigrants, and *braceros*, I learned the North Mexican dialect. With Mexicans I'll try to speak either Standard Mexican Spanish or the North Mexican dialect. From my parents and Chicanos living in the Valley, I picked up Chicano Texas Spanish, and I speak it with my mom, younger brother (who married a Mexican and who rarely mixes Spanish with English), aunts and other relatives.

15   With Chicanas from *Nuevo México* or *Arizona* I will speak Chicano Spanish a little, but often they don't understand what I'm saying. With most California Chicanas I speak entirely in English (unless I forget). When I first moved to San Francisco, I'd rattle off something in Spanish, unintentionally embarrassing them. Often it is only with another Chicana *tejana* that I can talk freely.

Words distorted by English are known as anglicisms or *pochismos*. The *pocho* is an anglicized Mexican or American of Mexican origin who speaks Spanish with an accent characteristic of North Americans and who distorts and reconstructs the language according to the influence of English.[4] Tex-Mex, or Spanglish, comes most naturally to me. I may switch back and forth from English to Spanish in the same sentence or in the same word. With my sister and my brother Nune and with Chicano *tejano* contemporaries I speak in Tex-Mex.

From kids and people my own age I picked up *Pachuco*. *Pachuco* (the language of the zoot suiters[5]) is a language of rebellion, both against Standard

---

4   [Anzaldúa's note]   R.C. Ortega, *Dialectología Del Barrio*, trans. Hortencia S. Alwan (Los Angeles, CA: R.C. Ortega Publisher & Bookseller, 1977), 132.

5   *zoot suiters*   Zoot suits—suits with wide legs and long, shoulder-padded jackets— are associated with Black and Chicano cultural pride.

Spanish and Standard English. It is a secret language. Adults of the culture and outsiders cannot understand it. It is made up of slang words from both English and Spanish. *Ruca* means girl or woman, *vato* means guy or dude, *chale* means no, *simón* means yes, *churo* is sure, talk is *periquiar*, *pigionear* means petting, *que gacho* means how nerdy, *ponte águila* means watch out, death is called *la pelona*. Through lack of practice and not having others who can speak it, I've lost most of the *Pachuco* tongue.

Chicano Spanish

Chicanos, after 250 years of Spanish/Anglo colonization have developed significant differences in the Spanish we speak. We collapse two adjacent vowels into a single syllable and sometimes shift the stress in certain words such as *maíz/maiz*, *cohete/cuete*. We leave out certain consonants when they appear between vowels: *lado/lao*, *mojado/mojao*. Chicanos from South Texas pronounced *f* as *j* as in *jue* (*fue*). Chicanos use "archaisms," words that are no longer in the Spanish language, words that have been evolved out. We say *semos*, *truje*, *haiga*, *ansina*, and *naiden*. We retain the "archaic" *j*, as in *jalar*, that derives from an earlier *h*, (the French *halar* or the Germanic *halon* which was lost to standard Spanish in the 16th century), but which is still found in several regional dialects such as the one spoken in South Texas. (Due to geography, Chicanos from the Valley of South Texas were cut off linguistically from other Spanish speakers. We tend to use words that the Spaniards brought over from Medieval Spain. The majority of the Spanish colonizers in Mexico and the Southwest came from Extremadura—Hernán Cortés was one of them—and Andalucía. Andalucians pronounce *ll* like a *y*, and their *d*'s tend to be absorbed by adjacent vowels: *tirado* becomes *tirao*. They brought *el lenguaje popular, dialectos y regionalismos*.[6])

Chicanos and other Spanish speakers also shift *ll* to *y* and *z* to *s*.[7] We leave out initial syllables, saying *tar* for *estar*, *toy* for *estoy*, *hora* for *ahora* (*cubanos* and *puertorriqueños* also leave out initial letters of some words). We also leave out the final syllable such as *pa* for *para*. The intervocalic *y*, the *ll* as in *tortilla*, *ella*, *botella*, gets replaced by *tortia* or *tortiya*, *ea*, *botea*. We add an additional syllable at the beginning of certain words: *atocar* for *tocar*, *agastar* for *gastar*. Sometimes we'll say *lavaste las vacijas*, other times *lavates* (substituting the *ates* verb ending for the *aste*).

---

6 [Anzaldúa's note]   Eduaredo Hernandéz-Chávez, Andrew D. Cohen, and Anthony F. Beltramo, *El Lenguaje de los Chicanos*: *Regional and Social Characteristics of Language Used by Mexican Americans* (Arlington, VA: Center for Applied Linguistics, 1975), 39.

7 [Anzaldúa's note]   Hernandéz-Chávez, xvii.

20   We use anglicisms, words borrowed from English: *bola* from ball, *carpeta* from carpet, *máchina de lavar* (instead of *lavadora*) from washing machine. Tex-Mex argot, created by adding a Spanish sound at the beginning or end of an English word such as *cookiar* for cook, *watchar* for watch, *parkiar* for park, and *rapiar* for rape, is the result of the pressures on Spanish speakers to adapt to English.

We don't use the word *vosotros/as* or its accompanying verb form. We don't say *claro* (to mean yes), *imagínate*, or *me emociona*, unless we picked up Spanish from Latinas, out of a book, or in a classroom. Other Spanish-speaking groups are going through the same, or similar, development in their Spanish.

LINGUISTIC TERRORISM

Deslenguadas. Somos los del español deficiente. We are your linguistic nightmare, your linguistic aberration, your linguistic *mestizaje*, the subject of your *burla*. Because we speak with tongues of fire we are culturally crucified. Racially, culturally and linguistically *somos huérfanos*—we speak an orphan tongue.

Chicanas who grew up speaking Chicano Spanish have internalized the belief that we speak poor Spanish. It is illegitimate, a bastard language. And because we internalize how our language has been used against us by the dominant culture, we use our language differences against each other.

Chicana feminists often skirt around each other with suspicion and hesitation. For the longest time I couldn't figure it out. Then it dawned on me. To be close to another Chicana is like looking into the mirror. We are afraid of what we'll see there. *Pena.* Shame. Low estimation of self. In childhood we are told that our language is wrong. Repeated attacks on our native tongue diminish our sense of self. The attacks continue throughout our lives.

Chicanas feel uncomfortable talking in Spanish to Latinas, afraid of their censure. Their language was not outlawed in their countries. They had a whole lifetime of being immersed in their native tongue; generations, centuries in which Spanish was a first language, taught in school, heard on radio and TV, and read in the newspaper.

25   If a person, Chicana or Latina, has a low estimation of my native tongue, she also has a low estimation of me. Often with *mexicanas y latinas* we'll speak English as a neutral language. Even among Chicanas we tend to speak English at parties or conferences. Yet, at the same time, we're afraid the other will think we're *agringadas* because we don't speak Chicano Spanish. We oppress each other trying to out-Chicano each other, vying to be the "real" Chicanas, to

speak like Chicanos. There is no one Chicano language just as there is no one Chicano experience. A monolingual Chicana whose first language is English or Spanish is just as much a Chicana as one who speaks several variants of Spanish. A Chicana from Michigan or Chicago or Detroit is just as much a Chicana as one from the Southwest. Chicano Spanish is as diverse linguistically as it is regionally.

By the end of this century, Spanish speakers will comprise the biggest minority group in the U.S., a country where students in high schools and colleges are encouraged to take French classes because French is considered more "cultured." But for a language to remain alive it must be used.[8] By the end of this century, English, and not Spanish, will be the mother tongue of most Chicanos and Latinos.

So, if you want to really hurt me, talk badly about my language. Ethnic identity is twin skin to linguistic identity—I am my language. Until I can take pride in my language, I cannot take pride in myself. Until I can accept as legitimate Chicano Texas Spanish, Tex-Mex and all the other languages I speak, I cannot accept the legitimacy of myself. Until I am free to write bilingually and to switch codes[9] without having always to translate, while I still have to speak English or Spanish when I would rather speak Spanglish, and as long as I have to accommodate the English speakers rather than having them accommodate me, my tongue will be illegitimate.

I will no longer be made to feel ashamed of existing. I will have my voice: Indian, Spanish, white. I will have my serpent's tongue[10]—my woman's voice, my sexual voice, my poet's voice. I will overcome the tradition of silence.

> My fingers
> move sly against your palm
> Like women everywhere, we speak in code ....
> —Melanie Kaye/Kantrowitz[11]

---

8 [Anzaldúa's note] Irena Klepfisz, "Secular Jewish Identity: Yidishkayt in America," in *The Tribe of Dina* Kaye/Kantrowitz and Klepfisz, eds., 43.

9 *switch codes* Alternate between languages, or between styles of language, within one conversation.

10 *serpent's tongue* In "Entering into the Serpent," an earlier chapter of *Borderlands/La Frontera*, Anzaldúa examines the history of the snake's association with Mesoamerican goddesses linked to femininity, sexuality, creation, and death. Snakes are also symbolic in the Bible: a serpent persuades Eve, the first woman, to eat the fruit forbidden to her by God, which leads to the expulsion of the first people from the paradise of Eden (see Genesis 3).

11 [Anzaldúa's note] Melanie Kaye/Kantrowitz, "Sign," in *We Speak In Code: Poems and Other Writings* (Pittsburgh, PA: Motheroot Publications, Inc., 1980), 85.

"VISTAS," CORRIDOS, Y COMIDA: MY NATIVE TONGUE

In the 1960s, I read my first Chicano novel. It was *City of Night* by John Rechy, a gay Texan, son of a Scottish father and a Mexican mother. For days I walked around in stunned amazement that a Chicano could write and could get published. When I read *I Am Joaquín*[12] I was surprised to see a bilingual book by a Chicano in print. When I saw poetry written in Tex-Mex for the first time, a feeling of pure joy flashed through me. I felt like we really existed as a people. In 1971, when I started teaching High School English to Chicano students, I tried to supplement the required texts with works by Chicanos, only to be reprimanded and forbidden to do so by the principal. He claimed that I was supposed to teach "American" and English literature. At the risk of being fired, I swore my students to secrecy and slipped in Chicano short stories, poems, a play. In graduate school, while working toward a Ph.D., I had to "argue" with one advisor after the other, semester after semester, before I was allowed to make Chicano literature an area of focus.

30   Even before I read books by Chicanos or Mexicans, it was the Mexican movies I saw at the drive-in—the Thursday night special of $1.00 a carload—that gave me a sense of belonging. "*Vámonos a las vistas*," my mother would call out and we'd all—grandmother, brothers, sister and cousins—squeeze into the car. We'd wolf down cheese and bologna white bread sandwiches while watching Pedro Infante in melodramatic tearjerkers like *Nosotros los pobres*, the first "real" Mexican movie (that was not an imitation of European movies). I remember seeing *Cuando los hijos se van* and surmising that all Mexican movies played up the love a mother has for her children and what ungrateful sons and daughters suffer when they are not devoted to their mothers. I remember the singing-type "westerns" of Jorge Negrete and Miguel Aceves Mejía. When watching Mexican movies, I felt a sense of homecoming as well as alienation. People who were to amount to something didn't go to Mexican movies, or *bailes* or tune their radios to *bolero*, *rancherita*, and *corrido* music. The whole time I was growing up, there was *norteño* music sometimes called North Mexican border music, or Tex-Mex music, or Chicano music, or *cantina* (bar) music. I grew up listening to *conjuntos*, three- or four-piece bands made up of folk musicians playing guitar, *bajo sexto*, drums and button accordion, which Chicanos had borrowed from the German immigrants who had come to Central Texas and Mexico to farm and build breweries. In the Rio Grande Valley, Steve Jordan and Little Joe Hernández were popular, and Flaco Jiménez was the accordion king. The rhythms of Tex-Mex music are those of the polka,

---

12 [Anzaldúa's note] Rodolfo, Gonzales, *I Am Joaquín / Yo Soy Joaquín* (New York, NY: Bantam Books, 1972). It was first published in 1967.

also adapted from the Germans, who in turn had borrowed the polka from the Czechs and Bohemians.

I remember the hot, sultry evenings when *corridos*—songs of love and death on the Texas-Mexican borderlands—reverberated out of cheap amplifiers from the local *cantinas* and wafted in through my bedroom window.

Corridos first became widely used along the South Texas/Mexican border during the early conflict between Chicanos and Anglos. The *corridos* are usually about Mexican heroes who do valiant deeds against the Anglo oppressors. Pancho Villa's song, "*La cucaracha*," is the most famous one. *Corridos* of John F. Kennedy and his death are still very popular in the Valley. Older Chicanos remember Lydia Mendoza, one of the great border *corrido* singers who was called *la Gloria de Tejas*. Her "*El tango negro*," sung during the Great Depression, made her a singer of the people. The everpresent *corridos* narrated one hundred years of border history, bringing news of events as well as entertaining. These folk musicians and folk songs are our chief cultural mythmakers, and they made our hard lives seem bearable.

I grew up feeling ambivalent about our music. Country-western and rock-and-roll had more status. In the 50s and 60s, for the slightly educated and *agringado* Chicanos, there existed a sense of shame at being caught listening to our music. Yet I couldn't stop my feet from thumping to the music, could not stop humming the words, nor hide from myself the exhilaration I felt when I heard it.

There are more subtle ways that we internalize identification, especially in the forms of images and emotions. For me food and certain smells are tied to my identity, to my homeland. Woodsmoke curling up to an immense blue sky; woodsmoke perfuming my grandmother's clothes, her skin. The stench of cow manure and the yellow patches on the ground; the crack of a .22 rifle and the reek of cordite. Homemade white cheese sizzling in a pan, melting inside a folded *tortilla*. My sister Hilda's hot, spicy *menudo*, *chile colorado* making it deep red, pieces of *panza* and hominy floating on top. My brother Carito barbequing *fajitas* in the backyard. Even now and 3,000 miles away, I can see my mother spicing the ground beef, pork and venison with *chile*. My mouth salivates at the thought of the hot steaming *tamales* I would be eating if I were home.

SI LE PREGUNTAS A MI MAMÁ, "¿QUÉ ERES?"

"Identity is the essential core of who we are as individuals, the conscious experience of the self inside."
—Kaufman[13]

35   *Nosotros los* Chicanos straddle the borderlands. On one side of us, we are constantly exposed to the Spanish of the Mexicans, on the other side we hear the Anglos' incessant clamoring so that we forget our language. Among ourselves we don't say *nosotros los americanos, o nosotros los españoles, o nosotros los hispanos*. We say *nosotros los mexicanos* (by *mexicanos* we do not mean citizens of Mexico; we do not mean a national identity, but a racial one). We distinguish between *mexicanos del otro lado* and *mexicanos de este lado*. Deep in our hearts we believe that being Mexican has nothing to do with which country one lives in. Being Mexican is a state of soul—not one of mind, not one of citizenship. Neither eagle nor serpent,[14] but both. And like the ocean, neither animal respects borders.

> *Dime con quien andas y te diré quien eres.*
> (Tell me who your friends are and I'll tell you who you are.)
> —Mexican saying

Si le preguntas a mi mamá, "¿Qué eres?" te dirá, "Soy mexicana." My brothers and sister say the same. I sometimes will answer *"soy mexicana"* and at others will say *"soy Chicana" o "soy tejana."* But I identified as *"Raza"* before I ever identified as *"mexicana"* or "Chicana."

As a culture, we call ourselves Spanish when referring to ourselves as a linguistic group and when copping out. It is then that we forget our predominant Indian genes. We are 70–80% Indian.[15] We call ourselves Hispanic[16] or Spanish-American or Latin American or Latin when linking ourselves to other Spanish-speaking peoples of the Western hemisphere and when copping out.

---

13 [Anzaldúa's note] Gershen Kaufman, *Shame: The Power of Caring* (Cambridge, MA: Schenkman Books, Inc. 1980), 68.

14 *eagle nor serpent* The Mexican coat of arms depicts an eagle eating a snake, and the bald eagle is the national animal of the United States.

15 [Anzaldúa's note] John R. Chávez, *The Lost Land: The Chicano Images of the Southwest* (Albuquerque, NM: University of New Mexico Press, 1984), 88–90.

16 [Anzaldúa's note] "Hispanic" is derived from *Hispanis* (*España*, a name given to the Iberian Peninsula in ancient times when it was a part of the Roman Empire) and is a term designated by the U.S. government to make it easier to handle us on paper.

We call ourselves Mexican-American[17] to signify we are neither Mexican nor American, but more the noun "American" than the adjective "Mexican" (and when copping out).

Chicanós and other people of color suffer economically for not acculturating. This voluntary (yet forced) alienation makes for psychological conflict, a kind of dual identity—we don't identify with the Anglo-American cultural values and we don't totally identify with the Mexican cultural values. We are a synergy of two cultures with various degrees of Mexicanness or Angloness. I have so internalized the borderland conflict that sometimes I feel like one cancels out the other and we are zero, nothing, no one. *A veces no soy nada ni nadie. Pero hasta cuando no lo soy, lo soy.*

When not copping out, when we know we are more than nothing, we call ourselves Mexican, referring to race and ancestry; *mestizo* when affirming both our Indian and Spanish (but we hardly ever own our Black ancestry); Chicano when referring to a politically aware people born and/or raised in the U.S.; *Raza* when referring to Chicanos; *tejanos* when we are Chicanos from Texas.

Chicanos did not know we were a people until 1965 when Cesar Chavez[18] and the farmworkers united and *I Am Joaquín* was published and *la Raza Unida*[19] party was formed in Texas. With that recognition, we became a distinct people. Something momentous happened to the Chicano soul—we became aware of our reality and acquired a name and a language (Chicano Spanish) that reflected that reality. Now that we had a name, some of the fragmented pieces began to fall together—who we were, what we were, how we had evolved. We began to get glimpses of what we might eventually become.

40

Yet the struggle of identities continues, the struggle of borders is our reality still. One day the inner struggle will cease and a true integration take place. In the meantime, *tenemos que hacerla lucha. ¿Quién está protegiendo los ranchos de mi gente? ¿Quién está tratando de cerrar la fisura entre la india y el blanco en nuestra sangre? El Chicano, sí, el Chicano que anda como un ladrón en su propia casa.*

---

17 [Anzaldúa's note]   The Treaty of Guadalupe Hidalgo created the Mexican-American in 1848.

18   *Cesar Chavez*   Iconic Chicano activist best known as a founder of the National Farm Workers Association, which evolved into the influential United Farm Workers union.

19   *la Raza Unida*   Chicano political party that arose in the 1970s.

Los Chicanos, how patient we seem, how very patient. There is the quiet of the Indian about us.[20] We know how to survive. When other races have given up their tongue, we've kept ours. We know what it is to live under the hammer blow of the dominant *norteamericano* culture. But more than we count the blows, we count the days the weeks the years the centuries the eons until the white laws and commerce and customs will rot in deserts they've created, lie bleached. *Humildes* yet proud, *quietos* yet wild, *nosotros los mexicanos*-Chicanos will walk by the crumbling ashes as we go about our business. Stubborn, persevering, impenetrable as stone, yet possessing a malleability that renders us unbreakable, we, the *mestizas* and *mestizos*, will remain.

(1987)

Questions

1. How does the opening anecdote about Anzaldúa's experience at the dentist frame the rest of the piece?

2. Anzaldúa writes in both English and Spanish in this piece. What is your reaction to this? Why do you think she writes in both languages?

3. Why are Chicano books and Mexican films important to Anzaldúa?

4. How is Anzaldúa's experience of being Chicano inflected by her experience of gender?

5. Anzaldúa writes that "*Nosotros los* Chicanos straddle the borderlands" (paragraph 35).

   a. What does it mean to "straddle a borderland"?

   b. In what way or ways do Chicanos straddle the borderlands?

   c. Do you occupy any borderlands, literally or metaphorically, in your life? To what extent do borderlands play a role in your own identity or experience?

6. In paragraph 13, Anzaldúa makes a list of "some of the languages" Chicanos speak. Following her example, make a list of the languages and language forms you speak. How different are they? Where do you speak each of them? How much privilege does each form carry?

---

20 [Anzaldúa's note] Anglos, in order to alleviate their guilt for dispossessing the Chicano, stressed the Spanish part of us and perpetrated the myth of the Spanish Southwest. We have accepted the fiction that we are Hispanic, that is Spanish, in order to accommodate ourselves to the dominant culture and its abhorrence of Indians. Chávez, 88–91.

7. Anzaldúa writes that Chicanos are "Neither eagle nor serpent, but both" (paragraph 35). Explain this metaphor.

8. Read "If Black English Isn't a Language, Then Tell Me, What Is?" by James Baldwin (also in this anthology). What are the parallels between Baldwin's and Anzaldúa's arguments? How are they different?

9. An image of Anishinaabekwe artist Rebecca Belmore's sculpture *Mixed Blessings* is included in this anthology's color insert.

   a. Compare Belmore's sculpture with Anzaldúa's essay. What does each creator's work say about her experience as a marginalized person?

   b. How do Anzaldúa's and Belmore's pieces each depict the relationship between identity and self-expression? What (if anything) do these depictions have in common, and how (if at all) do they differ?

Leslie Marmon Silko

Language and Literature from a Pueblo Indian Perspective

Leslie Marmon Silko—a writer of fiction and poetry as well as non-fiction—draws in much of her writing on her experience growing up on the Laguna Pueblo Reservation in New Mexico; her essays examine colonialism, women's issues, and racism in the United States from a variety of angles. This essay, which began as a speech and first appeared in English Literature: Opening Up the Canon *(1979), is organized to mirror the patterns and construction of Pueblo stories.*

❧

Where I come from, the words most highly valued are those spoken from the heart, unpremeditated and unrehearsed. Among the Pueblo people,* a written speech or statement is highly suspect because the true feelings of the speaker remain hidden as she reads words that are detached from the occasion and the audience. I have intentionally not written a formal paper because I want you to hear and to experience English in a structure that follows patterns from the oral tradition. For those of you accustomed to being taken from point A to point B to point C, this presentation may be somewhat difficult to follow. Pueblo expression resembles something like a spider's web with many little threads radiating from the center, crisscrossing each other. As with the web, the structure emerges as it is made and you must simply listen and trust, as the Pueblo people do, that meaning will be made.

My task is a formidable one: I ask you to set aside a number of basic approaches that you have been using, and probably will continue to use, and instead, to approach language from the Pueblo perspective, one that embraces the whole of creation and the whole of history and time.

What changes would Pueblo writers make to English as a language for literature? I have some examples of stories in English that I will use to address this question. At the same time, I would like to explain the importance of story-telling and how it relates to a Pueblo theory of language.

So I will begin, appropriately enough, with the Pueblo Creation story, an all-inclusive story of how life began. In this story, Tséitsínako, Thought Woman, by thinking of her sisters, and together with her sisters, thought of everything that is. In this way, the world was created. Everything in this world was a part of the original creation; the people at home understood that far away there were other human beings, also a part of this world. The Creation story even includes a prophecy, which describes the origin of European and African peoples and also refers to Asians.

This story, I think, suggests something about why the Pueblo people are 5 more concerned with story and communication and less concerned with a particular language. There are at least six, possibly seven, distinct languages among the twenty pueblos[1] of the southwestern United States, for example, Zuñi and Hopi. And from mesa[2] to mesa there are subtle differences in language. But the particular language spoken isn't as important as what a speaker is trying to say, and this emphasis on the story itself stems, I believe, from a view of narrative particular to the Pueblo and other Native American peoples—that is, that language is story.

I will try to clarify this statement. At Laguna Pueblo,[3] for example, many individual words have their own stories. So when one is telling a story, and one is using words to tell the story, each word that one is speaking has a story of its own, too. Often the speakers or tellers will go into these word-stories, creating an elaborate structure of stories within stories. This structure, which becomes very apparent in the actual telling of a story, informs contemporary Pueblo writing and storytelling as well as the traditional narratives. This perspective on narrative—of story within story, the idea that one story is only the beginning of many stories, and the sense that stories never truly end—represents an important contribution of Native American cultures to the English language.

Many people think of storytelling as something that is done at bedtime, that it is something done for small children. But when I use the term *storytelling*, I'm talking about something much bigger than that. I'm talking about something that comes out of an experience and an understanding of that original view of creation—that we are all part of a whole; we do not differentiate or fragment stories and experiences. In the beginning, Tséitsínako, Thought Woman, thought of all things, and all of these things are held together as one holds many things together in a single thought.

---

1   *pueblos*   Towns of the Pueblo people.

2   *mesa*   Hill with a flat top.

3   *Laguna Pueblo*   Territory of the Laguna Pueblo people, a Puebloan tribe in west-central New Mexico.

So in the telling (and you will hear a few of the dimensions of this telling) first of all, as mentioned earlier, the storytelling always includes the audience, the listeners. In fact, a great deal of the story is believed to be inside the listener; the storyteller's role is to draw the story out of the listeners. The storytelling continues from generation to generation.

Basically, the origin story constructs our identity—within this story, we know who we are. We are the Lagunas. This is where we come from. We came this way. We came by this place. And so from the time we are very young, we hear these stories, so that when we go out into the world, when one asks who we are, or where we are from, we immediately know: we are the people who came from the north. We are the people of these stories.

10   In the Creation story, Antelope says that he will help knock a hole in the earth so that the people can come up, out into the next world. Antelope tries and tries; he uses his hooves, but is unable to break through. It is then that Badger says, "Let me help you." And Badger very patiently uses his claws and digs a way through, bringing the people into the world. When the Badger clan people think of themselves, or when the Antelope people think of themselves, it is as people who are of this story, and this is our place, and we fit into the very beginning when the people first came, before we began our journey south.

Within the clans there are stories that identify the clan. One moves, then, from the idea of one's identity as a tribal person into clan identity, then to one's identity as a member of an extended family. And it is the notion of "extended family" that has produced a kind of story that some distinguish from other Pueblo stories, though Pueblo people do not. Anthropologists and ethnologists have, for a long time, differentiated the types of stories the Pueblos tell. They tended to elevate the old sacred, and traditional stories and to brush aside family stories, the family's account of itself. But in Pueblo culture, these family stories are given equal recognition. There is no definite, present pattern for the way one will hear the stories of one's own family, but it is a very critical part of one's childhood, and the storytelling continues throughout one's life. One will hear stories of importance to the family—sometimes wonderful stories—stories about the time a maternal uncle got the biggest deer that was ever seen and brought it back from the mountains. And so an individual's identity will extend from the identity constructed around the family—"I am from the family of my uncle who brought in this wonderful deer and it was a wonderful hunt."

Family accounts include negative stories, too; perhaps an uncle did something unacceptable. It is very important that one keep track of all these stories—both positive and not so positive—about one's own family and other families. Because even when there is no way around it—old Uncle Pete *did* do a terrible thing—by knowing the stories that originate in other families, one is able to deal with terrible sorts of things that might happen within one's own family. If a member of the family does something that cannot be excused, one always knows stories about similar inexcusable things done by a member of another family. But this knowledge is not communicated for malicious reasons.* It is very important to understand this. Keeping track of all the stories within the community gives us all a certain distance, a useful perspective, that brings incidents down to a level we can deal with. If others have done it before, it cannot be so terrible. If others have endured, so can we.

The stories are always bringing us together, keeping this whole together, keeping this family together, keeping this clan together. "Don't go away, don't isolate yourself, but come here, because we have all had these kinds of experiences." And so there is this constant pulling together to resist the tendency to run or hide or separate oneself during a traumatic emotional experience. This separation not only endangers the group but the individual as well—one does not recover by oneself.

Because storytelling lies at the heart of Pueblo culture, it is absurd to attempt to fix the stories in time. "When did they tell the stories?" or "What time of day does the storytelling take place?"—these questions are nonsensical from a Pueblo perspective, because our storytelling goes on constantly: as some old grandmother puts on the shoes of a child and tells her the story of a little girl who didn't wear her shoes, for instance, or someone comes into the house for coffee to talk with a teenage boy who has just been in a lot of trouble, to reassure him that someone else's son has been in that kind of trouble, too. Storytelling is an ongoing process, working on many different levels.

Here's one story that is often told at a time of individual crisis (and I want   15 to remind you that we make no distinctions between types of story—historical, sacred, plain gossip—because these distinctions are not useful when discussing the Pueblo *experience* of language). There was a young man who, when he came back from the war in Vietnam, had saved up his army pay and bought a beautiful red Volkswagen. He was very proud of it. One night he drove up to a place called the King's Bar right across the reservation line. The bar is notorious for many reasons, particularly for the deep *arroyo*[4] located behind it. The young man ran in to pick up a cold six-pack, but he forgot to put on his emergency brake. And his little red Volkswagen rolled back into the *arroyo* and was all smashed up. He felt very bad about it, but within a few days everybody had come to him with stories about other people who had lost cars and family members to that *arroyo*, for instance, George Day's station wagon, with his mother-in-law and kids inside. So everybody was saying, "Well, at least your mother-in-law and kids weren't in the car when it rolled in," and one can't argue with that kind of story. The story of the young man and his smashed-up Volkswagen was now joined with all the other stories of cars that fell into that *arroyo*.

---

4   *arroyo* Spanish: dry creek bed with steep sides.

Now I want to tell you a very beautiful little story. It is a very old story that is sometimes told to people who suffer great family or personal loss. This story was told by my Aunt Susie. She is one of the first generation of people at Laguna who began experimenting with English—who began working to make English speak for us—that is, to speak from the heart. (I come from a family intent on getting the stories told.)

As you read the story, I think you will hear that. And here and there, I think, you will also hear the influence of the Indian school[5] at Carlisle, Pennsylvania, where my Aunt Susie was sent (like being sent to prison) for six years.

This scene is set partly in Acoma,[6] partly in Laguna. Waithea was a little girl living in Acoma and one day she said, "Mother, I would like to have some *yashtoah* to eat." *Yashtoah* is the hardened crust of corn mush that curls up. *Yashtoah* literally means "curled up." She said, "I would like to have some *yashtoah*," and her mother said, "My dear little girl, I can't make you any *yashtoah* because we haven't any wood, but if you will go down off the mesa, down below, and pick up some pieces of wood and bring them home, I will make you some *yashtoah*." So Waithea was glad and ran down the precipitous cliff of Acoma mesa. Down below, just as her mother had told her, there were pieces of wood, some curled, some crooked in shape, that she was to pick up and take home. She found just such wood as these.

She brought them home in a little wicker basket. First she called to her mother as she got home, "*Nayah, deeni!* Mother, upstairs!" The Pueblo people always called "upstairs" because long ago their homes were two, three stories, and they entered from the top. She said, "*Deeni!* upstairs!" and her mother came. The little girl said, "I have brought the wood you wanted me to bring." And she opened her little wicker basket to lay out the pieces of wood but here they were snakes. They were snakes instead of crooked sticks of wood. And her mother said, "Oh my dear child, you have brought snakes instead!" She said, "Go take them back and put them back just where you got them." And the little girl ran down the mesa again, down below to the flats. And she put those snakes back just where she got them. They were snakes instead and she was very hurt about this and so she said, "I'm not going home. I'm going to *Kawaik*, the beautiful lake place, *Kawaik*, and drown myself in the lake, *byn'yah'nah* [the "west lake"]. I will go there and drown myself."

---

5   *Indian school*   Residential school where Native American children were forced to adopt Euro-American culture. Between 1879 and 1918 over 12,000 children attended the Carlisle Indian Industrial School, the first federally funded boarding school of its kind in the US.

6   *Acoma*   Territory of the Pueblo tribe west of Albuquerque, New Mexico.

So she started off, and as she passed the Enchanted Mesa near Acoma she   20
met an old man, very aged, and he saw her running, and he said, "My dear
child, where are you going?" "I'm going to Kawaik and jump into the lake
there." "Why?" "Well, because," she said, "my mother didn't want to make any
yashtoah for me." The old man said, "Oh, no! You must not go my child. Come
with me and I will take you home." He tried to catch her, but she was very light
and skipped along. And every time he would try to grab her she would skip
faster away from him.

The old man was coming home with some wood strapped to his back and
tied with yucca. He just let the strap go and let the wood drop. He went as fast
as he could up the cliff to the little girl's home. When he got to the place where
she lived, he called to her mother. "*Deeni!*"

"Come on up!" And he said, "I can't. I just came to bring you a message.
Your little daughter is running away. She is going to *Kawaik* to drown herself
in the lake there." "Oh my dear little girl!" the mother said. So she busied herself with making the *yashtoah* her little girl liked so much. Corn mush curled
at the top. (She must have found enough wood to boil the cornmeal and make
the *yashtoah*.)

While the mush was cooking off, she got the little girl's clothing, her *manta*
dress[7] and buckskin moccasins and all her other garments, and put them in a
bundle—probably a yucca bag. And she started down as fast as she could on
the east side of Acoma. (There used to be a trail there, you know. It's gone now,
but it was accessible in those days.) She saw her daughter way at a distance and
she kept calling: "Stsamaku! My daughter! Come back! I've got your *yashtoah*
for you." But the little girl would not turn. She kept on ahead and she cried:
"My mother, my mother, she didn't want me to have any *yashtoah*. So now I'm
going to *Kawaik* and drown myself." Her mother heard her cry and said, "My
little daughter, come back here!" "No," and she kept a distance away from her.
And they came nearer and nearer to the lake. And she could see her daughter
now, very plain. "Come back, my daughter! I have your *yashtoah*." But no, she
kept on, and finally she reached the lake and she stood on the edge.

She had tied a little feather in her hair, which is traditional (in death they
tie this feather on the head). She carried a feather, the little girl did, and she tied
it in her hair with a piece of string, right on top of her head she put the feather.
Just as her mother was about to reach her, she jumped into the lake. The little
feather was whirling around and around in the depths below. Of course the
mother was very sad. She went, grieved, back to Acoma and climbed her mesa
home. She stood on the edge of the mesa and scattered her daughter's clothing,

---

7   *manta dress*   Dress made of a rectangular piece of cloth wrapped and secured at the
waist with a sash.

the little moccasins, the *yashtoah*. She scattered them to the east, to the west, to the north, to the south. And the pieces of clothing and the moccasins and *yashtoah*, all turned into butterflies. And today they say that Acoma has more beautiful butterflies: red ones, white ones, blue ones, yellow ones. They came from this little girl's clothing.

25   Now this is a story anthropologists would consider very old. The version I have given you is just as Aunt Susie tells it. You can occasionally hear some English she picked up at Carlisle—words like "precipitous." You will also notice that there is a great deal of repetition, and a little reminder about *yashtoah*, and how it is made. There is a remark about the cliff trail at Acoma—that it was once there, but is there no longer. This story may be told at a time of sadness or loss, but within this story many other elements are brought together. Things are not separated out and categorized; all things are brought together. So that the reminder about the *yashtoah* is valuable information that is repeated—a recipe, if you will. The information about the old trail at Acoma reveals that stories are, in a sense, maps, since even to this day there is little information or material about trails that is passed around with writing. In the structure of this story the repetitions are, of course, designed to help you remember. It is repeated again and again, and then it moves on.

    The next story I would like to tell is by Simon Ortiz, from Acoma Pueblo. He is a wonderful poet who also works in narrative. One of the things I find very interesting in this short story is that if you listen very closely, you begin to hear what I was talking about in terms of a story never beginning at the beginning, and certainly never ending. As the Hopis sometimes say, "Well, it has gone this far for a while." There is always that implication of a continuing. The other thing I want you to listen for is the many stories within one story. Listen to the kinds of stories contained within the main story—stories that give one a family identity and an individual identity, for example. This story is called "Home Country":

> "Well, it's been a while. I think in 1947 was when I left. My husband had been killed in Okinawa[8] some years before. And so I had no more husband. And I had to make a living. O I guess I could have looked for another man but I didn't want to. It looked like the war had made some of them into a bad way anyway. I saw some of them come home like that. They either got drunk or just stayed around a while or couldn't seem to be satisfied anymore with what was there. I guess now that I think about it, that happened to me although I wasn't in the war not in the Army or even much off the reservation just that several years at the

---

8   *Okinawa* Japanese island where American and Japanese forces fought each other during World War II.

Indian School. Well there was that feeling things were changing not only the men the boys, but things were changing.

"One day the home nurse the nurse that came from the Indian health service was at my mother's home my mother was getting near the end real sick and she said that she had been meaning to ask me a question. I said what is the question. And the home nurse said well your mother is getting real sick and after she is no longer around for you to take care of, what will you be doing you and her are the only ones here. And I said I don't know. But I was thinking about it what she said made me think about it. And then the next time she came she said to me Eloise the government is hiring Indians now in the Indian schools to take care of the boys and girls I heard one of the supervisors saying that Indians are hard workers but you have to supervise them a lot and I thought of you well because you've been taking care of your mother real good and you follow all my instructions. She said I thought of you because you're a good Indian girl and you would be the kind of person for that job. I didn't say anything I had not ever really thought about a job but I kept thinking about it.

"Well my mother she died and we buried her up at the old place the cemetery there it's real nice on the east side of the hill where the sun shines warm and the wind doesn't blow too much sand around right there. Well I was sad we were all sad for a while but you know how things are. One of my aunties came over and she advised me and warned me about being too sorry about it and all that she wished me that I would not worry too much about it because old folks they go along pretty soon life is that way and then she said that maybe I ought to take in one of my aunties kids or two because there was a lot of them kids and I was all by myself now. But I was so young and I thought that I might do that you know take care of someone but I had been thinking too of what the home nurse said to me about working. Hardly anybody at our home was working at something like that no woman anyway. And I would have to move away.

"Well I did just that. I remember that day very well. I told my aunties and they were all crying and we all went up to the old highway where the bus to town passes by every day. I was wearing an old kind of bluish sweater that was kind of big that one of my cousins who was older had got from a white person a tourist one summer in trade for something she had made a real pretty basket. She gave me that and I used to have a picture of me with it on it's kind of real ugly. Yeah that was the day I left wearing a baggy sweater and carrying a suitcase that someone gave me too I think or maybe it was the home nurse there wasn't much in it anyway either. I was scared and everybody seemed to be sad I was so young and skinny then. My aunties said one of them who was real fat you make sure you eat now make your own tortillas drink the milk and stuff like candies is no good she learned that from the nurse. Make sure you got your letter my auntie said. I had it folded into my purse. Yes I have one too a brown one that my husband when he was still alive one time on furlough he brought it on my birthday it was a nice purse and still looked new because I never used it.

"The letter said that I had a job at Keams Canyon[9] the boarding school there but I would have to go to the Agency first for some papers to be filled and that's where I was going first. The Agency. And then they would send me out to Keams Canyon. I didn't even know where it was except that someone of our relatives said that it was near Hopi.[10] My uncles teased me about watching out for the Hopi men and boys don't let them get too close they said well you know how they are and they were pretty strict too about those things and then they were joking and then they were not too and so I said aw they won't get near to me I'm too ugly and I promised I would be careful anyway.

"So we all gathered for a while at my last auntie's house and then the old man my grandfather brought his wagon and horses to the door and we all got in and sat there for a while until my auntie told her father okay father let's go and shook his elbow because the poor old man was old by then and kind of going to sleep all the time you had to talk to him real loud. I had about ten dollars I think that was a lot of money more than it is now you know and when we got to the highway where the Indian road which is just a dirt road goes off the pave road my grandfather reached into his blue jeans and pulled out a silver dollar and put it into my hand. I was so shocked. We were all so shocked. We all looked around at each other we didn't know where the old man had gotten it because we were real poor two of my uncles had to borrow on their accounts at the trading store for the money I had in my purse but there it was a silver dollar so big and shrinking in my grandfather's hand and then in my hand.

"Well I was so shocked and everybody was so shocked that we all started crying right there at the junction of that Indian road and the pave highway I wanted to be a little girl again running after the old man when he hurried with his long legs to the cornfields or went for water down to the river. He was old then and his eye was turned gray

---

9   *Keams Canyon*   Area in Navajo County, Arizona.
10   *Hopi*   Territory of the Hopi, a Puebloan tribe, in northeastern Arizona.

and he didn't do much anymore except drive the wagon and chop a little bit of wood but I just held him and I just held him so tightly.

"Later on I don't know what happened to the silver dollar it had a date of 1907 on it but I kept it for a long time because I guess I wanted to have it to remember when I left my home country. What I did in between then and now is another story but that's the time I moved away,"

is what she said.[11]

There are a great many parallels between Pueblo experiences and those of African and Caribbean peoples—one is that we have all had the conqueror's language imposed on us. But our experience with English has been somewhat different in that the Bureau of Indian Affairs schools were not interested in teaching us the canon* of Western classics. For instance, we never heard of Shakespeare. We were given Dick and Jane,[12] and I can remember reading that the robins were heading south for the winter. It took me a long time to figure out what was going on. I worried for quite a while about our robins in Laguna because they didn't leave in the winter, until I finally realized that all the big textbook companies are up in Boston and their robins do go south in the winter. But in a way, this dreadful formal education freed us by encouraging us to maintain our narratives. Whatever literature we were exposed to at school (which was damn little), at home the storytelling, the special regard for telling and bringing together through the telling, was going on constantly.

And as the old people say, "If you can remember the stories, you will be all right. Just remember the stories." When I returned to Laguna Pueblo after attending college, I wondered how the storytelling was continuing (anthropologists say that Laguna Pueblo is one of the more acculturated pueblos[13]), so I visited an English class at Laguna Acoma High School. I knew the students had cassette tape recorders in their lockers and stereos at home, and that they listened to Kiss and Led Zeppelin and were all informed about popular culture in general. I had with me an anthology of short stories by Native American writers, *The Man to Send Rain Clouds*. One story in the book is about the killing of a state policeman in New Mexico by three Acoma Pueblo men in the early 1950s.[14] I asked the students how many had heard this story and steeled

---

11 [Silko's note] Simon J. Ortiz, *Howabah Indians* (Tucson: Blue Moon Press, 1978).

12 *Dick and Jane* Books that taught young children to read. Popular in American schools from the 1930s into the 1960s, these readers featured the characters Dick and Jane.

13 *more acculturated pueblos* Areas where cultural assimilation has been widely adopted.

14 [Silko's note] See Simon J. Ortiz, "The Killing of a State Cop," in *The Man to Send Rain Clouds*, ed. Kenneth Rosen (New York: Viking Press, 1974), 101–108.

myself for the possibility that the anthropologists were right, that the old traditions were indeed dying out and the students would be ignorant of the story. But instead, all but one or two raised their hands—they had heard the story, just as I had heard it when I was young, some in English, some in Laguna.

One of the other advantages that we Pueblos have enjoyed is that we have always been able to stay with the land. Our stories cannot be separated from their geographical locations, from actual physical places on the land. We were not relocated like so many Native American groups who were torn away from their ancestral land. And our stories are so much a part of these places that it is almost impossible for future generations to lose them—there is a story connected with every place, every object in the landscape.

30   Dennis Brutus[15] has talked about the "yet unborn" as well as "those from the past," and how we are still *all* in this place, and language—the storytelling—is our way of passing through or being with them, or being together again. When Aunt Susie told her stories, she would tell a younger child to go open the door so that our esteemed predecessors might bring in their gifts to us. "They are out there," Aunt Susie would say. "Let them come in. They're here, they're here with us *within* the stories."

A few years ago, when Aunt Susie was 106, I paid her a visit, and while I was there she said, "Well, I'll be leaving here soon. I think I'll be leaving here next week, and I will be going over to the Cliff House."[16] She said, "It's going to be real good to get back over there." I was listening, and I was thinking that she must be talking about our house at Paguate Village, just north of Laguna. And she went on, "Well, my mother's sister (and she gave her Indian name) will be there. She has been living there. She will be there and we will be over there, and I will get a chance to write down these stories I've been telling you." Now you must understand, of course, that Aunt Susie's mother's sister, a great storyteller herself, has long since passed over into the land of the dead. But then I realized, too, that Aunt Susie wasn't talking about death the way most of us do. She was talking about "going over" as a journey, a journey that perhaps we can only begin to understand through an appreciation for the boundless capacity of language that, through storytelling, brings us together, despite great distances between cultures, despite great distances in time.

(1979)

---

15 *Dennis Brutus*   Dennis Vincent Brutus (1924–2009) was a South African journalist, poet, and activist. He is known for his efforts to have that country, which was still under the apartheid government, banned from the 1964 Olympic Games.

16 *Cliff House*   Dwelling built in a cliff along a high canyon wall.

Questions

1. Near the beginning of this piece Silko makes the following statement:
    "I have intentionally not written a formal paper because I want you
    to hear and to experience English in a structure that follows patterns
    from the oral tradition" (paragraph 1). How is Silko's piece like—and
    unlike—a typical academic essay in the Western tradition? What (if
    anything) is Silko able to communicate that might not have been
    communicated as effectively in a typical academic essay?

2. Choose one of the stories incorporated into this piece and explain its
    significance in the context of the piece as a whole.

3. Read the first part of Eden Robinson's *The Sasquatch at Home*
    (included in this anthology). Compare the approach to language and
    narrative taken by Robinson with that taken in Silko's piece.

4. When discussing the Pueblo experience of language, Silko guards
    against making distinctions between types of story—historical,
    sacred, or plain gossip (paragraph 15). How (if at all) do these
    distinctions help you as a reader? How (if at all) do they limit your
    experience of a piece of writing/storytelling?

YIYUN LI

TO SPEAK IS TO BLUNDER

*Yiyun Li is a Chinese American writer raised in Beijing whose novels
and short stories have gained international renown. Her memoir
essay "To Speak Is to Blunder," reprinted below, was published in*
The New Yorker *in January 2017. It is an excerpted version of a
chapter from Li's first nonfiction book,* Dear Friend, from My Life I
Write to You in Your Life*, which was published in February 2017.*

❧

In a dream the other night, I was back in Beijing, at the entrance of my family's apartment complex, where a public telephone, a black rotary,[1] had once been guarded by the old women from the neighborhood association. They used to listen without hiding their disdain or curiosity while I was on the phone with friends; when I finished, they would complain about the length of the conversation before logging it in to their book and calculating the charge. In those days, I accumulated many errands before I went to use the telephone, lest my parents notice my extended absence. My allowance—which was what I could scrimp and save from my lunch money—was spent on phone calls and stamps and envelopes. Like a character in a Victorian novel, I checked our mail before my parents did and collected letters to me from friends before my parents could intercept them.

In my dream, I asked for the phone. Two women came out of a front office. I recognized them: in real life, they are both gone. No, they said; the service is no longer offered, because everyone has a cell phone these days. There was nothing extraordinary about the dream—a melancholy visit to the past in this manner is beyond one's control—but for the fact that the women spoke to me in English.

Years ago, when I started writing in English, my husband asked if I understood the implication of the decision. What he meant was not the practical concerns, though there were plenty: the nebulous hope of getting published; the lack of a career path as had been laid out in science, my first field of postgraduate study in America; the harsher immigration regulation I would face

---

1 *rotary* Landline phone with a round dial.

as a fiction writer. Many of my college classmates from China, as scientists, acquired their green cards under a National Interest Waiver. An artist is not of much importance to any nation's interest.

My husband, who writes computer programs, was asking about language. Did I understand what it meant to renounce my mother tongue?*

Nabokov[2] once answered a question he must have been tired of being asked: "My private tragedy, which cannot, indeed should not, be anybody's concern, is that I had to abandon my natural language, my natural idiom." That something is called a tragedy, however, means it is no longer personal. One weeps out of private pain, but only when the audience swarms in and claims understanding and empathy do people call it a tragedy. One's grief belongs to oneself; one's tragedy, to others.

I often feel a tinge of guilt when I imagine Nabokov's woe. Like all intimacies, the intimacy between one and one's mother tongue can be comforting and irreplaceable, yet it can also demand more than what one is willing to give, or more than one is capable of giving. If I allow myself to be honest, my private salvation, which cannot and should not be anybody's concern, is that I disowned my native language.

In the summer and autumn of 2012, I was hospitalized in California and in New York for suicide attempts, the first time for a few days, and the second time for three weeks. During those months, my dreams often took me back to Beijing. I would be standing on top of a building—one of those gray, Soviet-style apartment complexes—or I would be lost on a bus traveling through an unfamiliar neighborhood. Waking up, I would list in my journal images that did not appear in my dreams: a swallow's nest underneath a balcony, the barbed wires at the rooftop, the garden where old people sat and exchanged gossip, the mailboxes at street corners—round, green, covered by dust, with handwritten collection times behind a square window of half-opaque plastic.

Yet I have never dreamed of Iowa City, where I first landed in America, in 1996, at the age of twenty-three. When asked about my initial impression of the place, I cannot excavate anything from memory to form a meaningful answer. During a recent trip there from my home in California, I visited a neighborhood that I used to walk through every day. The one-story houses, which were painted in pleasantly muted colors, with gardens in the front enclosed by white picket fences, had not changed. I realized that I had never described them to others or to myself in Chinese, and when English was established as my language they

5

2   *Nabokov*   Vladimir Nabokov (1899–1977) was a Russian novelist and poet. He wrote his first nine novels in Russian, and then wrote in English from 1941 on. He also translated his own works from Russian to English and vice versa.

had become everyday mundanities. What happened during my transition from one language to another did not become memory.

People often ask about my decision to write in English. The switch from one language to another feels natural to me, I reply, though that does not say much, just as one can hardly give a convincing explanation as to why someone's hair turns gray on one day but not on another. But this is an inane analogy, I realize, because I do not want to touch the heart of the matter. Yes, there is something unnatural, which I have refused to accept. Not the fact of writing in a second language—there are always Nabokov and Conrad[3] as references, and many of my contemporaries as well—or that I impulsively gave up a reliable career for writing. It's the absoluteness of my abandonment of Chinese, undertaken with such determination that it is a kind of suicide.

10 The tragedy of Nabokov's loss is that his misfortune was easily explained by public history. His story—of being driven by a revolution into permanent exile[4]—became the possession of other people. My decision to write in English has also been explained as a flight from my country's history. But unlike Nabokov, who had been a published Russian writer, I never wrote in Chinese. Still, one cannot avoid the fact that a private decision, once seen through a public prism, becomes a metaphor. Once, a poet of Eastern European origin and I—we both have lived in America for years, and we both write in English—were asked to read our work in our native languages at a gala. But I don't write in Chinese, I explained, and the organizer apologized for her misunderstanding. I offered to read Li Po or Du Fu or any of the ancient poets I had grown up memorizing, but instead it was arranged for me to read poetry by a political prisoner.

A metaphor's desire to transcend diminishes any human story; its ambition to illuminate blinds those who create metaphors. In my distrust of metaphors I feel a kinship with George Eliot:[5] "We all of us, grave or light, get our thoughts entangled in metaphors, and act fatally on the strength of them." My abandonment of my first language is personal, so deeply personal that I resist any interpretation—political or historical or ethnographical. This, I know, is what my husband was questioning years ago: was I prepared to be turned into a symbol by well-intentioned or hostile minds?

---

3   *Conrad*   Joseph Conrad (1857–1924) was a Polish-British writer. English was only one of his languages, but Conrad used it for all of his literary work.

4   *permanent exile*   Nabokov fled Russia after the Bolshevik Revolution of 1917, emigrating to Western Europe. In 1940, Nabokov and his family moved to the United States to avoid Nazi persecution. He never returned to Russia.

5   *George Eliot*   Pen name for Mary Anne Evans (1819–80), an English writer, essayist, and translator. The quotation is from her classic novel *Middlemarch* (1871–72).

Chinese immigrants of my generation in America criticize my English for not being native enough. A compatriot, after reading my work, pointed out, in an e-mail, how my language is neither lavish nor lyrical, as a real writer's language should be: you write only simple things in simple English, you should be ashamed of yourself, he wrote in a fury. A professor—an American writer—in graduate school told me that I should stop writing, as English would remain a foreign language to me. Their concerns about ownership of a language, rather than making me as impatient as Nabokov, allow me secret laughter. English is to me as random a choice as any other language. What one goes toward is less definitive than that from which one turns away.

Before I left China, I destroyed the journal that I had kept for years and most of the letters written to me, those same letters I had once watched out for, lest my mother discover them. What I could not bring myself to destroy I sealed up and brought with me to America, though I will never open them again. My letters to others I would have destroyed, too, had I had them. These records, of the days I had lived time and time over, became intolerable now that my time in China was over. But this violent desire to erase a life in a native language is only wishful thinking. One's relationship with the native language is similar to that with the past. Rarely does a story start where we wish it had, or end where we wish it would.

One crosses the border to become a new person. One finishes a manuscript and cuts off the characters. One adopts a language. These are false and forced frameworks, providing illusory freedom, as time provides illusory leniency when we, in anguish, let it pass monotonously. "To kill time," an English phrase that still chills me: time can be killed but only by frivolous matters and purposeless activities. No one thinks of suicide as a courageous endeavor to kill time.

During my second hospital stay, in New York, a group of nursing students 15 came to play bingo one Friday night. A young woman, another patient, asked if I would join her. Bingo, I said, I've never in my life played that. She pondered for a moment, and said that she had played bingo only in the hospital. It was her eighth hospitalization when I met her; she had taken middle-school courses for a while in the hospital, when she was younger, and, once, she pointed out a small patch of fenced-in green where she and other children had been let out for exercise. Her father often visited her in the afternoon, and I would watch them sitting together playing a game, not attempting a conversation. By then, all words must have been inadequate, language doing little to help a mind survive time.

Yet language is capable of sinking a mind. One's thoughts are slavishly bound to language. I used to think that an abyss is a moment of despair becoming interminable; but any moment, even the direst, is bound to end. What's abysmal is that one's erratic language closes in on one like quicksand: "You are nothing. You must do anything you can to get rid of this nothingness." We can kill time, but language kills us.

"Patient reports feeling ... like she is a burden to her loved ones"—much later, I read the notes from the emergency room. I did not have any recollection of the conversation. A burden to her loved ones: this language must have been provided to me. I would never use the phrase in my thinking or my writing. But my resistance has little to do with avoiding a platitude. To say "a burden" is to grant oneself weight in other people's lives; to call them "loved ones" is to fake one's ability to love. One does not always want to be subject to self-interrogation imposed by a cliché.

When Katherine Mansfield[6] was still a teenager, she wrote in her journal about a man next door playing "Swanee River"[7] on a cornet, for what seemed like weeks. "I wake up with the 'Swannee River,' eat it with every meal I take, and go to bed eventually with 'all de world am sad and weary' as a lullaby." I read Mansfield's notebooks and Marianne Moore's[8] letters around the same time, when I returned home from New York. In a letter, Moore described a night of fund-raising at Bryn Mawr.[9] Maidens in bathing suits and green bathing tails on a raft: "It was Really most realistic ... way down upon the Swanee River."

I marked the entries because they reminded me of a moment I had forgotten. I was nine, and my sister thirteen. On a Saturday afternoon, I was in our apartment and she was on the balcony. My sister had joined the middle-school choir that year, and in the autumn sunshine she sang in a voice that was beginning to leave girlhood. "Way down upon the Swanee River. Far, far away. That's where my heart is turning ever; That's where the old folks stay."

20   The lyrics were translated into Chinese. The memory, too, should be in Chinese. But I cannot see our tiny garden with the grapevine, which our father cultivated and which was later uprooted by our wrathful mother, or the bamboo fence dotted with morning glories, or the junk that occupied half the balcony— years of accumulations piled high by our hoarder father—if I do not name these things to myself in English. I cannot see my sister, but I can hear her sing the lyrics in English. I can seek to understand my mother's vulnerability and cruelty, but language is the barrier I have chosen. "Do you know, the moment

---

6   *Katherine Mansfield*   Modernist short story writer (1888–1923) from New Zealand.

7   *"Swanee River"*   Song written by Stephen Foster in 1851. Also known as "Old Folks at Home," the song is written from the perspective of an American slave who repines at being sold to a different plantation.

8   *Marianne Moore*   American Modernist poet (1887–1972).

9   *Bryn Mawr*   Private women's liberal arts college in Pennsylvania, founded in 1885.

I die your father will marry someone else?" my mother used to whisper to me when I was little. "Do you know that I cannot die, because I don't want you to live under a stepmother?" Or else, taken over by inexplicable rage, she would say that I, the only person she had loved, deserved the ugliest death because I did not display enough gratitude. But I have given these moments—what's possible to be put into English—to my characters. Memories, left untranslated, can be disowned; memories untranslatable can become someone else's story.

Over the years, my brain has banished Chinese. I dream in English. I talk to myself in English. And memories—not only those about America but also those about China; not only those carried with me but also those archived with the wish to forget—are sorted in English. To be orphaned from my native language felt, and still feels, like a crucial decision.

When we enter a world—a new country, a new school, a party, a family or a class reunion, an army camp, a hospital—we speak the language it requires. The wisdom to adapt is the wisdom to have two languages: the one spoken to others, and the one spoken to oneself. One learns to master the public language not much differently from the way that one acquires a second language: assess the situations, construct sentences with the right words and the correct syntax, catch a mistake if one can avoid it, or else apologize and learn the lesson after a blunder. Fluency in the public language, like fluency in a second language, can be achieved with enough practice.

Perhaps the line between the two is, and should be, fluid; it is never so for me. I often forget, when I write, that English is also used by others. English is my private language. Every word has to be pondered before it becomes a word. I have no doubt—can this be an illusion?—that the conversation I have with myself, however linguistically flawed, is the conversation that I have always wanted, in the exact way I want it to be.

In my relationship with English, in this relationship with the intrinsic distance between a nonnative speaker and an adopted language that makes people look askance, I feel invisible but not estranged. It is the position I believe I always want in life. But with every pursuit there is the danger of crossing a line, from invisibility to erasure.

There was a time when I could write well in Chinese. In school, my essays were used as models; in the Army, where I spent a year of involuntary service between the ages of eighteen and nineteen, our squad leader gave me the choice between drafting a speech for her and cleaning the toilets or the pigsties— I always chose to write. Once, in high school, I entered an oratory contest. Onstage, I saw that many of the listeners were moved to tears by the poetic and insincere lies I had made up; I moved myself to tears, too. It crossed my mind that I could become a successful propaganda writer. I was disturbed by this. A young person wants to be true to herself and to the world. But it did not occur

25

to me to ask: Can one's intelligence rely entirely on the public language; can one form a precise thought, recall an accurate memory, or even feel a genuine feeling, with only the public language?

My mother, who loves to sing, often sings the songs from her childhood and youth, many of them words of propaganda from the nineteen-fifties and sixties. But there is one song she has reminisced about all her life because she does not know how to sing it. She learned the song in kindergarten, the year Communism took over her home town; she can remember only the opening line.

There was an old woman in the hospital in New York who sat in the hall-way with a pair of shiny red shoes. I feel like Dorothy,* she said as she showed me the shoes, which she had chosen from the donations to patients. Some days, her mind was lucid, and she would talk about the red shoes that hurt her feet but which she could not part with, or the medication that made her brain feel dead and left her body in pain. Other days, she talked to the air, an endless conversation with the unseen. People who had abandoned her by going away or dying returned and made her weep.

I often sat next to this lonesome Dorothy. Was I eavesdropping? Perhaps, but her conversation was beyond encroachment. That one could reach a point where the border between public and private language no longer matters is frightening. Much of what one does—to avoid suffering, to seek happiness, to stay healthy—is to keep a safe space for one's private language. Those who have lost that space have only one language left. My grandmother, according to my mother and her siblings, had become a woman who talked to the unseen before she was sent to the asylum to die. There's so much to give up: hope, freedom, dignity. A private language, however, defies any confinement. Death alone can take it away.

Mansfield spoke of her habit of keeping a journal as "being garrulous … I must say nothing affords me the same relief." Several times, she directly addressed the readers—her posterity—in a taunting manner, as though laughing at them for taking her dead words seriously. I would prefer to distrust her. But it would be dishonest not to acknowledge the solace of reading her words. It was in the immediate weeks after the second hospitalization. My life was on hold. There were diagnoses to grapple with, medications to take, protocols to implement, hospital staff to report to, but they were there only to eliminate an option. What to replace it with I could not see, but I knew it was not within any-one's capacity to answer that. Not having the exact language for the bleakness I felt, I devoured Mansfield's words like thirst-quenching poison. Is it possible that one can be held hostage by someone else's words? What I underlined and reread: Are they her thoughts or mine?

There is nought to do but WORK, but how can I work when this awful weakness makes even the pen like a walking stick?

There is something profound & terrible in this eternal desire to establish contact.

It is astonishing how violently a big branch shakes when a silly little bird has left it. I expect the bird knows it and feels immensely arrogant.

One only wants to feel sure of another. That's all.

I realize my faults better than anyone else could realize them. I know exactly where I fail.

Have people, apart from those far away people, ever existed for me? Or have they always failed me, and faded because I denied them reality? Supposing I were to die, as I sit at this table, playing with my indian paper knife[10]—what would be the difference. No difference at all. Then why don't I commit suicide?

When one thinks in an adopted language, one arranges and rearranges words that are neutral, indifferent even.

When one remembers in an adopted language, there is a dividing line in that remembrance. What came before could be someone else's life; it might as well be fiction.

What language, I wonder, does one use to feel? Or does one need a language to feel? In the hospital in New York, one of my doctors asked me to visit a class studying minds and brains. Two medical students interviewed me, following a script. The doctor who led the class, impatient with their tentativeness, sent them back to their seats and posed questions more pointed and unrelenting. To answer him, I had to navigate my thoughts, and I watched him and his students closely, as I was being watched. When he asked about feelings, I said it was beyond my ability to describe what might as well be indescribable.

If you can be articulate about your thoughts, why can't you articulate your feelings? the doctor asked.

It took me a year to figure out the answer. It is hard to feel in an adopted language, yet it is impossible in my native language.

Often I think that writing is a futile effort; so is reading; so is living. Loneliness is the inability to speak with another in one's private language. That emptiness is filled with public language or romanticized connections.

---

10 *paper knife* Knife used for cutting open letters or slitting open the uncut leaves of paper in a book.

After the dream of the public telephone, I remembered a moment in the Army. It was New Year's Eve, and we were ordered to watch the official celebration on CCTV.[11] Halfway through the program, a girl on duty came and said that there was a long-distance call for me.

It was the same type of black rotary phone as we had back at the apartment complex, and my sister was on the line. It was the first long-distance call I had received in my life, and the next time would be four years later, back in Beijing, when an American professor phoned to interview me. I still remember the woman, calling from Mount Sinai Hospital in New York City, asking questions about my interests in immunology, talking about her research projects and life in America. My English was good enough to understand half of what she said, and the scratching noises in the background made me sweat for the missed half.

What did my sister and I talk about on that New Year's Eve? In abandoning my native language, I have erased myself from that memory. But erasing, I have learned, does not stop with a new language, and that, my friend, is my sorrow and my selfishness. In speaking and in writing in an adopted language, I have not stopped erasing. I have crossed the line, too, from erasing myself to erasing others. I am not the only casualty in this war against myself.

In an ideal world, I would prefer to have my mind reserved for thinking, and thinking alone. I dread the moment when a thought trails off and a feeling starts, when one faces the eternal challenge of eluding the void for which one does not have words. To speak when one cannot is to blunder. I have spoken by having written—this piece or any piece—for myself and against myself. The solace is with the language I chose. The grief, to have spoken at all.

(2017)

Questions

1. What would the author lose or gain by choosing to write in Chinese instead of English?

2. The author describes herself as being engaged in a "war against myself" (paragraph 38). What does this mean? How does it relate to her choice to cease speaking and writing her first language?

---

11 *CCTV* China Central Television, the state television broadcaster of the Communist Party of China.

3. The author states that "What happened during my transition from one language to another did not become memory" (paragraph 8). How does language impact your memories? Choose a memory you have and examine the role language has played in shaping and storing that memory.

4. What distinction does the author draw between public and private language? Do you experience public and private language differently? If so, how? If not, why not?

5. What, for the author, is the relationship between language and identity?

6. Read the selection from Gloria Anzaldúa's *Borderlands/La Frontera* included in this anthology. Compare and contrast the ways Anzaldúa and Li see the role of language in identity formation.

IF BLACK ENGLISH ISN'T A LANGUAGE, THEN TELL ME, WHAT IS?

Although he spent most of his adult life in France, James Baldwin, born in New York City's historically Black neighborhood of Harlem, made a profound intellectual contribution to the American Civil Rights Movement through both fiction and nonfiction. From his position as an expatriate writer, Baldwin was able to give essential insight into the system of racial prejudice that shaped all aspects of life in his home country. The following essay, which Baldwin wrote at his home in the French village of St. Paul de Vence, was first published in the New York Times *Books section in 1979.*

❧

The argument concerning the use, or the status, or the reality, of black English is rooted in American history and has absolutely nothing to do with the question the argument supposes itself to be posing. The argument has nothing to do with language itself but with the *role* of language. Language, incontestably, reveals the speaker. Language, also, far more dubiously, is meant to define the other—and, in this case, the other is refusing to be defined by a language that has never been able to recognize him.

People evolve a language in order to describe and thus control their circumstances, or in order not to be submerged by a reality that they cannot articulate. (And, if they cannot articulate it, they *are* submerged.) A Frenchman living in Paris speaks a subtly and crucially different language from that of the man living in Marseilles; neither sounds very much like a man living in Quebec; and they would all have great difficulty in apprehending what the man from Guadeloupe, or Martinique, is saying, to say nothing of the man from Senegal—although the "common" language of all these areas is French. But each has paid, and is paying, a different price for this "common" language, in which, as it turns out, they are not saying, and cannot be saying, the same things: They each have very different realities to articulate, or control.

What joins all languages, and all men, is the necessity to confront life, in order, not inconceivably, to outwit death: The price for this is the acceptance, and achievement, of one's temporal identity.[1] So that, for example, though it is not taught in the schools (and this has the potential of becoming a political issue) the south of France still clings to its ancient and musical Provençal, which resists being described as a "dialect." And much of the tension in the Basque countries, and in Wales,[2] is due to the Basque and Welsh determination not to allow their languages to be destroyed. This determination also feeds the flames in Ireland for among the many indignities the Irish have been forced to undergo at English hands is the English contempt for their language.

It goes without saying, then, that language is also a political instrument, means, and proof of power. It is the most vivid and crucial key to identity: It reveals the private identity, and connects one with, or divorces one from, the larger, public, or communal identity. There have been, and are, times, and places, when to speak a certain language could be dangerous, even fatal. Or, one may speak the same language, but in such a way that one's antecedents are revealed, or (one hopes) hidden. This is true in France, and is absolutely true in England: The range (and reign) of accents on that damp little island make England coherent for the English and totally incomprehensible for everyone else. To open your mouth in England is (if I may use black English) to "put your business in the street": You have confessed your parents, your youth, your school, your salary, your self-esteem, and, alas, your future.

Now, I do not know what white Americans would sound like if there had never been any black people in the United States, but they would not sound the way they sound. *Jazz*, for example, is a very specific sexual term, as in *jazz me, baby*, but white people purified it into the Jazz Age. *Sock it to me*, which means, roughly, the same thing, has been adopted by Nathaniel Hawthorne's descendants[3] with no qualms or hesitations at all, along with *let it all hang out* and *right on! Beat to his socks* which was once the black's most total and

5

---

1   *temporal identity*   Identity as manifested in time (during earthly, rather than eternal, life).

2   *Basque countries*   Area in the western Pyrenees mountains made up of the Basque Country and Navarre in Spain and the Northern Basque Country in France;   *tension ... Wales*   The peoples of Wales and of the Basque Country have their own distinctive languages and cultures within the larger country that governs them (England and Spain, respectively). In both cases, political tension and conflict surrounds these peoples' efforts to achieve self-governance as a means of preserving cultural identities.

3   *Nathaniel Hawthorne's descendants*   Hawthorne (1804–64) was a nineteenth-century white American writer. He was descended from Puritans who immigrated to America in the early seventeenth century. His work explores themes of inherited guilt, sin, and evil.

despairing image of poverty, was transformed into a thing called the Beat Generation,[4] which phenomenon was, largely, composed of *uptight*, middle-class white people, imitating poverty, trying to *get down*, to get *with it*, doing their *thing*, doing their despairing best to be *funky*, which we, the blacks, never dreamed of doing—we *were* funky, baby, like *funk* was going out of style.

Now, no one can eat his cake, and have it, too,* and it is late in the day to attempt to penalize black people for having created a language that permits the nation its only glimpse of reality, a language without which the nation would be even more *whipped* than it is.

I say that the present skirmish is rooted in American history, and it is. Black English is the creation of the black diaspora.[5] Blacks came to the United States chained to each other, but from different tribes: Neither could speak the other's language. If two black people, at that bitter hour of the world's history, had been able to speak to each other, the institution of chattel slavery[6] could never have lasted as long as it did. Subsequently, the slave was given, under the eye, and the gun, of his master, Congo Square,[7] and the Bible—or, in other words, and under these conditions, the slave began the formation of the black church, and it is within this unprecedented tabernacle that black English began to be formed. This was not, merely, as in the European example, the adoption of a foreign tongue, but an alchemy that transformed ancient elements into a new language: *A language comes into existence by means of brutal necessity, and the rules of the language are dictated by what the language must convey.*

There was a moment, in time, and in this place, when my brother, or my mother, or my father, or my sister, had to convey to me, for example, the danger in which I was standing from the white man standing just behind me, and to convey this with a speed, and in a language, that the white man could not possibly understand, and that, indeed, he cannot understand, until today. He cannot afford to understand it. This understanding would reveal to him too much about himself, and smash that mirror before which he has been frozen for so long.

---

4 *Beat Generation* Literary movement in the 1950s that rejected mainstream American culture, seeking to escape materialism and find spiritual and sexual liberation.

5 *black diaspora* People with ancestral roots in Africa who now live in other places.

6 *chattel slavery* System in which enslaved people are considered the property of their enslavers, as are any chiildren born to the enslaved.

7 *Congo Square* Open space in what is now Louis Armstrong Park in Tremé, New Orleans, where, in 1817, the mayor gave permission for enslaved people to gather on Sundays. Hundreds would come to dance, sing, make music, and attend voodoo ceremonies. The gatherings were notable for the bringing together of many traditional practices (and languages) of the various tribes from which the participants had been taken. The meetings in Congo Square dwindled in the decade preceding Emancipation, but its dances, music, and rituals evolved into jazz and are still present in various forms in New Orleans today.

Now, if this passion, this skill, this (to quote Toni Morrison[8]) "sheer intelligence," this incredible music, the mighty achievement of having brought a people utterly unknown to, or despised by "history"—to have brought this people to their present, troubled, troubling, and unassailable and unanswerable place—if this absolutely unprecedented journey does not indicate that black English is a language, I am curious to know what definition of language is to be trusted.

A people at the center of the Western world, and in the midst of so hostile   10
a population, has not endured and transcended by means of what is patronizingly called a "dialect." We, the blacks, are in trouble, certainly, but we are not doomed, and we are not inarticulate because we are not compelled to defend a morality that we know to be a lie.

The brutal truth is that the bulk of white people in America never had any interest in educating black people, except as this could serve white purposes. It is not the black child's language that is in question, it is not his language that is despised: It is his experience. A child cannot be taught by anyone who despises him, and a child cannot afford to be fooled. A child cannot be taught by anyone whose demand, essentially, is that the child repudiate his experience, and all that gives him sustenance, and enter a limbo in which he will no longer be black, and in which he knows that he can never become white. Black people have lost too many black children that way.

And, after all, finally, in a country with standards so untrustworthy, a country that makes heroes of so many criminal mediocrities, a country unable to face why so many of the nonwhite are in prison, or on the needle,* or standing, futureless, in the streets—it may very well be that both the child, and his elder, have concluded that they have nothing whatever to learn from the people of a country that has managed to learn so little.

(1979)

Questions

1. Look up how linguists define "dialect" and "language." Why does Baldwin view the label "dialect" as insulting when applied to the language spoken by Black Americans? Do you agree with him?

2. Baldwin writes that Black language "permits the nation its only glimpse of reality" (paragraph 6). What does this mean?

---

8   *Toni Morrison*   Prominent African American writer and Nobel prize winner (1931–2019), best known for her novel *Beloved* (1998).

3. Baldwin offers many reasons why Black Americans developed a unique language in America. Summarize three of them. Are there others that you can think of that aren't mentioned here?

4. Research the Beat Generation. Why does Baldwin disapprove of this movement?

5. In the closing paragraphs of the essay, Baldwin moves from his discussion of language to that of education. What point does this essay make about the connection between the two?

6. According to Baldwin, how can language give power, and how can it limit power? How does this relate to its function as the "key to identity" (paragraph 4)?

7. Consider the last paragraph of this essay. Does this paragraph suggest that Baldwin is hopeful about the future of race relations in America? Why or why not?

8. Research a relatively recent borrowing from Black language into white speech (consider, for example, "to throw shade," "yas"/"yas queen," or "bae"). Given the history of the word you researched, do you think non-Black people ought not to use it? Why or why not?

WILLIAM BRENNAN

JULIE WASHINGTON'S QUEST TO GET SCHOOLS TO RESPECT AFRICAN-AMERICAN ENGLISH

Speech pathologist Julie Washington's areas of interest include the status of African-American English as a dialect, its use by children in schools, and its relationship to students' academic success. This article from The Atlantic *by journalist William Brennan discusses Washington's work on the value of "code-switching," or the ability to fluidly move between different modes of speech, and the potentially life-changing significance of this skill for a wide body of elementary school students.*

☙

Studying African-American vernacular English wasn't Julie Washington's plan. But one day in the fall of 1990, her speech-pathology doctorate fresh in hand, she found herself sitting with a little girl at a school outside Detroit. The two were reading the classic P.D. Eastman picture book *Are You My Mother?*, which tells the tale of a lost hatchling trying to find its way home. The girl—4 years old, homeless, and a heavy speaker of the dialect known as African-American English, or AAE—listened attentively as Washington read:

"Are you my mother?" the baby bird asked the cow.
"How could I be your mother?" said the cow. "I am a cow."

Washington closed the book and asked the girl to recount the story from memory. The girl hesitated, then launched into it. "She goes, 'Is you my mama? I ain't none a yo' mama!'" Washington recalls. "She did the whole thing in dialect." Washington found the girl's retelling deft and charming, and she left the classroom smiling.

Only later, sitting in her office at the University of Michigan, did Washington have the flash of insight that would redirect her career. "As a scientist, I stepped back and thought about what that girl had to do," Washington told me recently, while waiting to address a gathering of linguists at the University of Wisconsin at Madison. "She had to listen to a story in a dialect she doesn't really use herself, understand the meaning, hold the story in her memory, recode it in her own dialect, and then say it all back to me." The girl's "translation" of the book might not sound like much, but translating it? "That's *hard*," Washington said, especially for a young child. The experience convinced her that dialect was playing a significant and unrecognized role in the reading achievement of millions of children—and very likely contributing to the persistence of the black-white gap in test scores.

In the decades since, Washington, now a professor of communications sciences and disorders at Georgia State, has devoted her career to exploring the challenges that speakers of African-American English face in the classroom. Not all African American students speak the dialect, but most do. Teaching kids to "code-switch" between their home dialect and the dialect spoken at school, Washington has come to believe, is an important step toward creating a more level playing field. She is not, of course, the first person to make this argument. Linguists pioneered the case for code-switching in the 1960s, and over the years at least half a dozen programs have sought to teach speakers of AAE how to speak standard English in the classroom. Most of them, however, have provoked furious backlash and quickly met their end.

5 The most notorious of these controversies occurred in 1996, when the school board of Oakland, California, approved the use of "Ebonics"[1] as a tool for reading instruction. The board had hoped to raise students' scores by teaching kids to code-switch. But the prospect of encouraging the dialect in the classroom elicited national, and near-universal, censure. As the White House and editorialists for the country's top newspapers condemned the plan, several states banned the use of AAE in education, and Oakland's superintendent was called before the U.S. Senate. The school board's program was never implemented, and the word *Ebonics* became a national punch line. New research by scholars like Washington, however, suggests an interesting possibility: Maybe Oakland was onto something.

Washington grew up in an all-black part of Seattle, at the height of the civil-rights movement, surrounded by African-American English and fascinated by language from an early age. As a young girl, she played a game with herself, eavesdropping on her mother's phone calls and trying to guess who was on the other end. She found that she could always tell just by listening to the different ways her mother spoke after saying "Hello?" Her father was a high-school

---

1   *Ebonics*   Another term for African-American Vernacular English, understood as a separate language rather than simply a dialect. The word was coined in the 1970s by psychology professor Robert Williams.

history teacher and her mother was a gospel singer; like many middle-class parents in the neighborhood, they held AAE in low regard—they considered the dialect a barrier to "mainstream" success—and forbade Washington and her siblings from speaking it in the house. But Washington picked it up from friends. Today she code-switches effortlessly and unremarkably.

At the conference in Madison, linguists threw around phrases such as *auxiliary alternation* and *diachronic precursor*, speaking an academic code Washington avoids. She mostly kept her distance, skipping talks with boring titles; she lacks a linguist's tolerance for obscure grammatical disputes, declaring herself more interested in "functional" matters. ("Oh my *God*," she remarked after one particularly pedantic lecture.) As she waited to deliver her own talk, on the language and literacy of African American children, she walked me through one of her career's guiding questions: Why don't all kids learn to code-switch as easily as she did?

Like speakers of any nonstandard dialect, from Swiss German to Cypriot Greek, most speakers of African-American English do learn to code-switch naturally, Washington explained. "Some start during kindergarten, then we see a big wave at the end of first grade and another at the end of second. Then you get to third grade and it's over." At that point, about a third of them still can't speak the standard dialect, and "code-switching isn't going to happen unless you teach it. We *know* those kids will have trouble." By the end of fourth grade, "switching" students—that is, students who are proficient in both their home dialect and standard English—score at least a full academic year ahead of their nonswitching classmates in reading.

Why exactly does speaking a nonstandard dialect stymie* kids as they're learning to read? In his seminal 1972 book, *Language in the Inner City*, the linguist William Labov advanced the reigning theory. A teacher writes a word on the blackboard—something simple, like *told* or *past*—sounding it out letter by letter as she does. For a speaker of standard English, the lesson is clear: The four letters represent the four sounds that make up the word. But the rule is more complex for AAE speakers. In the black vernacular,* many consonant clusters—such as the *-ld* in *told*, and the *-st* in *past*—aren't fully pronounced when they appear at the end of a word. A speaker of African-American English is likely to say *told* the same as *toll* (or even *toe*), and *past* the same as *pass*. The profusion of homonyms* obscures the fundamental sound-to-letter principle: AAE-speaking kids are presented with an enormous number of words that are all pronounced the same yet spelled in nonsensically different ways. To help kids grasp the dialect of the classroom, Labov wrote, teachers should employ "the methods used in teaching English as a foreign language."

10   Labov's recommendation was largely overlooked outside his field. But last June, Washington completed a four-year study of almost 1,000 low-income elementary-school students in a southern city—the most extensive study ever of the dialect's role in education—which led her to a similar conclusion. Strikingly, she discovered that African American students' lagging growth in reading was accounted for almost entirely by the low scores of the students who speak the heaviest dialect. And location mattered: The majority of kids in the city she studied, Washington found, use a regional variety of AAE that is especially far from standard English. This suggests to her that children who speak one of the dialect's "really dense" varieties are having an experience in the classroom not unlike that of, say, native Spanish speakers.

Compounding these challenges is the fact that most AAE speakers have teachers who are hostile to their dialect. In an illuminating investigation published in 1973 (but, according to several linguists I spoke with, still reflective of classroom conditions today), Ann McCormick Piestrup portrayed the AAE speaker's experience as one of incessant interruption. Black children at the California schools Piestrup studied often answered questions correctly, only to be pounced on for irrelevant differences of pronunciation or grammar. This climate had a drastic effect: As time went on, Piestrup saw students withdraw into "moody silences"; when they did speak, their voices were soft and hesitant. The interrupted students had the lowest reading scores of any children Piestrup observed.

The social effects of this type of classroom environment have been acknowledged for decades, but what's come to concern researchers more recently is the extent to which dialect differences between student and teacher increase the student's cognitive load.* "What does it do to your response times when you have to stop and interpret something before you can move on?" Washington asks. "Over the course of a school day, those moments have to add up."

In this way, Washington believes that dialect may very well account for a significant part of the black-white literacy gap. At the start of kindergarten, she notes, research finds a relatively small academic gap between black and white children, and what little gap exists can be entirely explained by controlling for socioeconomic status. Yet by first grade, the gap between them has widened considerably. If recent research on the effects of mismatched dialects is right, Washington reasons, one way to narrow the gap is to help kids learn the dialect of school, while also helping schools accept the dialect students bring with them.

To this end, one group of researchers has developed a code-switching curriculum called ToggleTalk, which has met with modest success; last year, the Los Angeles Unified School District, the country's second-largest school system, implemented it in a few dozen classrooms. (Teachers in the district have also requested lessons meant for speakers of Chicano English, a Spanish-influenced dialect used by a large minority of students there.) But getting code-switching lessons into schools remains a challenge.

As Washington learned early in her career, even seemingly benign conversations about African-American English can be fraught—and often, it's speakers of the dialect who most fiercely resist efforts to incorporate it into the classroom. In preparation for one of her first studies of AAE, she sent out consent forms to parents, describing her goal of studying "the role Black English plays in children's oral language." Weeks passed, and not a single form came back. Eventually, Washington called a parents' night and asked why no one had signed the form. Two dozen parents stared at her in silence until, Washington told me, one mother erupted: "How dare you say we talk different than other people! What the hell is 'black English'? We don't speak 'black English'!"

"You do," Washington said, and to make her point, she code-switched. "I think I said, 'Look, we ain't got no business doin' this,'" she recalled. The room burst into laughter. "Okay, we do speak like that," the mother granted. "But we don't like you calling it that." It was a lesson Washington never forgot: The dialect was so stigmatized that even among people who spoke it every day, she needed to tread carefully.

A new insight of Washington's might offer a new path forward, however. In presenting code-switching lessons as a way to ward off catastrophic reading failure, she says, advocates have failed to convey the upsides of speaking African-American English. In a recent paper, Washington points to research showing that fluent speakers of two dialects might benefit from some of the cognitive advantages that accrue to speakers of two languages. She hopes that this line of thinking might at last persuade teachers and parents alike to buy in. "We see value in speaking two languages," Washington told me. "But we don't see value in speaking two dialects. Maybe it's time we did."

Washington believes that programs used to strengthen bilingual students' grasp of English grammar could provide a stealthy way of slipping code-switching lessons into the classroom. "Many of the features covered for students who speak another language are exactly the same ones that cause African-American English speakers trouble," she said. She has seen firsthand the ways such curricula can benefit kids who speak the dialect. At one elementary school she studied in Michigan, teachers implemented a bilingual curriculum for the majority-black student body and saw a 75 percent increase in the number of students who passed state reading tests.

15

Despite such results, code-switching remains a tough sell, even in academia. Some linguists I spoke with said they'd come to see code-switching lessons as well intentioned but ultimately marginalizing—a linguistic version of "separate but equal." Washington told me she understands their concerns, and faults some code-switching programs for focusing too much on the "harms" of not being able to code-switch. But she said she refuses to lose sight of the children, usually poor and black, whose futures are on the line. Until and unless "the places these kids might want to go to learn, work, and live" change fundamentally, she told me, "you're handicapping them by not teaching them the two codes."

(2018)

Questions

1. In your own words, summarize Julie Washington's arguments in favor of teaching code-switching in the classroom. What evidence does she provide for her recommendations?

2. Why do you think the notion of identifying "African-American English" as a distinct dialect—and of recognizing it as such in the classroom—has been so controversial? What is your perspective on the matter?

3. Do your own research to find out some ways that linguists determine whether a particular mode of speech counts as a distinct dialect or not. Keeping these approaches in mind, identify a few dialects (standard or nonstandard) you sometimes use, read, hear, or otherwise encounter in media or in person. How privileged—or underprivileged—is each of these dialects?

4. Read James Baldwin's essay "If Black English Isn't a Language, Then Tell Me, What Is?" (also included in this anthology).

   a. Washington calls African American English a "dialect"—something Baldwin argues against. What is implied by calling African American English a dialect, and what is implied by calling it a language? Which term (if either) should be used?

   b. How (if at all) does African American English reflect the experiences of the people who speak it? How does speaking it shape their experiences? Answer with reference to both Brennan's and Baldwin's articles.

FORMING THE SELF

ROLAND BARTHES

from MYTHOLOGIES[1]

TOYS

In his book Mythologies *(1957), Roland Barthes argues that any*
activity or material thing that is culturally meaningful—from steak
and fries to the Tour de France—can be interpreted much as one
might interpret a written text. "[A] photograph will be a kind of
speech for us in the same way as a newspaper article," he writes;
"even objects will become speech if they mean something." Central
to this approach to analysis is the concept of the "sign," which
is any unit that communicates meaning (for example, a word,
an emoji, a facial expression, or a photograph). Below, Barthes
interprets toys as signs; another essay from Mythologies *elsewhere*
in this anthology discusses "Soap-Powders and Detergents."

℘

French toys: one could not find a better illustration of the fact that the adult
Frenchman sees the child as another self. All the toys one commonly sees
are essentially a microcosm of the adult world; they are all reduced copies of
human objects, as if in the eyes of the public the child was, all told, nothing but
a smaller man, a homunculus[2] to whom must be supplied objects of his own
size.

Invented forms are very rare: a few sets of blocks, which appeal to the
spirit of do-it-yourself, are the only ones which offer dynamic forms. As for
the others, French toys *always mean something*, and this something is always
entirely socialized, constituted by the myths or the techniques of modern adult
life: the Army, Broadcasting, the Post Office, Medicine (miniature instrument-
cases, operating theaters for dolls), School, Hair-Styling (driers for permanent-
waving), the Air Force (Parachutists), Transport (trains, Citroens, Vedettes,
Vespas,[3] petrol-stations), Science (Martian toys).

---

1   *Mythologies*   Translated by Annette Lavers, 1972.
2   *homunculus*   Little or miniature man.
3   *Citroens, Vedettes, Vespas*   European cars and scooters.

The fact that French toys *literally* prefigure the world of adult functions obviously cannot but prepare the child to accept them all, by constituting for him, even before he can think about it, the alibi of a Nature which has at all times created soldiers, postmen and Vespas. Toys here reveal the list of all the things the adult does not find unusual: war, bureaucracy, ugliness, Martians, etc. It is not so much, in fact, the imitation which is the sign of an abdication, as its literalness: French toys are like a Jivaro head,[4] in which one recognizes, shrunken to the size of an apple, the wrinkles and hair of an adult. There exist, for instance, dolls which urinate; they have an esophagus, one gives them a bottle, they wet their nappies;[5] soon, no doubt, milk will turn to water in their stomachs. This is meant to prepare the little girl for the causality of housekeeping, to "condition" her to her future role as mother. However, faced with this world of faithful and complicated objects, the child can only identify himself as owner, as user, never as creator; he does not invent the world, he uses it: there are, prepared for him, actions without adventure, without wonder, without joy. He is turned into a little stay-at-home householder who does not even have to invent the mainsprings of adult causality;* they are supplied to him readymade: he has only to help himself, he is never allowed to discover anything from start to finish. The merest set of blocks, provided it is not too refined, implies a very different learning of the world: then, the child does not in any way create meaningful objects, it matters little to him whether they have an adult name; the actions he performs are not those of a user but those of a demiurge.[6] He creates forms which walk, which roll, he creates life, not property: objects now act by themselves, they are no longer an inert and complicated material in the palm of his hand. But such toys are rather rare: French toys are usually based on imitation, they are meant to produce children who are users, not creators.

The bourgeois* status of toys can be recognized not only in their forms, which are all functional, but also in their substances. Current toys are made of a graceless material, the product of chemistry, not of nature. Many are now moulded from complicated mixtures; the plastic material of which they are made has an appearance at once gross and hygienic, it destroys all the pleasure, the sweetness, the humanity of touch. A sign which fills one with consternation is the gradual disappearance of wood, in spite of its being an ideal material because of its firmness and its softness, and the natural warmth of its touch. Wood removes, from all the forms which it supports, the wounding quality of

---

4 *Jivaro head* The Jivaroan people of northern Peru and eastern Ecuador are known for shrinking the heads severed on annual head-hunting expeditions. The heads are shrunk to about the size of a large apple.

5 *nappies* Diapers.

6 *demiurge* Maker or creator of worlds.

angles which are too sharp, the chemical coldness of metal. When the child handles it and knocks it, it neither vibrates nor grates, it has a sound at once muffled and sharp. It is a familiar and poetic substance, which does not sever the child from close contact with the tree, the table, the floor. Wood does not wound or break down; it does not shatter, it wears out, it can last a long time, live with the child, alter little by little the relations between the object and the hand. If it dies, it is in dwindling, not in swelling out like those mechanical toys which disappear behind the hernia of a broken spring. Wood makes essential objects, objects for all time. Yet there hardly remain any of these wooden toys from the Vosges, these fretwork[7] farms with their animals, which were only possible, it is true, in the days of the craftsman. Henceforth, toys are chemical in substance and color; their very material introduces one to a coenaesthesis[8] of use, not pleasure. These toys die in fact very quickly, and once dead, they have no posthumous life for the child.

(1957)

Questions

1. What, according to Barthes, is wrong with the materials used to make children's toys today? Why would he rather see wood used instead? Do you agree with his suggestion that wood is a better material for toys?

2. According to Barthes, what kinds of toys make children into "users"? How do they do this? What are the social repercussions of giving children these toys? How do they preserve the status quo, particularly in regard to class?

3. What toys did you play with most as a child? To what extent do Barthes' observations regarding toys apply to your childhood experiences? How (if at all) did the toys you played with shape you?

4. In *Mythologies*, Barthes looks closely at cultural artifacts and interprets them as signs, showing how these artifacts perpetuate social ideologies and hierarchies. Choose a contemporary artifact and interpret it in a similar way (what values does it represent? How is it advertised? How does using it affect you? Does it perpetuate or challenge the status quo? How?).

---

7   *Vosges* Mountainous area of eastern France with a thriving wood industry; *fretwork* Type of intricate woodworking.

8   *coenaesthesis* Feeling of existence that arises from sensory information.

IVAN COYOTE

from TOMBOY SURVIVAL GUIDE

TOMBOYS STILL

Writer, filmmaker, and performer Ivan Coyote is known for their humorous and heartfelt approach to storytelling. Coyote, whose gender is nonbinary, reflects on the evolution of their identity in their 2016 memoir, Tomboy Survival Guide; *the following story appeared in that memoir.*

❦

Linda Gould was a friend of my mom's. Linda was from somewhere not here, somewhere not the Yukon, she had family down south and she had raven black hair. One time I asked my mom why Linda's name was Linda Gould but her husband was still called Don Dixon. My mom told me that some women chose not to take their husband's last name when they got married. It was 1974 and this impressed me for reasons I did not fully comprehend just yet.

Linda and Don lived in a rented house next to the clay cliffs downtown, and had one wall in their living room covered in that mural type of wallpaper, depicting a picture of a forest of giant pine trees. Linda wouldn't let Don paint over that wallpaper or tear it down; she said it reminded her of California.

I was a Yukon kid and had never seen a real tree that big in my life, I could only imagine them.

Linda played hockey, and she also coached a girl's ringette team. As soon as I turned five years old I was allowed to join up. I had never really heard of the game called ringette but wanted to be good at it because Linda was good at it. It turned out ringette was kind of like hockey light, but only girls played it. It wasn't as much fun as hockey looked like it was, but I kept going to practices because my mom had spent all that money on skates and a helmet for me. There were barely enough girls to make one team so we never got to play a real game, we mostly skated around and practiced stopping. That's the truth, and also a metaphor. Some of the girls came in figure skates, but not me.

5   One day Don Dixon showed up early at practice and watched us run a passing drill for a while. He told Linda after practice that I was already a better skater than half the boys on the Squirts team he coached and so did I want to come and play with the boys? he asked.

I didn't even have to think before I said yes. My mom said hold on, she had to talk it over with my dad, who was only half listening because he was reading that book *Shogun*[1] and it was a super good book he said, and my mom said yes, I guess, you can play hockey, but be careful out there. Linda taught me how to do a slap shot and told me never to skate with my head down. I was the only girl playing in the Whitehorse Minor Hockey League for eleven years after that. I made it all the way up to junior hockey. Left wing.

When I turned sixteen they wouldn't let me play hockey with the boys anymore. I was now a legal liability, they told my parents, and the minor hockey league just couldn't afford that kind of insurance, and besides, what if I got hurt, the boys were so much bigger now, plus body-checking. Come and play on the women's team with us, Linda said, and so I did.

That was how I met Donna Doucette, who played defense and worked as a bartender at the Kopper King on the Alaska Highway. Donna Doucette wore her long brown hair in a whip-like braid that swung between her shoulder blades when she skated back hard for the puck. I think I pretty much fell in love with Donna Doucette the first time I saw her spit perfectly through the square holes in the face mask on her helmet. She just curled her tongue into a tube and horked unapologetically right through her mask. It shot like a bullet, about fifteen feet, straight out onto the ice. I had never seen a woman do anything like that before, I could only imagine the back-of-the-head slap my gran would lay on me if I ever dared to spit anywhere in public, much less turn it into an art form like Donna Doucette did.

I remember hearing her playing fastball one midnight sunny summer evening; I was playing softball on the field next to the women's league. All the women on my hockey team played ball together in the summer; like serious fast pitch, they were not fooling around. Hockey was for sport but fast pitch was for keeps. Donna Doucette played shortstop and would spare no skin to make a catch, and she spat all over the goddamn place out there on the field too, and cussed and catcalled. Hey batter batta batta swing batta batta.* I remember her in silhouette, bobbing back and forth on the toes of her cleats, all backlit by the sun and gum a-chew, a mouthy shadow, punching the pocket of her gloved hand with her red-nailed fingertips coiled into a fist.

That's the thing about Linda and Donna. They weren't like me. Linda wore   10
sapphire studs in her ears and a red red dress to our Christmas party. Donna swore and stole third base wearing what my mother claimed to be too much eye makeup for daylight hours, which even back then I thought was kind of harsh, it being summer in the Yukon and it never really getting dark and all.

---

1   *Shogun*   1975 novel by James Clavell.

Donna and Linda. My memories of them are sharp, hyper-focused. I was paying attention to every detail of them, I was searching them for clues to who I wanted to be, but I already knew I couldn't be like them. I wanted something else. Something close to what they had. They hinted at a kind of freedom, a kind of just not giving a fuck what anyone said about them that made me want things I didn't know the words for.

Theresa Turner drove her two-stroke dirt bike to school every day we were in grade eleven, appearing out of the willows and trailing a tail of dust as she gunned the throttle and skidded to a stop by the tree line at the edge of our high school parking lot. She would dismount and stomp her kickstand down with the heel of her buckled biker boot and shake her mane of mahogany ringlets loose from under her helmet and strut in her skin-tight Levi 501s past the heads smoking cigarettes by the back double doors to the wood shop. Fuck you looking at? she would sneer at them. This for some reason made them blush, and pretend they weren't watching her ass swing as the door hissed shut behind her. I was old enough by then to be full-on smitten.

Carolyn O'Hara was Theresa Turner's very best friend from Cedar. Cedar was a suburb of the pulp mill town of Nanaimo where I was living with my grandmother. Theresa Turner and Carolyn O'Hara had grown up out there together and had known each other all their lives. They also knew all about all the boys from the rural working class outskirts of Nanaimo. Knew all the boys who had to skip school in the fall to bring in the hay and miss entire weeks in the spring when the lambs came.

They knew all about the boys with the jean jacket vests with ZZ Top or Judas Priest[2] album covers recreated in ballpoint ink. Houses of the Holy.[3] The boys whose older brothers were doing time.*

15 Carolyn O'Hara had a necklace strung of these diamonds in the rough, these boys who would punch locker doors and prick the skin in between their forefinger and thumb and rub ink into it in the shape of a broken heart all for the love of Carolyn O'Hara. She had her brother who died in a motorcycle accident's acoustic guitar and she would play "Walk on the Wild Side" by Lou Reed at lunch. I remember her swinging her honey-brown hair in the sun in the front seat of Eddie Bartolo's midnight blue Nova with the windows rolled down and saying, "So what if I am on the rag, you asshole. I'd like to see you go to gym class and do your fucking flexed arm hang exercises if you'd been bleeding out of your ass like it's going out of goddamn style for the last three fucking days. You going to smoke that thing or pass it on, you selfish bastard?"

---

2   *ZZ Top ... Judas Priest*   Bands that became popular in the early 1970s.

3   *Houses of the Holy*   1973 album by Led Zeppelin.

Carolyn O'Hara could out-swear even Theresa Turner, it's why they were the perfect pair. Carolyn O'Hara was gorgeous. Could have been a model, everybody said so, but she was very practical and took the dental hygienist's program up at the college right after we graduated.

I ran into Theresa one day about five years ago, on my way to Vancouver Island for a gig. Theresa was wearing false eyelashes and an orange reflective vest at the same time, which I thought was awesome. Hugged me hard and told me she had been working for BC Ferries for seventeen years now, doing what my gran had always said was a good, clean, union job if you liked people. Said Carolyn O'Hara had opened her own dog grooming business. A real cool place where you can drop your dog off to get groomed, or rent a big tub and wash your own dog in the back. She said they were both happy, they still kept in real good touch, in fact they were going for mani-pedis for their fortieth birthdays just next week.

Mia Telerico. Fall of 1992, she had just moved to town from Toronto. I met her in my friend's coffee shop on the Drive, she smoked Du Maurier Light King Size and I smoked Player's Light regulars. I, for reasons unexamined by me at the time, I guess I was trying to impress her, so I spontaneously leapt up and did a dramatic reading for her of *The Cat in the Hat*, and we briefly became lovers, and then, so far, life-long friends. Mia Telerico said in my kitchen one night that first winter, It's E-Talian, not Eye-Talian, you sound like a redneck if you say it wrong, and then she showed me how to peel a bunch of garlic all at once by crushing it with the side of the butcher knife.

How many ways do I love Mia Telerico? I love that she refinishes furniture and owns all her own power tools and that it takes hours for her curls to dry so she has special hair-washing days, because washing her hair is like, a thing, right, and she is missing part of a finger from an accident she had cleaning the chain on her motorcycle and she is tough as nails but with the softest heart and bosom, can I even use the word "bosom" anymore? I don't know. Her hugs feel better than nearly anything is all I'm saying, and when she lets me rest my head there for a second I feel so untouchable, so unhurtable somehow, so magically protected by her soft cheek and rough hands ever capable. I called her just now and left a message asking her if it was okay if I called her a femme tomboy, how does she feel about me pinning those words on her femme tomboy, but really, all I'm trying to do here is broaden the joining, I tell her voice mail. All I want to do is honor all the femme tomboys I have ever loved, and thank them for showing me the possibilities. Anyway. Mia's father was from Malta and her mother is Italian and her dad was a janitor and her ma worked in a chocolate factory just like I Love Lucy and Ethel[4] except less funny and for decades until it wrecked her back.

20   I left Mia Telerico a message but I haven't heard back yet. I hear through the grapevine that she is going through a breakup and, well, I guess I am too, and both of us, we take these things pretty hard, artist's hearts pumping just beneath the skin of our chests like they do.

(2016)

Questions

1. What is a "femme tomboy"? Identify an individual from this piece who might be considered a femme tomboy and explain what (if any) behaviors, physical attributes, and/or other markers of gender justify this description.

2. Near the end of this piece Coyote writes, "All I want to do is honor all the femme tomboys I have ever loved, and thank them for showing me the possibilities." What "possibilities" are they referring to?

3. How in this piece is gender expression affected by class?

4. Coyote does not introduce the term "femme tomboy" until the end of the piece. What do they accomplish by introducing this term? How would the piece have been different if they introduced the term at the beginning of the piece instead?

5. Coyote attempts to contact Mia Telerico about describing her as a "femme tomboy" in this piece. How—if at all—are writers of memoir morally obligated to regard the way their subjects are impacted by appearing in published writing?

---

4   *I Love Lucy and Ethel*   Reference to a popular episode of the *I Love Lucy* sitcom (1951–57), in which Lucy and Ethel struggle to keep up with the assembly line in a chocolate factory.

EDEN ROBINSON

from THE SASQUATCH AT HOME: TRADITIONAL PROTOCOLS AND STORYTELLING

This piece is an excerpt from the 2010 Canadian Literature Centre Kreisel Lecture, an annual lecture delivered at the University of Alberta by an important Canadian writer. The presentation excerpted here, by fiction writer Eden Robinson, was published in print form in 2011. Her lecture was divided into three parts; the following is the first of the three.

❧

My name is Eden Robinson. My mother is Heiltsuk[1] from Bella Bella and my father is Haisla from Kitimaat village, both small reserves* on the northwest coast of British Columbia. My maternal grandmother's family was originally from Rivers Inlet. Since both sides of my family are matrilineal, technically, my clan name should have come from my mother's side and I should belong to the Eagle Clan. When I was ten years old, my father's family decided to give me and my sister Beaver Clan names at a Settlement Feast for a chief of the Beaver Clan who had died a year earlier.

When a chief died, his body was embalmed in a Terrace funeral home and then he was brought back to his house where he lay for at least three days, attended around the clock by family members or people hired by his family to keep him safe from harm as he rested in the living room. Community members paid respects by visiting him in his home and at his memorial. After the funeral itself, the Thank You Supper was held for people who had helped out emotionally, financially and organizationally. After a year of planning and

---

1 [Robinson's note]   The Heiltsuk Nation's main reserve is Waglisla, BC, which is more commonly referred to as Bella Bella, the name given it by Spanish explorers. Kitamaat Village is known by its residents simply as the Village and was at first a winter camp and, later, a Methodist mission. It is currently the main reserve for the Haisla Nation. The reserve is also referred to as C'imotsa, "snag beach," because of all the stumps and logs that decorate the waterfront.

preparation, the family announced the date of the Settlement Feast and finally, of the headstone moving. Modern feasts are truncated affairs lasting six hours at the most. Much of the dancing has gone but the important dirges are sung, names are distributed and re-distributed to clan members, and people from the community are gifted according to status and involvement with the family. In general, headstone moving is considered an affair of the immediate family and close friends. Space in the graveyard is tight and imposing yourself on the family's grief is considered the height of rudeness.

You aren't supposed to attend a feast or a potlatch without an Indian[2] name and since we were living in Kitimaat Village, my mother, although annoyed, for the sake of convenience agreed to let us become Beaver Clan. My younger sister and I received our names at the Settlement Feast. Towards the end of the evening, we were told to go and line up with other children receiving names. I mostly remember being embarrassed to be standing in front of everyone and having no idea what I was supposed to do. One of my aunts told me if I wanted to learn more about my name, I should go visit my grandmother, my ma-ma-oo.[3]

The next day, we went to ma-ma-oo's house. She told my sister that her name was Sigadum'na'x, which meant Sent Back Chief Lady. A long time ago, a marriage was arranged between a high-ranking lady from up the line[4] and a Haisla chief. They fell deeply in love. Unfortunately, his other four wives became extremely jealous and kept trying to poison her. He couldn't divorce them because they came from powerful families and insulting them in this way would mean, at the very least, nasty feuds. So despite his feelings, he decided to send his love back to her home to save her life. He couldn't divorce her without causing her shame, so he made her a chief. I've since learned two other versions of the story behind my sister's name, but I like this one the best.

5   "Wow," I said when I heard the story. "What does my name mean?"

"Big lady."

"Um, what else does it mean?"

Ma-ma-oo paused. "Biiiiiig lady."

---

2   [Robinson's note]   Indian, aboriginal, First Nations, native Canadian are used interchangeably in the context of this essay and most of my work. [In Canada the use of the words "Indian" and "Native" to describe First Nations people is controversial; some consider these words to be tainted by association with racist stereotypes, while some First Nations people continue to identify with both or either of the terms—and with Indian in particular, as it is used by the Canadian government for the designation of "Indian Status."]

3   [Robinson's note]   Pronounced *ma*-MAH-*ew*.

4   *up the line*   North.

I paused. Names come loaded with rights and histories. Within the Beaver Clan, the name of the Chief of All Haislas (Jasee) is hotly contested and has started many family quarrels. My father is one of the younger sons of a high-ranking family, so my siblings and I receive noble names, but nothing that garners too much prestige and thus requires extensive feasting or that can get me into too much trouble. Implied in my name, Wiwltxº, therefore, is a high rank as it was obtained through marriage and only given to women of noble birth. I was disappointed in my name, and it has nothing to do with rank: I had story envy. No heartbroken women were standing beside rivers with their long hair unbound as they sang their sadness to the world. Unfortunately, to change my name I'd have to throw a feast. Putting up a feast is like a cross between organizing a large wedding and a small conference. Family politics aside, the sheer cost will run you $5000 if you cheap out and just invite the chiefs and gift them to witness your event. But then your name would be marred by your miserliness and people would remember how poorly you'd done things long after you'd died. A real feast starts at $10,000 and goes up very, very quickly.

My aunts also gave my mother a name not long after she'd married my father. My mother had just returned to Bella Bella from residential school[5] in Port Alberni. Meanwhile, in the Village, my father was under pressure from his family to get married. At thirty-three years old, they were worried he was going to be an embarrassing bachelor forever. Ma-ma-oo was trying to arrange a marriage with someone suitable. My father decided to go fishing instead.

My maternal grandmother lived in a house near the docks in Bella Bella. One day my mother was looking out the front picture window when she saw my father coming up the gangplank. According to Gran, Mom said, "That's the man I'm going to marry." Mom's version is that she simply asked if she knew who he was.

They met later that night at a jukebox joint[6] held in a house. My father was a hottie and all the girls wanted to dance with him, but he only wanted to dance with my mother. They were getting along so well, they lost track of time. Back then, the air raid siren left over from a World War II naval base would sound and mark the time when the generator was shut off. The streets

10

_____

5   *residential school*   Boarding school which many Aboriginal Canadian children were required to attend regardless of their parents' wishes. The purpose of the schools was to sever children's ties to their own communities and cultures and force them to adopt Euro-Canadian culture and language. Students were given a substandard education, poorly cared for, and often abused. The system was at its largest during the first half of the twentieth century, but the last residential school did not close until 1996.

6   *jukebox joint*   Informal gathering often featuring food, drink, dancing, and gambling.

went dark. Mom's house was on the other side of the reserve. Dad offered to walk her home.

My father took my mother back to the Village after they were married. Dad's family was upset because mom was twelve years younger than Dad. She was annoyed that they thought she was too young for Dad and expressed her opinion forcefully. My aunts gifted her with an Indian name so she could attend the feasts in the Village. Mom's new name Halh.qala.ghum.ne'x, meant Sea Monster Turning the Other Way. Although it lacks the romance of my sister's name, I like the attitude it suggests and hope to inherit it.

I had been introduced to the concept of nusa[7] as a child, but had never really understood it until my trip to Graceland[8] with my mother. In 1997, I received £800 for winning the Royal Society of Literature's Winifred Holtby Memorial Prize.[9] After taxes and currency exchange, it worked out to $2000 CAD. One of my coworkers at the time suggested I put it into our RRSPs or at the very least a GIC,[10] but I had always wanted a black leather couch.[11] I spent a few weeks searching for just the right couch and anxiously awaited its delivery. Once it was in my apartment, it seemed monolithic. And it squeaked. And it felt sticky when it was hot. I returned it the next day, deciding what I really wanted was a tropical vacation.

I flipped through travel magazines, trying to insert myself into the happy, sunny pictures. Overwhelmed by the choices, I phoned my mother. I asked her if she could go anywhere in the world, where would she go?

"Graceland," Mom said.

"Really?"

"I would go in a heartbeat."

I was impressed by her certainty. "Okay."

She laughed and we chatted a bit longer. I spent the rest of the evening surfing the Internet for cheap flights and a passable hotel. There were some incredible deals on flights, but the cheapest ones had multiple connections.

---

7   [Robinson's note]   *Nusa*: the traditional way of teaching children Haisla *nuyem*, or protocols.

8   *Graceland*   Site of the home of musician Elvis Presley (1935–77) in Memphis, Tennessee.

9   *Royal ... Prize*   Annual award for a distinguished work of fiction, non-fiction, or poetry. Robinson won for her short story collection *Traplines* (1996).

10   *RRSPs*   Registered Retirement Savings Plans; *GIC*   Guaranteed Investment Certificate, a form of low-risk investment.

11   [Robinson's note]   I don't know why. I think it's because when I was a child, having a black leather couch was like wearing red lipstick or smoking skinny cigarettes—somehow it transformed you into a sophisticated grown-up.

Mom hated flying, especially takeoffs and landings, so the fewer of those we could get away with the better. The Days Inn at Graceland promised Presley-inspired décor, a guitar-shaped pool and a twenty-four-hour Elvis movie channel. The shoulder season rates were great and it was right beside Graceland, so we wouldn't have to rent a car or grab a cab to get there.

"Hey, how'd you like to spend your birthday in Graceland?" I said.

There was a prolonged silence over the phone. "Are you kidding?"

"I just wanted to make sure you really wanted to go because everything's non-refundable."

Another silence. "You're serious."

"Yeah, we've got a couple of options for flights, but I think our best bet is a connection out of Seattle."

"I don't think I can afford that."

I explained about the Royal Society prize money and the black leather couch and the desire to go somewhere I've never been before.

"That seems like a lot of money," she said.

"Do you want to go to Graceland?"

"Well, yes."

"Then let's go."

Dad wasn't interested in going to Graceland with us, so it was just Mom and me. Dad had his heart set on driving from Kitimaat to the 100th Anniversary of the Klondike Gold Rush[12] in Dawson City. Mom hates driving vacations, so she said she'd save her money for Graceland, which Dad said sounded like a glorified shopping trip. We drove up to Dawson that July in his denim-blue standard Ford F-150, but that is a story for another time.

Mom hadn't traveled much, except to visit her grandchildren in Ontario and her mother in Vancouver. Three weeks before we were scheduled to leave, her fears about flying were not soothed by the infamous crash of Swiss Air 111[13] near Peggy's Cove in Nova Scotia and the near constant media coverage of the wreckage and grieving relatives.

At that point, a series of hurricanes marched across the Gulf States, causing widespread damage and flooding. I had a shaky grasp of American geography, so trying to convince Mom that our plane would not be blown out of the sky was difficult.

"It's a sign," Mom said.

---

12 *Klondike Gold Rush* Period (1896–99) during which a large number of people searching for gold migrated to what would become the Yukon Territory, in northwestern Canada.

13 *Swiss Air 111* In 1998 all 229 people aboard this flight from New York to Geneva, Switzerland, were killed when it crashed into the Atlantic Ocean.

"It's not a sign."

"We aren't meant to go."

"The tickets are non-refundable."

And then our airline pilots went on strike. Which was probably why the tickets had been dirt cheap. Another airline offered to carry their rival's passengers, but things were still iffy when mom flew into the Vancouver airport to meet up with me. From her pale complexion and bug-eyed expression, I knew the only things that could have got her on that plane were a) her grandchildren or b) Graceland.

40   We landed in Memphis at night. The cab ride to the hotel was quiet. We were both exhausted. I think I was expecting a longer ride because the blue billboard announcing our arrival at Graceland seemed abrupt. After dragging our luggage to our room, I asked if she wanted to look around or just pass out.

"I'm going to the gates," Mom said.

We passed an Elvis-themed strip mall called Graceland Plaza. We peered in at the closed stores and then crossed the street. The Manor[14] was lit by floodlights. It seemed smaller than I'd been expecting. A stone wall surrounding it was covered in graffiti left there by fans, who were invited by a sign to use the black Sharpies provided to leave a note or signature. We took pictures of each other, and then other tourists took pictures of us together, looking shell-shocked.*

In the morning, we went straight to the ticket counter and bought the Platinum Tour, which included all four Elvis museums and the Manor. Mom wanted to go straight to the Manor. We were given audio headsets, which would guide us through the rooms. I put my headphones on. Mom left hers hanging around her neck, ignoring the flow of traffic and irritated glances as she slowly made her way through the entrance.

I turned my Walkman[15] on and began the tour. Halfway through the first room, I realized Mom wasn't with me. I found her staring at a white bedroom with purple furniture. I was about to explain the headphones to her when I realized she was trembling.

45   "This is his mother's room," she said.

We spent a week in Memphis, and I got the immersion course in Elvis. But there, at that moment, while Mom was telling me stories about Elvis and his mother, I was glad we'd come here together. You should not go to Graceland without an Elvis fan. It's like Christmas without kids—you lose that sense of wonder. The Manor wasn't that impressive if you just looked at it as a house. More importantly, as we walked slowly through the house and she touched the

---

14 *The Manor* Mansion at Graceland.

15 *Walkman* Portable cassette or CD player.

walls, everything had a story, and history. In each story was everything she valued and loved and wanted me to remember and carry with me.[16]

This is nusa.

(2010)

Questions

1. What is nusa? What does Robinson's description of her visit to Graceland show us about nusa?

2. In this lecture, how does Robinson represent the relationship between tradition and contemporary life?

3. The Pueblo writer Leslie Marmon Silko says the following in the introduction to her essay "Language and Literature from a Pueblo Indian Perspective," also in this anthology:

    > For those of you accustomed to being taken from point A to point B to point C, this presentation may be somewhat difficult to follow. Pueblo expression resembles something like a spider's web with many little threads radiating from the center, crisscrossing each other. As with the web, the structure emerges as it is made and you must simply listen and trust, as the Pueblo people do, that meaning will be made.

    Though Silko is of course speaking of her own tradition, aspects of this approach to communication are common to some other Aboriginal North American cultures. To what extent does Silko's introduction describe the approach taken in Robinson's lecture?

4. Why is Robinson disappointed by her Indian name? What is the significance of this disappointment in the context of her lecture?

---

16 [Robinson's note]   To commemorate our trip, I wrote in a scene in *Monkey Beach* where my character took off for Graceland when he found out Elvis died.

JENNY ZHANG

HOW IT FEELS

*Jenny Zhang is an Asian American writer, poet, and performer.
"How It Feels" was published in* Poetry Magazine *in July 2015 as
part of a special section exploring poetry's relationship to teenage
angst. Nominated for a National Magazine Award, the piece
examines poetry, emotional excess, suicide, depression, and the
work of artist Tracey Emin.*

❧

There was a girl in my middle school no one really liked. She told everyone
her uncle had sexually abused her and that she had an older boyfriend who
was a freshman at Yale, and yes, they did more than kiss. People said terrible
things about her—that she was lying about her uncle, that she just wanted the
attention, that her boyfriend was made up, that she had never seen a penis in
her life, that the reason why she so frequently stared into space with her mouth
hanging open was so she could remind everyone what her "blowjob face"
looked like.

At the end of the year, she didn't come to school for a few days in a row.
The rumor was that she tried to kill herself with a plastic spoon (the especially
cruel said it was a plastic spork* she got from the lunchroom). It was officially
(unofficially?) the most hilarious and pathetic attempt at suicide anyone had
ever heard of. I didn't find it funny, but I did rush home after hearing about it,
grabbed a spoon from the kitchen, locked myself in my bedroom, and there, sitting on my bed, I pretended to slit my wrists with the spoon, pushing it against
my vein. Is this at all meaningful? I wondered.

Remember in the teen flick *Heathers*,[1] when Shannen Doherty's character,
Heather 2.0, informs Winona Ryder's character, Veronica, that the school's
numero uno loser Martha Dumptruck attempted suicide and failed? When even
one's failure to live is a failure ... is there anything more poetic?

In the movie, Heather rushes into Veronica's living room during "pâté-
hour" and announces gleefully, "Veronica, have you heard? We were doing

---

1   *Heathers*   Dark comedy (1988) about murder among a clique of popular high school
students, three of whom are named Heather.

Chinese at the food fair when it comes over the radio that Martha Dumptruck tried to buy the farm.* She bellyflopped in front of a car wearing a suicide note."

"Is she dead?" Veronica asks, horrified.   5

"No, that's the punchline. She's alive and in stable condition. Just another case of a geek trying to imitate the popular people in the school and failing miserably."

Do popular kids write poetry? The popular kids in my high school were the cliché teen movie jocks and cheerleaders who bitched and moaned through every poetry segment we did in English class. "This is just weird and makes no sense," was a constant refrain.

Or: "Yo, this person needs to chill out. It's just a tree/bird/building/urn/ body of water. Like it's really not that big of a deal."

Darkness is acceptable and even attractive so long as there is a threshold that is not crossed. But most people I know who suffer, suffer relentlessly and unendingly no matter what sort of future is proposed ("it'll get better/it won't always be this like/you will start to heal/I know it's such a cliché but you really will come out of this stronger in the end").

Why is it so humiliating to go on and on about something that means a lot to   10
you only to be told, "Wow, you spend *a lot* of time thinking about stuff, don't you?"

Or: "So, you're one of those people who analyzes everything, huh?"

Or: "That's kind of dark."

Or worse: "Um ... OK."

My school's Martha Dumptruck frequently submitted poems to our literary journal of which I was on the editorial board. I thought her poetry was terrible. I was so embarrassed for her. What I knew about poetry in high school was that it was both hard to understand and completely open to interpretation. I was told that a poem could really mean anything. Poems could have grammatical mistakes, they could give a fuck about narrative or the space-time continuum or reality as we knew it. Poetry was an attempt to dig into the buried stuff inside a person's psyche. It used dream logic instead of the logic of our waking lives. Poems were sputtered by demons not sprung out of morality. In other words, poems were *deep shit*, and they were also anything at all (this became clearer the further I strayed from my high school's poetry curriculum): a single word (lighght), symbols and signs (Hannah Weiner's code poems), phrases that a child learning to speak might say (a rose is a rose is a rose[2]), words that have been uttered a zillion times (I love thee/you), a blank page, a collage, an erasure, a Google spam filter, whatever. But if that was the case, if poems could be anything at all, then why is the default to cringe whenever someone writes a poem about their feelings? Even worse if that someone is a teenager? Even worse if that someone is no longer a teenager but nonetheless thinks about themselves with the kind of intensity that is only acceptable between the ages of thirteen and nineteen?

15 Last year, someone commented on my Instagram that I had a responsibility to the young (mostly) women and men who were using the hashtag #noonecares. The comment was under a picture of me standing on the pier of the Williamsburg waterfront, days before I slipped into the kind of bland, unexciting-to-describe, low-grade depression that I mostly masked from my friends and family by not leaving my apartment and making excuses to duck out of every social obliga-tion. It was several weeks of lying in bed, holding in my shit and piss for hours until I reached the tipping point (leakage happened occasionally) because I was too depressed to get out of bed—the thought of moving across the room and down the hallway to get to the bathroom seemed like a particular kind of hell that I could not agree to.

A few months later, when I was no longer in the I'd-rather-shit-my-pants-a-little-than-climb-out-of-bed phase of my depression, I became curious about what having little-to-no will to live looked like for other people. I browsed the hashtag I had used in the caption of my photo, "First taste of daylight in 72 hours #noonecares," and quickly spiraled into the territory of self-harm hashtags: from #noonecares to #noonecaresifidie, #wanttodie, #whatsthepoint, #depressed, #hurting, #help, #ihatemyself. I scrolled through the photos for as long as I could stomach it, which was not long as it was primarily pictures of slashed up arms, razors floating in the toilet with captions like, "the last of my stash ... if I get 100 likes tonight, I'll flush them."

Why are some people's feelings so repellent and others so madly allur-ing? As a fourteen-year-old, I wanted to be someone who was destined to die beautifully like Shakespeare's Juliet[3]—freshly fucked, dead before ever having

---

2   *lighght*   Controversial 1965 poem by Aram Saroyan, consisting of the single word "lighght" printed on an otherwise blank page; *Hannah Weiner's code poems*   Hannah Weiner's public art show *The Language of Things* (1968) featured poetry written using The International Code of Signals. It was first performed in Central Park, New York, by US Coast Guard members using flags, lights, and foghorns; *a rose ... a rose*   Phrase from Gertrude Stein's poem "Sacred Emily" (1913).

3   *Juliet*   Character in William Shakespeare's tragic play *Romeo and Juliet* (1597); she and her forbidden lover, Romeo, kill themselves.

the chance to know what it's like to despise the person you once loved. She died just as her love for Romeo was ascending, becoming heavenly. In the throes of love, infinity seemed like a good idea. Pain looked so good on her. It immortalized her. Juliet was my suicide idol—hers was a suicide to aspire to and I couldn't even get close. Like so many other fourteen-year-old girls, I was told that my problems were minor, my tragedies imaginary, and worst of all—I was told I hadn't lived enough to really want to die.

The failure to move someone with what you think is the tragedy of your existence. I don't know, or just another way of saying #noonecares.

That thing where we imagine what would happen if we died and our dead, needy souls could float above our own funeral, watching the people who didn't love us as we wanted to be loved, in attendance, weeping, blaming themselves for not having tried harder to save us, for not having been more generous, more attentive. Why does it give us such satisfaction to imagine them saying, "I should have been better to you. I should have never treated you this way."

When a young person dies, they are forever immortalized, forever grieved, but what happens when we are too old to die young? Or if we can't commit to dying a physical death but still want to reap the joys of being mourned, which I guess is just some way of saying: I need proof that my existence matters.

20

There was this other kid who was universally picked on in my high school. He had epilepsy and talked with his mouth a little crooked. The jocks (there were jocks) would purposefully bump into him in the hallway, knocking his books onto the ground and kicking them so he had to scramble to pick them all up again.

"We're just having some fun," they said whenever a teacher came out to investigate. No one really had the energy to stop the momentum of cruelty anyway. Then, during my senior year, it was announced over the loudspeaker that he had suffered a severe seizure in his sleep the night before and died.

Everything is embarrassing, everything seems like a facsimile of the real thing, whatever that might be, if it even exists. My whole high school went into mourning. I lost track of the red faces, the number of students who wanted to share their personal story of how he touched their lives, what a good person he was, how he represented the spirit of our school and our town. It was an exciting day ... to be so close to something so genuinely tragic, a rare instance where showing feelings in public was a good thing, as valuable as being an asshole had been the day before.

When someone dies, we go searching for poetry. When a new chapter of life starts or ends—graduations, weddings, inaugurations, funerals—we insist on poetry. The occasion for poetry is always a grand one, leaving us little people with our little lives bereft of elegies and love poems.

25
But I want elegies while I'm still alive, I want rhapsodies though I've never seen Mount Olympus.[4] I want ballads, I want ugly, grating sounds, I want repetition, I want white space, I want juxtaposition and metaphor and meditation and all caps and erasure and blank verse and sonnets and even center-aligned italicized poems that rhyme, and most of all—feelings.

When I was a teenager, every little moment called for poetry. I mean, I'm still this way, except at my age it's considered inappropriate and embarrassing, if not downright creepy.

The first time I was exposed to Tracey Emin[5] I was twenty-four and discussing misspellings and typos with my boyfriend at the time who had brought home a bunch of Tracey Emin art books from the library. Her work often contains "mistakes," like her monoprint[6] that says, "retier softly" in little kid chicken scratch above a drawing of a naked girl on her knees. We loved her sloppiness. We loved how little she seemed to process her emotions before turning them into art. "I'd rather eat processed food than have processed emotions," I wrote once in my notebook after reading a transcript of her film, *How It Feels*, where she describes in great detail the trauma of her first abortion: "I felt something slip and as it slipped I put my hand there and what I held between my thigh and the palm of my hand was a fetus, kind of mashed-up fetus ..."

We loved the crudeness of her drawings and embroideries and monoprints and neons.[7] I loved her self-absorption. I found it so incredibly generous—to be just as ugly as anyone but to emphasize that ugliness over and over again, to let yourself be the subject of your art and to take all the pummeling and the eye-rolling and the cruel remarks and the who cares? and the that's not art that's just a scorned woman unable to let go. Her pain was so alluring to me. I stared at the pictures of her depressed bed[8] with the sheets all bunched up and stained with her bodily fluids and dried up menstrual blood and the psychic

---

4   *Mount Olympus*   Home of the gods in Greek mythology.

5   *Tracey Emin*   English artist (b. 1963).

6   *monoprint*   Print made using a technique that produces only a single image (whereas most printing techniques can produce multiple copies).

7   *neons*   Artworks made from neon light tubes.

8   *her depressed bed*   Emin is best known for *My Bed* (1998), a controversial piece displaying her actual bed as it appeared after she spent several days in the room while experiencing extreme depression.

weight of psychic bedsores from not being able to lift oneself out of there. I had a bed too and it had been the site of my depression so many times in my life. I slept on my own dried blood as well and wore the same underwear so many days in a row that the discharge from my cunt had built up and become so thick that it essentially glued my pubic hair to my underwear and every time I had to pee and pull down my panties I would give myself like a little unintentional bikini wax.

My boyfriend and I were particularly enthralled with Tracey because at the time we were courting each other with misspellings and typos. It was the early years of auto-correct on phones. We both had flip-phones whose range of saved words were much more limited than iPhones now. "I miss you baby and my twat is still ringing" became "I miss you bikes and my twat is still ringing." "Come home and I'll make you ramen" became "Come home and I'll make you robb." "I will wait for you after class my pamplemousse" became "I will wait for you after class my samplenourse." "I miss you bikes" was mistyped one time as "I miss you bikers." "Bikers I'm preparing a very good robb for us" became "bikespspspspspspspspsp I'm preparing a very good robb for us" because I accidentally hit the *s* key too long. We built our private little world through these mistakes, and like everyone else falling in love we tried to become one entity, impenetrable through our arsenal of inside jokes, through a language that other people could not understand or use.

The year I fell in love, I wrote a story about my relationship with my little brother and sent it to my mom. She wrote back:

30

> I just finished read whole story. It is very funny and touchable, plus nice pictures. you should e-mail this to Johnny too. I was laughed a lot. I wish I can translate this to Chinese. Maybe oneday I will.

> Love,
> Mom

I rarely have the impulse to correct someone's mistake, or misspelling, or mispronunciation, or misusage. Every time my mom speaks in English, she makes a mistake. She pronounces tissue "tee-shoe" and once, in the middle of the night, when she was sick with the flu she woke violently sneezing and asked my dad to get her a "tee-shoe," and so he got up and pulled a T-shirt from the drawer, thinking she was cold. Later, I tried to teach both of them how to "correctly" pronounce "tissue" and "T-shirt" and I truly, truly, truly felt like a scumbag.

But I have to get back to Tracey Emin and her misspellings and her intensity and her nakedness. I mean her literal nakedness and her emotional nakedness, both subject to such revulsion and praise and fascination and snap judgment and boredom and ugly patronizing and overt cringing. I look at the photo from her show *I've Got It All* where she's sitting on the floor, legs bent and spread, wearing chains around her neck and little messy braids tucked behind her ear. She's shoving bills and coins and miscellaneous bits of junky flotsam and jetsam.* Her tits look unbelievably good and her legs look tired and she's looking down at all this garbage and bills and the moment captured is in a sense so completely trashy and gleeful and celebratory and excessive and weird, but in another sense, the photo is so much that it becomes a statement against allowing others to tell your story, against those who would insist on your victimhood. When I look at that photo, I don't pity her at all. I love her. She is the first poet I have loved.

And her scratched out poems are the greatest poems I know. One of her monoprints is a drawing of a naked girl standing in front of a nondescript black puddle, and next to it, the words:

> pethetic
> little
> thing

Aren't we? At least those of us who still risk revealing ourselves in public?

In *How It Feels*, Tracey narrates through a voiceover her struggle to make art after her abortion:

> Ah ... I gave up painting, I gave up art, I gave up believing, I gave up faith. I had what I called my emotional suicide, I gave up a lot of friendships with people, I just gave up believing in life really and it's taken me years to actually start loving and believing again. I realized that there was a greater idea of creativity. Greater than anything I could make just with my mind or with my hands, I realized there was something ... the essence of creativity, that moment of conception, the whole importance, the whole being of everything and I realized that if I was going to make art it couldn't be about ... it couldn't be about a fuckin' picture. It couldn't be about something visual. It had to be about where it was really coming from and because of the abortion and because of conceiving, I had a greater understanding of where things really came from and where they actually ended up so I couldn't tolerate, or, or, err, I just felt it would be unforgivable of me to start making things, filling the world up with more crap. There's no reason for that. But if I couldn't fill the world up with someone which I could love for

ever and ever and ever then there was no way I could fill the world up with just like menial things. That's art.

I guess that is what is so embarrassing about being a poet, that you might be filling the world up with more crap. That your pathetic little thing is not interesting to anyone but yourself.

When the warehouse that housed her piece *Everyone I Have Ever Slept* **35** *With 1963–1995*—a tent with all the names of everyone she slept with embroidered on the inside—burned down, journalist Tom Lubbock wrote in *The Independent*,

> But it's odd to hear talk about irreplaceable losses. Really? You'd have thought that, with the will and the funding, many of these works were perfectly replaceable. It wouldn't be very hard for Tracey Emin to re-stitch the names of *Every One I Have Ever Slept With* onto a little tent (it might need some updating since 1995).

If even internationally recognized artists can be invalidated with just one, "um … OK," then what about the rest of us? #noonecares

The quote I kept seeing again and again in all of these Instagram self-harm and suicide hashtags: "No one cares unless you're pretty or dying." But there were others as well:

> I hope my last breath is a sigh of relief.

> disgusted by my own self

> I remember everything that you forgot

> do you ever feel worthless

> please please please let me die in my sleep

> This is how you make me feel, like a black mass of nothingness, an ugly space filled with my own sadness

> I fucked up I failed—it was my disaster—my choice—I just didn't expect to feel so bad—so foolish and so afraid of ever being touched.

All of these but especially the last one remind me of Tracey Emin's artwork. There's a part in her essay "You Left Me Breathing" where she writes about the dissolution of a relationship:

> You left me—you left me breathing—just half alive—curled up like some small baby seal, clubbed half to death—you left me alone—you left me breathing—half alive—

> Half alive is not dead—stains on the shore, blood seeping into the water, but definitely not dead. I tried to think of and remember the times when I had cried, not just tears that ran down my cheeks, but the breathless sobs of overwrought, uncontrollable emotion.

> I don't know if we, as a culture, feel compelled to extend much sympathy to those who are half alive. Half alive is not dead.

In her neons, Tracey Emin takes a material that has long been associated with seediness to communicate some very adolescent feelings. Neon is cheesy, neon is tacky, neon hangs over love motels off the highway that charge by the hour, neon blinks in the part of town where the riffraff linger, where ne'er-do-wells pass each other on street corners, where people who might be there one day and dead the next hang out. Tracey's neons hang out in galleries, glow bright in Times Square, and they cycle through a moving range of teeny emotions, from the hopeful, *Fantastic to Feel Beautiful Again*, to the moody, *Sorry Flowers Die*, to the bratty, *people like you need to fuck people like me*. Some of her neon messages are crossed out, *i know i know i know*, while others literally appear as indecipherable scribbles.

My favorite neon is the one that simply says:

> Just Love me

Is there anything so inadequate as the words "I love you"? Is there anything so perfectly capable as "I love you"?

40   "O!"* I said when my boss at my first real job working as an union organizer told me, "We don't do midriffs here." "O! Okay!" I said. "Don't get me wrong," she said, "you look great and you should show that off on your own time. But just as a rule, we don't do midriffs at work." "O!" I said when a boy I waited all year to meet again in Paris told me, "I want to elope with you," while we were on a train from Paris to Nice. We spent three days eating sandwiches from the garbage bins outside of cafes. We tried to go to an outdoor movie screening of *Terminator 3* on a cliff that overlooked the Mediterranean Sea,

but it was twenty euros to enter and we were nineteen short, so he hoisted me up onto a tree—"O!" I said, "I'm gonna fall,"—and took off my underwear and scrunched it up into the pocket of my dress because I had an urinary tract infection and needed to pee every twenty minutes, my diseased urine dribbling through the leafy branches. "O!" I said, "I hope I don't accidentally pee on someone's head." Afterward we said goodbye in the doorway of the studio I was subletting in the Bastille—he was leaving to go back to Scotland and I was leaving to go back to the US—and just as I was beginning to mourn what I had to leave behind, I heard a knock at the door and it was him again. "It would be easy to fall in love with someone like you ... difficult in fact not to," he said, granting me my lifelong wish of being my own protagonist in a movie. "O ... " I said, "I won't be able to forget you." "O!" I said when I saw my grandmother for the first time in three years, chilled by how old she looked this time, too old to dye her hair black like how she used to and how the hair dye she used was so cheap that it would run down her scalp and the little black drip marks would remain on her forehead for days. She was too old to curl her bangs by wrapping them around an empty can of Pepsi and then taking me and my brother out to the store to buy more with her Pepsi can roller on prominent display. O! I was mortified back then. "O!" I said when her nose started bleeding as soon as she saw my brother, and I noticed how small she was sitting in that wheelchair, how at every stage we occupy a different throne and hers now was that of a sick old person. "O!" I said, "you must," when she said she wanted to make one last trip to the United States to see us, even though I knew she would never make that trip. "O!" I said when she told me she likes to have conversations with me and my brother in her dreams. We come to her and we are just the age we were when she took care of us and lived with us in New York. "O! Yes, I remember," I say to every memory she details even though I do not remember any of it. "O!" I write in my poems sometimes with nothing to follow but it is wonderful to use that letter and that exclamation mark. It is wonderful to try and say anything.

O maybe no one really does care. Maybe it is humiliating to attempt anything.

I sincerely don't know why poetry can be mortifying but tattoos can be cool.

I think everyone wants to make something touchable, but most of us don't out of fear of being laughable. I'm not saying I'm fearless.

My mom used to ask her mom to touch her earlobes so she could fall asleep. When she immigrated to New York and could no longer fall asleep at her mother's house in Shanghai, she started asking me and my father. I remember one time I said, I don't get it, why do you like that? Let me show you, she

45

said, and she rubbed my earlobes until I couldn't help but close my eyes. I started to see differently. I think we were spooning.* Or I had my head in her lap and she was sitting upright against the bed. "Do you see how good it feels to be touched there?" she asked me. I did.

(2015)

Questions

1. What is the significance of the recurring use of the hashtag #noonecares in this piece?

2. At several points, Zhang's essay incorporates personal information that might be considered embarrassing. Choose one of these moments in the essay and discuss it. What cultural norms make the information embarrassing? What response does it evoke in you as a reader? What purpose (if any) does this moment serve in the essay as a whole?

3. An image of Tracey Emin's installation *My Bed* is reproduced in this anthology's color insert. Interpret the image with reference to Zhang's essay. How (if at all) do the observations Zhang makes illuminate Emin's installation?

4. Who (if anyone) in this essay do you as a reader feel encouraged to identify with? Who (if anyone) do you feel discouraged from identifying with? What aspects of the essay make you feel this way?

5. Discuss the use of the word "O!" near the end of the piece (see paragraph 40). What does the repetition of "O!" in this passage communicate? Why does Zhang spell "O" unconventionally (as opposed to "Oh!")?

6. In Zhang's view, what is the relationship between poetry and everyday life? What role, if any, does poetry play in your everyday life?

7. What does Zhang's essay suggest about what aspects of artistic expression are valued in Western culture—and what aspects are not?

BETTINA LOVE

from HIP HOP'S LI'L SISTAS SPEAK: NEGOTIATING HIP HOP IDENTITIES AND POLITICS IN THE NEW SOUTH

In her introduction to Hip Hop's Li'l Sistas Speak, *Bettina Love reflects on her experience growing up in the 1980s and links her personal development to the political and cultural forces that shaped that decade: "The phenomenon of Hip Hop emerged in the decade of Reaganomics—President Ronald Reagan's attack on the poor and disadvantaged. By manipulating Americans with fear slogans like 'War on Crime,' 'War on Drugs,' 'welfare queens,' and 'gang wars,'" Reagan helped "cultivate the brash, gritty, often rebellious sound and culture of Hip Hop." Her ethnographical study focuses on six young women negotiating twenty-first century Hip-Hop culture in Atlanta, Georgia, but Love continually supplements their accounts with reflections on her own experiences as a consumer of Hip Hop culture, as a Black educator, as a woman, and as a lesbian. The excerpts included here are from the final two chapters of the book.*

❧

CHAPTER SEVEN: THE BEAT OF HEGEMONY

The driving force of Hip Hop is its sound, the beat of the music that pulls you in as a listener. Every rapper knows that in order to have a hit record, the beat of the song must be audibly gratifying for the listener.... Hip Hop historians (Forman & Neal, 2004; George, 1999; Rose, 1994) write that the contemporary sound of Hip Hop started in New York City with the arrival of a Jamaican immigrant by the name of Clive Campbell, better known in the Hip Hop world as DJ Kool Herc. Herc grew up with the musical influence of reggae, which infused aspects of African and slave-era music with infectious rhythmic beats (Perkins, 1996). Rose states, "Time suspension via rhythmic breaks—points at which the bass lines are isolated and suspended—are important clues in explaining sources of pleasure in black music" (p. 67). The rhythmic patterns of Hip Hop are powerful, soulful, endearing, and rebellious all at the same time.

The beat of Hip Hop can be both freeing and repressive. For example, in 2005 one of the most hypersexual and misogynistic songs I have ever heard—and liked—was "Wait" by the Ying Yang Twins, an Atlanta-based group. Here is just a small fraction of the foul language within the song: "Fuck a bitch on da counter.... Fuck that bend over imma give you the dick.... Ay bitch! Wait 'til you see my dick.... Beat da pussy up" (Ying Yang Twins, 2005). I was not the only person fond of this song. In 2005, "Wait" reached number two on the *Billboard* charts in the rap category. The video for the song followed the sexist storyline of the record. At one point in the video, there are over twenty half-clothed women laying on top of and around the Ying Yang Twins as they sing "Beat da pussy up." Although I detested the lyrics of the song, the beat was controlling and influential and seemed to paralyze my ability to critically examine the song as it took over my body. Every time I heard the song on the radio or in the club, I thought to myself, "This record is so demeaning to both men and women." However, I was reluctant to turn the song off in my car because I was alone and not visually accountable to anyone for finding pleasure in a song that I knew was misogynistic. This is the contradictory space of Hip Hop feminism, as I was ideologically split by my love for Hip Hop music and culture and my desire to challenge patriarchy. So in an effort to reconcile my divided position as a Hip Hop feminist, I did sit down when the song was played at clubs I attended. This action, in some respect, made me feel both powerful and fake. I took a stand when people were watching, as my social politics were on display, but when I was alone I blasted the song, in love with the beat. Thus, no matter how uncomfortable I felt with the content of the song, the beat kept me drawn to it, and at times I ignored the lyrics. My noncritical position relating to the song, which stopped me from taking personal action to resist it, was common among many of my friends, both male and female. As a collective group, we all knew the song was misogynistic but found it enjoyable.

The teens in the study were no different than my friends and me in regard to enjoying misogynistic rap music. However, as a first-year doctoral student at the time, I was learning to understand rap as a "discourse"—a production of knowledge—and not just as a genre that I found entertaining (Foucault, 1980). Thus, using the words of Foucault and Hall, I began to view rap music and culture as representations that formed issues of power and knowledge and the question of the subject (Hall, 1997). Within rap, the subjects are the rappers and women of color who appear in rap videos, or the women who are cited in rap songs as bitches. Yet, according to Foucault, subjects are not autonomous and stable entities; subjects are produced within the "regime of truth," which operates by creating truths that are discursive, which in turn regulates social practices and what is deemed as knowledge and power (Foucault, 1980). For example, there is much discourse surrounding same-sex parents' inability to effectively parent. There is no evidence that this assumption is accurate. On the contrary, there are a good number of studies that contend that same-sex parents are effective parents (Pruett & Pruett, 2009). Nonetheless, the common discourse penalizes same-sex parents and gives power to heterosexual parents.... McLaren (1994) defines hegemony as "a struggle in which the powerful win the consent of those who are oppressed, with the oppressed unknowingly participating in their own oppression.... Within the hegemonic process, established meanings are often laundered of contradiction, contestation, and ambiguity" (pp. 182–183). By way of Foucault and Hall, I was learning how to be media literate....

But I was twenty-five years old with two degrees and working toward a third before I understood hegemony and its fluidity regarding Black popular culture. I never learned in high school that Hip Hop music and culture had been co-opted to create music and sounds that only highlighted the most demeaning notions of Blackness. As a youngster and young adult, I unknowingly consented to hypersexual, degrading, and misogynistic lyrics of rap. My consent often led to contradictory thinking, as I opposed the same music whose beat I enjoyed. My experience was no different than the girls in the study. Sad to say, it took a Ph.D. program to teach me media literacy.

THE BEAT GOES ON ...

Similar to my experiences with the beat of rap, the problematic lyrics and images of rap music were secondary to the beat of the music for the girls, even as the girls critiqued the music for its derogatory content.... In "Keepin' It Real: Black Youth, Hip-Hop Culture, and Black Identity," Clay (2003) recognized that "in conversations, many of the youth said that it was the 'beats,' not the lyrics, that are important to them about hip-hop" (p. 1346). Many of the teens in this study echoed Clay's findings that the beat drove them to listen to and accept degrading lyrics.

> They [male rappers] call us the "H" stuff and you get kind of offended, but I don't know why. We still listen and dance because we like the beat. (Star, Interview, 2007)

> When I first heard it [Plies, "Shawty"], I listened to the whole song. Then I just start laughing. I was like, he nasty. And like now ... I didn't listen to it, I listen to the beat. (Nicole, Interview, 2007)

You listen to it and if a boy come up to me and I like the song, and I can turn it off. (Lisa, Interview, 2007)

The teens referred to the beat for enjoyment, disregarding the messages, which is problematic because the music's messages take on a latent, secondary meaning in juxtaposition to the primacy of the beat. As the girls found pleasure in rap music because of the beat, they consented to degrading diatribes about Black culture and Black identity even as they brilliantly critiqued it. I read their consent to the misogynistic and sexually explicit lyrics as revealing a hegemonic structure at play within rap music and Black popular culture. Although the girls denounced the sexist lyrics by attempting to ignore them, they still danced and listened to the songs. Furthermore, the girls created methods of reconciling the contradictory space because they knew listening to the songs sent a message to their male counterparts regarding sex, which was a message the girls wanted to control. However, the beat of the songs made the girls disregard their better judgment.

For example, Lisa admitted that she would not listen to degrading songs if a male was present; this is insightful. Lisa feared that males would think she was promiscuous, which could have social ramifications.... Lisa knew that males would label her a freak or a ho,* much like the women in videos. Nevertheless, by listening to the song, Lisa consented to the message. Maxine too realized that male rappers degraded Black women in rap songs. Just like Lisa, however, she listened to the songs because of the beat. Nicole stated that she does not even listen to the lyrics of "Shawty" by Plies—she just listened to the beat of the song. "Shawty" is one of Plies's hit records, and the title track topped the *Billboard* charts for rap tracks. In the song, Plies states, "I told her I don't usually do this, I don't fuck on the first night, 'cause after I beat ya baby I'm liable to fuck up ya whole life. I gotta train her, now she suck me with ice" (Plies, 2007). Nicole knew that the song was vulgar, so she only listened for the beat. Nicole was not alone; Dee and Maxine also admitted that they did not know the song lyrics and at times only knew the chorus but enjoyed the beat.

So you don't think about it at all, just the beat. (Dee, Interview, 2007)

I don't like it, I just. I don't like it, I like the beat. I just don't like the fact that he's talking about it and all that. Like Soulja Boy—I like Soulja Boy—The real version is not good. I don't like it because it's talking about sex … um, degrading women. (Maxine, Interview, 2007)

Dee admitted that she does not think about the degrading lyrics because she knows how damaging the lyrics are. Her love of the beat superseded her position that the music was problematic. Above, Maxine referenced Soulja

Boy's hit song "Crank Dat." In the song Soulja Boy states, "Super soak that hoe. I'm too fresh off in this bitch.... And superman that bitch." "Crank Dat" is yet another song with an infectious beat and a memorable chorus but problematic lyrics. To "superman" a woman is to masturbate and then ejaculate on the back of a female. Maxine understood the coded language of the record, so she preferred to listen to the song for the beguiling beat.

All the girls liked to dance. Because it was a community center that focused on homework help, the environment restricted much of the music to their personal mp3 players or iPods. Therefore, the girls would pass around their mp3 players so everyone could hear the latest dance songs. Maxine spoke passionately about her dislike of rap music because of how it degrades women. When I asked her if she liked Soulja Boy's song "Crank Dat," she repeated the phrase, "I don't like it." Maxine tried to resist rap's message when the songs degraded women. At times during our interviews, Maxine told me that she refused to listen to music by Soulja Boy that was sexually explicit. According to my observations, though, Maxine's resistance was not consistent, much like mine as I enjoyed the Ying Yang Twins.

> Maxine loves to dance. She and Star know all the latest dances including the Soulja Boy, who has become extremely popular. Even though Maxine has stated she does not like Soulja Boy, she and Star dance to the song every time one of the students has it on their mp3 players. (Field notes, B. Love, 1/08)

My field notes and observations addressed many of the students' conflicted and contradictory ideological stances. Maxine wanted rap music to change. She stated that she did not like rap music that degrades women and is sexually explicit, but she continued to use Soulja Boy as a medium for social engagement.... Maxine's and the rest of the girls' consent to find enjoyment in some of rap's most debasing messages is an example of hegemony, as the girls, a marginalized group, consented to their own oppression. Storey (1998) stated that the relationship between popular culture and hegemony is the "site of struggle between the forces of 'resistance' of subordinate groups in society, and the forces of 'incorporation' of dominant groups in society" (p. 14).

The girls stated that they found the lyrics of rap music explicit and vulgar; however, their cell phone ring tones were the same songs they detested.... Each Internet music site provided the beat to the music in which they escaped while doing their homework or searching the Internet.

Some of my field notes address the beat of the music as a vital part of their day at the center.

> Dee and Lisa did their homework while listening to music today. They
> would bob their heads while doing their homework humming the beat
> of the song. They would smile at certain parts of the song and some-
> times smile at each other. (Field notes, B. Love, 2007)

The beat served as the background for many of their daily activities, especially homework. I observed students' dancing at times with no music playing,
just the beat they carried in their heads....

The beat influenced a resounding number of comments, which led the
youth to consent blindly to the messages. Even when the youth expressed their
dislike for the lyrics, the beat of the music kept them listening.

> It's just they cute. Like I don't know, I listen to the songs because I
> think how cute they is but they've got some songs on there that's nice,
> they're nice. I like the beat and stuff. (Lara, Interview, 2007)

> Yeah, but I don't like the words, I like the beat.... Sometimes you don't
> understand what they be saying, so fast. (Maxine, Interview, 2007)

15   Obviously, the teens maintained that the beat of a song was the driving
force behind why they listened to the song. Yet, they acknowledged the presence of the lyrics. They explained that they did not know many of the words
to a particular song and may not have liked the particular rapper but enjoyed
the beat. Adams and Fuller (2006) argued, "It is imperative that we as a society
move beyond the beat and seriously consider the effect that negative imagery
produced in misogynistic rap can have on the African American community
and society at large" (p. 955). The beat of the song masks the explicit lyrics of
rap music and the negative imagery consumed by youth who enjoy the songs.
Because the youth engaged with the beat, their ability to evaluate the lyrics was
challenged.

NOBODY WANTS TO BE LAME

The girls in the study were at the age where being accepted by their peers
was extremely important. Hip Hop music and culture were precursors to their
peers' accepting them. The girls believed there were social ramifications for
not liking the rap music of their peers or taking a stand against music they
found to be demeaning. The girls conceptualized rap's vulgar language as a
permanent fixture within rap and feared being seen as lame or as someone who
thought otherwise. When I asked Dee why she listened to music she thought
was belittling to women she stated, "What can I do, it's everywhere you go"
(Dee, informal interview, 2008). Dee is right; in Atlanta music that has a sexual

message can be heard just about everywhere. Moreover, if the lyrics cannot be heard, the beat is in the background. To be clear, I am not an advocate of censoring music that has sexual messages; I support the need for girls and boys to learn the tools to unpack sexual and degrading messages regarding women and hyper-macho stereotypes of masculinity....

Young girls need a space where they feel comfortable resisting demeaning notions of womanhood. They also need teachers who expose popular culture for its contrived messages built on stereotypes but do not demoralize youth choices to consume Hip Hop or any form of popular culture; this is a hard pedagogical technique but is needed, according to the experiences of the girls. For example, Lisa commented on the social repercussions associated with attempts to take action against the music when I asked her why she does not turn off songs she believes degrade women. Lisa stated, "If you say turn it off, then you lame" (Lisa, informal interview, 2008). Previously, Lisa had stated that she does not listen to sexually explicit music around males; however, here she has a fear of being viewed as uncool by her peers for turning off the music. Lisa wants to live above the peer pressure, but does not know how, which is evident by her words. Lisa is at odds because she is trying to fit in and take a stance in spaces that are overwhelmed with the music she is trying to challenge. Nicole passionately speculated, "Everyone dances to the music, how would it look if you don't dance"? (Nicole, informal interview, 2008). None of the girls ever tried resisting rap's misogynistic and sexually explicit lyrics by participating in some type of social action....

The pressure to conform to what society and rap music say Black men and women should be like is quite powerful and hegemonic. The girls ... feared the risk of being uncool—or to use Lisa's term, lame—if we rejected misogynistic rap music. Therefore, we enjoyed the beat and ignored our better judgment because of the fear of being an outcast. Fear was the driving force of our conformity; we wanted to fit in and be seen as cool. Learning the latest dance and listening to the most popular rap song were the cool things to do, and none of the girls, including myself years ago, felt powerful enough to resist Hip Hop's misogynistic messages....

Chapter Eight: Black Girls Resisting When No One Is Listening

Intuitively, the girls resisted Hip Hop's more pugnacious messages. A fundamental part of consuming popular culture is resisting popular culture. Hall (1981) argued, "Popular culture is one of the sites where this struggle for and against culture of the powerful is engaged: it is also the stake to be won or lost in the struggle. It is the arena of consent and resistance" (p. 65). I, however, argue that their resistance was undermined by rap's hegemonic force, which can be a normal outcome in today's mass media built on hegemonic race, class, gender, and political ideologies. Collins (2004) writes:

> All women engage an ideology that deems middle-class, heterosexual, White femininity as normative. In this context, Black femininity as a subordinated gender identity becomes constructed not just in relation to White women, but also in relation to multiple others, namely, all men, sexual outlaws (prostitutes and lesbians), unmarried women, and girls. These benchmarks construct a discourse of a hegemonic (White) femininity that becomes a normative yardstick for all femininities in which Black women typically are relegated to the bottom of the gender hierarchy. (p. 193)

20   The girls' resistance was never nurtured in classrooms, where conversations that problematize and critique rap in nonjudgmental disclosures took place, which are vital to their development. Their voices and experiences with rap were disregarded in classrooms and pushed to the margins. The complex issues of race, sexuality, class, and gender that are embedded within the music are dismissed by school officials as immature youth culture and music not worthy of classroom time. When I began to ask the girls to critique Hip Hop, their intellectual prowess was evident. The girls understood that the music did not always represent Black folks in constructive ways, specifically Black men, and that the messages within rap were problematic.

> Like they need to change what they talking about. They [rappers] probably not like that for real but they know that young people don't do that and want to sing it and stuff because of the beat and stuff and they doing it mostly because of money.... Future kids that doing drugs, so they're sending out future things so what the police and the government and the President is doing, building more jailhouses than schools and after school because people are going to drop out, they know people are going to drop out and go to jail. (Maxine, Interview, 2007)

> Like violence. Like they [rappers] be talking about how they got guns and then you know a teenager might think they can have guns, they [rappers] go get a gun to feel protected. They [rappers] talk about they might want to go to jail then come rap about how they was in jail. You know, like they be some of them songs have negative impact on children because they want to be just like the rappers. (Lisa, Interview, 2007)

> Yeah, talking about killing people and stuff. (Lara, Interview, 2007)

These comments make it apparent that the girls had the ability to negotiate not only rap but also social issues around the music and urban life. Maxine's notions that rap needs to change and her understandings of the social issues that plague the Black community were insightful in that she used contemporary politics to address some of the current sociopolitical issues Black America faces. The fact that Maxine thought in regard to future generations showed her keen intellect and concern for others. Maxine also understood the masked racism of the prison industrial complex. Moreover, the girls' comments about violence represented their ideological perspectives concerning rappers and gun use. Lisa linked rappers' gun use to the belief that rappers carrying guns may influence other youth to follow their example. Dyson (2007) stated, "There's a preoccupation with the gun because the gun is the central part of the iconography of the ghetto" (p. 91). Black youth's obsession with guns and violence, according to Dyson, is a staple of urban life. Lisa linked guns and violence to rap music and rappers. She spoke to the perpetual violence that takes place in urban communities because of the belief that males need a gun to be viewed as fully masculine. Lisa understood the large-scale significance of rap music.

When I asked the girls why they thought rappers rhymed about guns and violence, they all stated in some fashion that rappers do not care about the youth who listen to their music.

It is all about money basically. They [rappers] really don't care. Oh, they're [rappers] sending a bad message. (Lara, Interview, 2008)

They don't care about us. They care about the money. (Star, Interview, 2008)

They do it for money. (Nicole, Interview, 2008)

The girls state that rappers take on hardcore and hypersexual facades for financial gain. Their critique of rap speaks to the materialistic, bling-bling* culture of the music that glorifies conspicuous consumption above social issues that many scholars have unpacked (Basu, 2005; Love, 2010). A ... concrete example surrounding the girls' thoughts regarding rappers and their motives lies in their opinions of Atlanta-based rapper T.I. (Clifford Joseph Harris, Jr.) and his hardcore image. During the study, the police arrested T.I. on federal gun charges....

Not T.I., he got locked up. T.I., I like him but he is a bad influence so that's it. Because he's in jail. And what he did wasn't called for. Like he shouldn't have did it.... And he got everybody disappointed, all his fans and stuff.... Now what he's going to do time because he's in jail, he gone be there a while. (Star, Interview, 2008)

Something wrong with that boy; he think he tough. (Dee, Interview, 2008)

He actin' like that for the money. (Lara, Interview, 2008)

... Star looked upon T.I.'s message of violence and criminal activity as discreditable, and the fact that the rapper's stage persona became a reality disappointed her. Lara suggested that money was the primary reason for T.I.'s hardcore image. In an interview with Lisa, she accused T.I. of pretending to be dangerous and nefarious to sell records.

Lisa: He actin' like that to sell records.

Tina: Actin' like what?

Lisa: Like he a gangsta. Actin' hard. (Interview, 2008)

25   ... The girls critically examined the authenticity of T.I. and his music. These examinations of T.I., and Hip Hop music and culture in general, are important to the overall growth and well-being of Black girls and all youth. The dialogue that these girls engaged in created a space for them to resist rap's monolithic image of Black males.

However, conversations surrounding Black women did not produce the same outcome. When I asked the girls to examine Black women with a more critical lens, they relied heavily on how Black women react to the position of Black males. For example, Maxine felt that Black women dressed scantily in rap videos because they were attempting to gain the attention of males. Lisa, Dee, and Lara had views parallel to those of Maxine. The girls felt that Black women's choices were a reaction to what Black males wanted, as well as poor decision making in general. Conversely, the teens saw rap through multiple lenses of Black expression. In some cases the teens challenged rap's hegemonic messages, but in other cases the teens understood rap as essentialized[1] notions of Blackness and were unable to reject its images and sounds....

... When asked about what they thought it meant to be Black, all the youth stated that to be Black is to be beautiful, smart, athletic, and have the ability to dance. They essentialized their ideas of what it means to be Black on multiple levels depending on the question. The data showed that the teens contradicted themselves as they struggled to make meaning of images of Blackness that they understood as authentic, even when those images glorified degrading women. The teens resisted labeling the Black race as violent, but they accepted

---

1   *essentialized* I.e., based on the idea that the characteristics of Blackness are fundamental and unchanging (rather than being shaped by historical events, culture, and, therefore, changeable).

Black women who appeared in rap videos as hos and freaks. The postmodern condition allows these fluid and contradictory ideas because of the hybridizations of culture and the contradictory nature of Black popular culture (Hall, 1983). Their conclusions regarding the choices of Black women ... illustrate why Black girls need a space to question what it means to be a Black woman in conjunction with how Hip Hop, issues of class, race, politics, and body influence Black womanhood.

The data expressed within this book show that girls are engaging in the complicated and contradictory work of negotiating the space of Hip Hop music and culture but are doing the work alone. The girls were able to deconstruct Hip Hop's violent images in profound ways and question the lyrical content of rappers as juxtaposed to their own lives. Also, through questioning rappers' authenticity, the girls interrogated the monolithic image of male rappers as hardcore. Their critiques are insightful and have the power to become the foundation of revolutionary change and paradigm shifts in youth culture; however, these teens found no educational support to explore further rap's contrived and stereotypical messages....

(2012)

References[2]

Adams, T.M., & Fuller, D.B. (2006). The words have changed but the ideology remains the same: Misogynistic lyrics in rap music. *Journal of Black Studies*, 36(6), 938–957.

Basu, D. (2005). A critical examination of the political economy of the hip-hop industry. In C. Cecilia, J. Whitehead, P. Mason, & J. Stewart (Eds.), *African Americans in the US economy* (pp. 290–305). Lanham, MD: Rowman and Littlefield.

Clay, A. (2003). Keepin' it real: Black youth, hip-hop culture, and black identity. *American Behavioral Scientist*, 46(10), 1346.

Collins, P.H. (2004). *Black sexual politics: African Americans, gender, and the new racism*. New York: Routledge.

Dyson, M.E. (2007). *Know what l mean?: Reflections on hip hop*. New York: Basic Civitas Books.

Emdin, C. (2006). Affiliation and alienation: Hip-hop, rap, and urban science education. *Journal of Curriculum Studies*, 42(1), 1–25.

Forman, M., & Neal, M.A. (2004). *That's the joint!: The hip-hop studies reader*. New York: Routledge.

Foucault, M. (1980). *Power/Knowledge: Selected interviews and other writings, 1972–1977*. New York: Pantheon.

George, N. (1999). *Hip hop America*. New York: Penguin.

Hall, S. (1981). Notes on deconstructing the popular. *People's History and Socialist Theory, 233*, 227–240.

---

2 *References* References have been excerpted to reflect only those noted in the portion of Love's text reprinted here.

Hall, S. (1983). What is this black in black popular culture. In M. Wallace (Ed.), *Black popular culture*. Boston, MA: Beacon Press.

Hall, S. (1997). *Representation: Cultural representations and signifying practices*. London: Sage Publications.

Love, B.L. (2010). Commercial hip hop: The sounds and images of a racial project. In D. Alridge, J.B. Stewart, & V.P. Franklin (Eds.), *Message in the music: Hip hop, history, and pedagogy* (pp. 55–67). Washington, D.C.: Association for the Study of African American Life and History Press.

McLaren, P. (1994). Life in schools. *An introduction to critical pedagogy in the foundations of education*. Chicago: Addison-Wesley.

Perkins, W.E. (1996). *Droppin' science: Critical essays on rap music and hip hop culture*. Philadelphia, PA: Temple University Press.

Plies. (2007). Shawty. On *The real testament*. Big Gates/Slip-n-Slide Records.

Pruett, K., & Pruett, M. (2009). *Partnership parenting: How men and women parent differently—why it helps your kids and can strengthen your marriage*. New York: Da Capo Lifelong Books.

Rose, T. (1994). *Black noise: Rap music and black culture in contemporary America*. Hanover, NH, and London: Wesleyan University Press.

Storey, J. (1998). *An introduction to cultural theory and popular culture*. Athens, GA: University of Georgia Press.

Ying Yang Twins. (2005). Wait (The whisper song). On *United State of Atlanta*. TVT Records.

Questions

1. Love's book incorporates primary research in the form of interviews. What role does this research play in the argument she advances here?

2. Love critiques commercial rap as "only highlight[ing] the most demeaning notions of Blackness" and as "hypersexual, degrading, and misogynistic" (paragraph 4). To what extent is this an accurate characterization of commercial rap? To what extent is it unfairly reductive?

3. Love writes that "Maxine's and the rest of the girls' consent to find enjoyment in some of rap's most debasing messages is an example of hegemony, as the girls, a marginalized group, consented to their own oppression" (paragraph 10). Is this how you would interpret the interviews Love quotes in this selection? Why or why not?

4. Find a recent popular song by a Black male rapper. To what extent (if at all) does Love's critique of Hip Hop in general apply to the song you chose?

5. Find a recent popular song by a Black female rapper. To what extent (if at all) does Love's critique of Hip Hop in general apply to the song you chose?

POWER IN SPORTS

CLAUDIA RANKINE

from CITIZEN: AN AMERICAN LYRIC

In 2014, for the first time in the history of the National Book Critics Circle Awards, the same book was nominated in two different categories: Claudia Rankine's Citizen, *a short, heavily illustrated book exploring various aspects of African American experience in unconventional ways, was a finalist in the Criticism category, and the winner in the Poetry category.*

The excerpt included here is the second of the book's seven, unnamed chapters.

❧

Hennessy Youngman aka Jayson Musson, whose *Art Thoughtz* take the form of tutorials on YouTube, educates viewers on contemporary art issues. In one of his many videos, he addresses how to become a successful black artist, wryly suggesting black people's anger is marketable. He advises black artists to cultivate "an angry nigger exterior"* by watching, among other things, the Rodney King video[1] while working.

Youngman's suggestions are meant to expose expectations for blackness as well as to underscore the difficulty inherent in any attempt by black artists to metabolize real rage. The commodified anger his video advocates rests lightly on the surface for spectacle's sake. It can be engaged or played like the race card* and is tied solely to the performance of blackness and not to the emotional state of particular individuals in particular situations.

On the bridge between this sellable anger and "the artist" resides, at times, an actual anger. Youngman in his video doesn't address this type of anger: the anger built up through experience and the quotidian struggles against dehumanization every brown or black person lives simply because of skin color. This other kind of anger in time can prevent, rather than sponsor, the production of anything except loneliness.

---

1   *the Rodney King video*   Video footage from 3 March 1991 showed the violent beating of African American taxi driver Rodney King (1965–2012) by four white Los Angeles police officers. The event heightened awareness of racism in law enforcement, and the subsequent acquittal of the police officers prompted the 1992 Los Angeles Riots.

You begin to think, maybe erroneously, that this other kind of anger is really a type of knowledge: the type that both clarifies and disappoints. It responds to insult and attempted erasure simply by asserting presence, and the energy required to present, to react, to assert is accompanied by visceral disappointment: a disappointment in the sense that no amount of visibility will alter the ways in which one is perceived.

5   Recognition of this lack might break you apart. Or recognition might illuminate the erasure the attempted erasure triggers. Whether such discerning creates a healthier, if more isolated self, you can't know. In any case, Youngman doesn't speak to this kind of anger. He doesn't say that witnessing the expression of this more ordinary and daily anger might make the witness believe that a person is "insane."

And insane is what you think, one Sunday afternoon, drinking an Arnold Palmer,* watching the 2009 Women's US Open semifinal, when brought to full attention by the suddenly explosive behavior of Serena Williams.[2] Serena in HD before your eyes becomes overcome by a rage you recognize and have been taught to hold at a distance for your own good. Serena's behavior, on this particular Sunday afternoon, suggests that all the injustice she has played through all the years of her illustrious career flashes before her and she decides finally to respond to all of it with a string of invectives. Nothing, not even the repetition of negations ("no, no, no") she employed in a similar situation years before as a younger player at the 2004 US Open, prepares you for this. Oh my God, she's gone crazy, you say to no one.

What does a victorious or defeated black woman's body in a historically white space look like? Serena and her big sister Venus Williams brought to mind Zora Neale Hurston's[3] "I feel most colored when I am thrown against a sharp white background." This appropriated line, stenciled on canvas by Glenn Ligon, who used plastic letter stencils, smudging oil sticks, and graphite to transform the words into abstractions, seemed to be ad copy[4] for some aspect of life for all black bodies.

Hurston's statement has been played out on the big screen by Serena and Venus: they win sometimes, they lose sometimes, they've been injured, they've been happy, they've been sad, ignored, booed mightily (see Indian

---

2   *US Open* One of the four most important annual tennis tournaments, which together comprise the Grand Slam; *Serena Williams* African American tennis player (b. 1981), often considered the best female tennis player of all time.

3   *Zora Neale Hurston* African American writer (1891–1960), best known for her novel *Their Eyes Were Watching God* (1937). The quotation here appears in her 1928 essay "How It Feels to Be Colored Me."

4   *Glenn Ligon* African American artist (b. 1960); *ad copy* Text of an advertisement.

Wells,[5] which both sisters have boycotted for more than a decade), they've been cheered, and through it all and evident to all were those people who are enraged they are there at all—graphite against a sharp white background.

For years you attribute to Serena Williams a kind of resilience appropriate only for those who exist in celluloid. Neither her father nor her mother nor her sister nor Jehovah her God nor NIKE camp could shield her ultimately from people who felt her black body didn't belong on their court, in their world. From the start many made it clear Serena would have done better struggling to survive in the two-dimensionality of a Millet painting, rather than on their tennis court—better to put all that strength to work in their fantasy of her working the land, rather than be caught up in the turbulence of our ancient dramas, like a ship fighting a storm in a Turner[6] seascape.

The most notorious of Serena's detractors takes the form of Mariana Alves, the distinguished tennis chair umpire.[7] In 2004 Alves was excused from officiating any more matches on the final day of the US Open after she made five bad calls against Serena in her quarterfinal matchup against fellow American Jennifer Capriati. The serves and returns Alves called out were landing, stunningly unreturned by Capriati, inside the lines, no discerning eyesight needed. Commentators, spectators, television viewers, line judges, everyone could see the balls were good, everyone, apparently, except Alves. No one could understand what was happening. Serena, in her denim skirt, black sneaker boots, and dark mascara, began wagging her finger and saying "no, no, no," as if by negating the moment she could propel us back into a legible world. Tennis superstar John McEnroe,[8] given his own keen eye for injustice during his professional career, was shocked that Serena was able to hold it together after losing the match.

Though no one was saying anything explicitly about Serena's black body, you are not the only viewer who thought it was getting in the way of Alves's sight line. One commentator said he hoped he wasn't being unkind when he stated, "Capriati wins it with the help of the umpires and the line judges." A

10

---

5   *Indian Wells*   Tennis tournament held annually in Indian Wells, California. In 2001, the Williams sisters and their father Richard Williams were booed, and some in the crowd shouted racial slurs.

6   *Millet*   Jean-François Millet (1815–75), French painter best known for works depicting peasant farmers;   *Turner*   J.M.W. Turner (1775–1851), English painter known for his evocative landscapes. (Rankine includes reproductions of his painting *Slave Ship* and of a detail from the painting as the final images in *Citizen*.)

7   *chair umpire*   In tennis, person who holds final authority to decide questions and disputes during a match.

8   *John McEnroe*   American tennis player (b. 1959), often considered one of the all-time best players.

year later that match would be credited for demonstrating the need for the speedy installation of Hawk-Eye, the line-calling technology that took the seeing away from the beholder. Now the umpire's call can be challenged by a replay; however, back then after the match Serena said, "I'm very angry and bitter right now. I felt cheated. Shall I go on? I just feel robbed." And though you felt outrage for Serena after that 2004 US Open, as the years go by, she seems to put Alves, and a lengthening list of other curious calls and oversights, against both her and her sister, behind her as they happen.

Yes, and the body has memory. The physical carriage hauls more than its weight. The body is the threshold across which each objectionable call passes into consciousness—all the unintimidated, unblinking, and unflappable resilience does not erase the moments lived through, even as we are eternally stupid or everlastingly optimistic, so ready to be inside, among, a part of the games.

And here Serena is, five years after Alves, back at the US Open, again in a semifinal match, this time against Belgium's Kim Clijsters. Serena is not playing well and loses the first set. In response she smashes her racket on the court. Now McEnroe isn't stunned by her ability to hold herself together and is moved to say, "That's as angry as I've ever seen her." The umpire gives her a warning; another violation will mean a point penalty.

She is in the second set at the critical moment of 5–6 in Clijsters's favor, serving to stay in the match, at match point. The line judge employed by the US Open to watch Serena's body, its every move, says Serena stepped on the line while serving. What? (The Hawk-Eye cameras don't cover the feet, only the ball, apparently.) What! Are you serious? She is serious; she has seen a foot fault, one no one else is able to locate despite the numerous replays. "No foot fault, you definitely do not see a foot fault there," says McEnroe. "That's overofficiating for certain," says another commentator. Even the ESPN tennis commentator, who seems predictable in her readiness to find fault with the Williams sisters, says, "Her foot fault call was way off." Yes, and even if there had been a foot fault, despite the rule, they are rarely ever called at critical moments in a Grand Slam match because "You don't make a call," tennis official Carol Cox says, "that can decide a match unless it's flagrant."

15   As you look at the affable Kim Clijsters, you try to entertain the thought that this scenario could have played itself out the other way. And as Serena turns to the lineswoman and says, "I swear to God I'm fucking going to take this fucking ball and shove it down your fucking throat, you hear that? I swear to God!" As offensive as her outburst is, it is difficult not to applaud her for reacting immediately to being thrown against a sharp white background. It is difficult not to applaud her for existing in the moment, for fighting crazily against the so-called wrongness of her body's positioning at the service line.

She says in 2009, belatedly, the words that should have been said to the umpire in 2004, the words that might have snapped Alves back into focus, a focus that would have acknowledged what actually was happening on the court. Now Serena's reaction is read as insane. And her punishment for this moment of manumission[9] is the threatened point penalty resulting in the loss of the match, an $82,500 fine, plus a two-year probationary period by the Grand Slam Committee.

Perhaps the committee's decision is only about context, though context is not meaning. It is a public event being watched in homes across the world. In any case, it is difficult not to think that if Serena lost context by abandoning all rules of civility, it could be because her body, trapped in a racial imaginary, trapped in disbelief—code for being black in America—is being governed not by the tennis match she is participating in but by a collapsed relationship that had promised to play by the rules. Perhaps this is how racism feels no matter the context—randomly the rules everyone else gets to play by no longer apply to you, and to call this out by calling out "I swear to God!" is to be called insane, crass, crazy. Bad sportsmanship.

Two years later, September 11, 2011, Serena is playing the Australian Sam Stosur in the US Open final. She is expected to win, having just beaten the number-one player, the Dane Caroline Wozniacki, in the semifinal the night before. Some speculate Serena especially wants to win this Grand Slam because it is the tenth anniversary of the attack on the Twin Towers.[10] It's believed that by winning she will prove her red-blooded American patriotism and will once and for all become beloved by the tennis world (think Arthur Ashe[11] after his death). All the bad calls, the boos, the criticisms that she has made ugly the game of tennis—through her looks as well as her behavior—that entire cluster of betrayals will be wiped clean with this win.

One imagines her wanting to say what her sister would say a year later after being diagnosed with Sjögren's syndrome[12] and losing her match to shouts of "Let's go, Venus!" in Arthur Ashe Stadium: "I know this is not proper tennis etiquette, but this is the first time I've ever played here that the crowd has been

---

9   *manumission* Release from slavery.

10   *tenth anniversary ... Twin Towers* In the terrorist attacks by al-Qaeda on September 11, 2001, the Twin Towers of the World Trade Center in New York were destroyed; almost 3000 people died.

11   *Arthur Ashe* American tennis player (1943–93), winner of three Grand Slam tournaments. An African American, Ashe was often the target of racism during his lifetime, but he became almost universally revered after his death.

12   *Sjögren's syndrome* Autoimmune disorder which typically causes dry mouth, dry eyes, joint pain, and fatigue, as well as often being the cause of other complications.

behind me like that. Today I felt American, you know, for the first time at the US Open. So I've waited my whole career to have this moment and here it is."

20   It is all too exhausting and Serena's exhaustion shows in her playing; she is losing, a set and a game down. Yes, and finally she hits a great shot, a big forehand, and before the ball is safely past Sam Stosur's hitting zone, Serena yells, "Come on!" thinking she has hit an irretrievable winner. The umpire, Eva Asderaki, rules correctly that Serena, by shouting, interfered with Stosur's concentration. Subsequently, a ball that Stosur seemingly would not have been able to return becomes Stosur's point. Serena's reply is to ask the umpire if she is trying to screw her again. She remembers the umpire doing this to her before. As a viewer, you too, along with John McEnroe, begin to wonder if this is the same umpire from 2004 or 2009. It isn't—in 2004 it was Mariana Alves and in 2009 it was Sharon Wright; however, the use of the word "again" by Serena returns her viewers to other times calling her body out.

Again Serena's frustrations, her disappointments, exist within a system you understand not to try to understand in any fair-minded way because to do so is to understand the erasure of the self as systemic, as ordinary. For Serena, the daily diminishment is a low flame, a constant drip. Every look, every comment, every bad call blossoms out of history, through her, onto you. To understand is to see Serena as hemmed in as any other black body thrown against our American background. "Aren't you the one that screwed me over last time here?" she asks umpire Asderaki. "Yeah, you are. Don't look at me. Really, don't even look at me. Don't look my way. Don't look my way," she repeats, because it is that simple.

Yes, and who can turn away? Serena is not running out of breath. Despite all her understanding, she continues to serve up aces while smashing rackets and fraying hems. In the 2012 Olympics she brought home two of the three gold medals the Americans would win in tennis. After her three-second celebratory dance on center court at the All England Club, the American media reported, "And there was Serena ... Crip-Walking[13] all over the most lily-white place in the world.... You couldn't help but shake your head.... What Serena did was akin to cracking a tasteless, X-rated* joke inside a church.... What she did was immature and classless."

Before making the video *How to Be a Successful Black Artist*, Hennessy Youngman uploaded to YouTube *How to Be a Successful Artist*. While putting forward the argument that one needs to be white to be truly successful, he adds, in an aside, that this might not work for blacks because if "a nigger paints a

---

13   *Crip-Walking*   Dance move originated by the Los Angeles Crip gang in the 1970s.

flower it becomes a slavery flower, flower de *Amistad*,"[14] thereby intimating that any relationship between the white viewer and the black artist immediately becomes one between white persons and black property, which was the legal state of things once upon a time,* as Patricia Williams has pointed out in *The Alchemy of Race and Rights*: "The cold game of equality staring makes me feel like a thin sheet of glass.... I could force my presence, the real me contained in those eyes, upon them, but I would be smashed in the process."

Interviewed by the Brit Piers Morgan after her 2012 Olympic victory, Serena is informed by Morgan that he was planning on calling her victory dance "the Serena Shuffle"; however, he has learned from the American press that it is a Crip Walk, a gangster dance. Serena responds incredulously by asking if she looks like a gangster to him. Yes, he answers. All in a day's fun, perhaps, and in spite and despite it all, Serena Williams blossoms again into Serena Williams. When asked if she is confident she can win her upcoming matches, her answer remains, "At the end of the day, I am very happy with me and I'm very happy with my results."

Serena would go on to win every match she played between the US Open and the year-end 2012 championship tournament, and because tennis is a game of adjustments, she would do this without any reaction to a number of questionable calls. More than one commentator would remark on her ability to hold it together during these matches. She is a woman in love, one suggests. She has grown up, another decides, as if responding to the injustice of racism is childish and her previous demonstration of emotion was free-floating and detached from any external actions by others. Some others theorize she is developing the admirable "calm and measured logic" of an Arthur Ashe, who the sportswriter Bruce Jenkins felt was "dignified" and "courageous" in his ability to confront injustice without making a scene. Jenkins, perhaps inspired by Serena's new comportment, felt moved to argue that her continued boycott of Indian Wells in 2013, where she felt traumatized by the aggression of racist slurs hurled at her in 2001, was lacking in "dignity" and "integrity" and demonstrated "only stubbornness and a grudge." (Serena lifted her boycott in 2015, though Venus continues to boycott Indian Wells.)

Watching this newly contained Serena, you begin to wonder if she finally has given up wanting better from her peers or if she too has come across Hennessy's *Art Thoughtz* and is channeling his assertion that the less that is communicated the better. Be ambiguous. This type of ambiguity could also be diagnosed as dissociation and would support Serena's claim that she has had to split herself off from herself and create different personae.

25

---

14   *Amistad*   The reference is to *La Amistad*, a nineteenth-century schooner on which a slave revolt occurred in 1839.

Now that there is no calling out of injustice, no yelling, no cursing, no finger wagging or head shaking, the media decides to take up the mantle when on December 12, 2012, two weeks after Serena is named WTA[15] Player of the Year, the Dane Caroline Wozniacki, a former number-one player, imitates Serena by stuffing towels in her top and shorts, all in good fun, at an exhibition match. Racist? CNN* wants to know if outrage is the proper response.

It's then that Hennessy's suggestions about "how to be a successful artist" return to you: be ambiguous, be white. Wozniacki, it becomes clear, has finally enacted what was desired by many of Serena's detractors, consciously or unconsciously, the moment the Compton[16] girl first stepped on court. Wozniacki (though there are a number of ways to interpret her actions—playful mocking of a peer, imitation of the mimicking antics of the tennis player known as the joker, Novak Djokovic) finally gives the people what they have wanted all along by embodying Serena's attributes while leaving Serena's "angry nigger exterior" behind. At last, in this real, and unreal, moment, we have Wozniacki's image of smiling blond goodness posing as the best female tennis player of all time.

(2014)

Questions

1. Rankine frequently writes in the second person, referring to a "you" who observes and reflects upon Williams and her games. What purpose do these asides serve? Who is the "you" of whom she speaks?

2. Rankine discusses two types of anger at the beginning of the essay. How would you characterize them, and how are they different? What does Rankine say about anger and the body?

3. How does Rankine interpret Serena Williams's response during the 2009 US Open? How does she use the tennis match as a metaphor to make a larger argument?

4. The book from which this essay was drawn was a finalist for the National Book Award in two categories, Poetry and Criticism. What (if any) characteristics make it a work of criticism? Does this piece accomplish or communicate anything that neither poetry nor criticism could on their own?

5. An image of Serena Williams is included in this anthology's color insert. Compare the depiction of Williams in this photograph with the way she is presented in Rankine's piece.

---

15 *WTA* Women's Tennis Association.
16 *Compton* City in California, south of Los Angeles.

IRA BOUDWAY

NBA REFS LEARNED THEY WERE RACIST, AND THAT MADE THEM LESS RACIST

The following article, reporting on the results of a study by Devin Pope, Joseph Price, and Justin Wolfers, was posted on the Bloomberg news website 7 February 2014. The 2013 study that the article describes was a follow-up to a 2007 study—Price and Wolfers' "Racial Discrimination among NBA Referees." Both the 2007 and the 2013 studies were widely reported in the media.

In some scholarly disciplines there can be a long lag between initial publication of preliminary research results and final publication in a scholarly journal. In this case, both the 2007 study and the more recent one were initially published as working papers; the working paper presenting the research results discussed in Boudway's article appeared in December 2013 as "National Bureau of Economic Research Working Paper No. 19765," and also in February of 2014 in the Brookings Institution's Working Paper series. A revised version of the 2007 study was published in 2010 in The Quarterly Journal of Economics; *a revised version of the follow-up study appeared in* Management Science *in 2018.*

❦

Seven years ago, a pair of scholars released a study of NBA* referees that found white officiating crews more likely to call fouls against black players—and, to a lesser degree, black officiating crews more likely to call fouls against white players. The study drew broad media attention and caused a small stir in the league. Then-Commissioner David Stern, questioned its validity in the *New York Times*, and players weighed in on sports-talk radio and ESPN.*

The same scholars, Justin Wolfers of the University of Michigan and Joseph Price of Brigham Young University, returned to the subject of racially biased referees in a working paper released in December with an astounding result. Once the results of the original study were widely known, the bias disappeared.

"When we conduct the same tests for own-race bias in the period immediately following the media coverage," they wrote, "we find none exists."

The original data set came from the 1991–2002 NBA seasons. In the new study, in which the original scholars worked with Devin Pope of the Booth School of Business, the authors looked both at a sample from the 2003–2006 seasons—after the original data but before the public attention—and from 2007–2010. From 2003 to 2006, the bias persisted at the same level, roughly an extra fifth of a foul every 48 minutes. But from 2007 to 2010, they found no significant bias in either direction.

In explaining why this happened, the authors argue that public awareness itself shaped referee behavior. The NBA, they wrote, did not increase the frequency of mixed-race officiating crews or otherwise take action after the release of the initial study:

> A phone conversation with NBA league administrators who oversee the NBA's officiating department suggests that the NBA did not take any specific action to eliminate referee discrimination. Specifically, the administrators to whom we spoke denied that the NBA spoke with the referees about the Price and Wolfers study. They also indicated that the study did not lead to a change in referee incentives or a change in the way they train their referees.

Simply knowing that bias was present and that other people knew, they wrote, made it go away:

> We argue that this dramatic decrease in bias is a causal result of the awareness associated with the treatment—the release and subsequent publicity surrounding the original academic study in 2007.

The study may hold implications for any organization looking to reduce group bias. In the realms of public policy and education, the focus is often on increased exposure and proximity to out groups. But bias, as the original referee study showed, can sometimes withstand proximity. The remedy might be to locate bigotry and bring it into the light. As Louis Brandeis famously wrote in 1913:[1] "Publicity is justly commended as a remedy for social and industrial diseases. Sunlight is said to be the best of disinfectants; electric light the most efficient policeman."

(2014)

---

[1] *Louis Brandeis ... 1913*   This well-known quotation from Brandeis (who later became a member of the Supreme Court), first appeared in *Harper's Weekly* magazine in an article entitled "What Publicity Can Do."

Questions

1. What are the findings of the study examining the 1991–2002 NBA seasons, and how do they compare to the same authors' findings regarding the 2003–2006 seasons? What about the 2007–2010 seasons? How do the authors account for the pattern of similarities and differences over time?

2. Do the reported findings adequately justify the title of this piece? What evidence does the article cite to prove the title's causal claim about learning and behavior?

3. What strategy does Boudway suggest for eliminating racial bias beyond the NBA? Under what (if any) circumstances do you think this strategy would be effective? Under what (if any) circumstances do you think it would be ineffective?

JONATHAN CAPEHART

TAKING A KNEE WITH COLIN KAEPERNICK AND STANDING WITH STEPHEN CURRY AGAINST TRUMP

Professional football player Colin Kaepernick initiated a movement when, in August 2016, as a protest against racial oppression and police brutality in the United States, he stopped standing during the national anthem. Individual players, and in some cases whole teams, gradually joined the protest through gestures such as kneeling, linking arms, or raising fists during the anthem. On 22 September 2017, President Trump responded by saying that the protesters should be "fired" from the NFL—a declaration which prompted a marked increase in the number of protests.

On the same day, Stephen Curry, widely considered one of the most skilled athletes in the NBA, publicly stated that he did not want to make the visit to the White House that his team, the Golden State Warriors, would have traditionally made as winners of the year's NBA championship. On 23 September, President Trump rescinded the invitation via tweet. The piece below appeared in the Washington Post*'s Opinion section the following day.*

❦

If you know me, you know I'm not a big sports fan. But President Trump's deplorable attacks against the Constitution's guarantee of freedom of speech have made me a fanatic for Stephen Curry and Colin Kaepernick, the National Basketball Association and the National Football League.

By now you are well aware of Trump's attacks. His foul-mouthed hit Friday on Kaepernick's taking a knee during the national anthem to protest the treatment of African Americans at the hands of police. His juvenile disinvitation of basketball champions the Golden State Warriors because of Curry's stated disinterest in making the traditional trip to the White House.

And as outrageous as Trump's words and actions are, the reaction of the sports world is most heartening. The Golden State Warriors took the presidential diss* in stride to announce that the team would still come to Washington. But the players will do something the president refuses to do. "In lieu of a visit to the White House," the team announced Saturday, "we have decided that we'll constructively use our trip to the nation's capital in February to celebrate equality, diversity and inclusion—the values that we embrace as an organization."

NFL Commissioner Roger Goodell refused to remain silent in the face of Trump's tantrum. "The NFL and our players are at our best when we help create a sense of unity in our country and our culture," he said Saturday. "Divisive comments like these demonstrate an unfortunate lack of respect for the NFL, our great game and all of our players, and a failure to understand the overwhelming force for good our clubs and players represent in our communities." Even Robert Kraft, the Trump-supporting owner of the New England Patriots, said in a statement he was "deeply disappointed by the tone of the comments made by the president on Friday."

From London to Boston to Oakland, athletes took a knee or locked arms 5 in response to ignorant hectoring from Trump. The Pittsburgh Steelers, Seattle Seahawks and Tennessee Titans stayed in their locker rooms during the national anthem before their respective games on Sunday. Whether taking a knee or standing while putting a hand on a teammate kneeling in protest, these athletes are filling the moral chasm created by a president whose sympathy and empathy are reserved for the "very fine people" among the white supremacists, Nazis and otherwise bigoted racists marching unmasked in Charlottesville.[1]

Let's not forget why Kaepernick kicked all this off in the first place. Here's what the still-out-of-work former San Francisco 49er told the media in August 2016 when he was still playing for the team.

> I'm going to continue to stand with the people that are being oppressed. To me, this is something that has to change. When there's significant change and I feel that flag represents what it's supposed to represent, and this country is representing people the way that it's supposed to, I'll stand.
>
> This stand wasn't for me. This is because I'm seeing things happen to people that don't have a voice, people that don't have a platform to talk and have their voices heard, and effect change. So I'm in the position where I can do that and I'm going to do that for people that can't.

---

1   *Charlottesville*   In Charlottesville, Virginia, on 12 August 2017, white nationalists opposed to the removal of Confederate monuments chanted a Nazi slogan and clashed violently with counterprotesters, murdering one. Following the incident, Trump delivered a series of self-contradictory statements. In one, he indicated that the protest had involved "some very fine people on both sides" and expressed support for the position of the white nationalists regarding the removal of monuments.

It's something that can unify this team. It's something that can unify this country. If we have these real conversations that are uncomfortable for a lot of people. If we have these conversations, there's a better understanding of where both sides are coming from.

I have great respect for the men and women that have fought for this country. I have family, I have friends that have gone and fought for this country. And they fight for freedom, they fight for the people, they fight for liberty and justice, for everyone. That's not happening. People are dying in vain because this country isn't holding their end of the bargain up, as far as giving freedom and justice, liberty to everybody. That's something that's not happening. I've seen videos, I've seen circumstances where men and women that have been in the military have come back and been treated unjustly by the country they fought for, and have been murdered by the country they fought for, on our land. That's not right.

Those who argue that doing any of this plays into Trump's hands politically are flat-out wrong. That's a demand that every American remain silent as rights they revere and rely on are chipped away by the creeping normalization of the reprehensible by this president. By that logic, fighting against injustice would be never okay.

Political considerations must take a backseat when character is at stake, when matters of conscience come into play, when standing up for one's beliefs is paramount. By speaking out, by taking a knee, by not bowing or buckling to pressure from as high as the Oval Office, Kaepernick and those now joining him are showing the power of our Constitution and the promise of our nation. They neither need nor deserve lectures on patriotism. Freedom of speech and freedom of expression are what make America great.*

(2017)

Questions

1. What is Capehart's stance on the importance of character? Why does character matter, even in sports?

2. Another article included in this anthology, "The Politicization of Everything: Everybody Loses in the Trump-NFL Brawl over the National Anthem," defends a view opposing the one adopted in this piece. The following questions address both pieces:

a. The *Wall Street Journal* article argues against "the politicization of the National Football League and the national anthem," while Capehart defends Kaepernick by saying that "[p]olitical considerations must take a backseat when character is at stake." How is each author using the concept of the "political"? To what extent do their usages overlap?

b. Identify what you consider to be the most persuasive point in each article. Drawing on these articles and/or your own invention, come up with a counterargument one might advance against each point you identified.

c. In response to these articles, write your own opinion piece on this topic. Your writing style should be suitable for publication in a newspaper.

3. An extensive quotation from Kaepernick makes up almost a third of Capehart's article. What is the rhetorical impact of this?

4. A photograph of a Nike billboard featuring Kaepernick is included in this anthology's color insert. What does Capehart's piece suggest about Kaepernick's reputation, and how (if at all) does Nike capitalize on this reputation for their billboard?

WALL STREET JOURNAL EDITORIAL BOARD

THE POLITICIZATION OF EVERYTHING: EVERYBODY LOSES IN THE TRUMP-NFL BRAWL OVER THE NATIONAL ANTHEM

During the 2016 football season, Colin Kaepernick, a quarterback for the San Francisco 49ers, abstained from standing during the national anthem as a protest against racial oppression in the United States. Other players began to follow his example, with some kneeling and others displaying raised fists or linked arms during the anthem. The protests continued into 2017, and the following article appeared in The Wall Street Journal's *Opinion section in September of that year, two days after President Trump stated that all participants in this form of protest should be "fired" from the NFL.*

Kaepernick was not employed by any NFL team for the following football seasons, which many suggested was a retaliation for his expression of his political views. He nonetheless continued his activism, and in early 2018 completed a "million dollar pledge" to donate a hundred thousand dollars a month for ten months to "organizations working in oppressed communities."

❧

Healthy democracies have ample room for politics but leave a larger space for civil society and culture that unites more than divides. With the politicization of the National Football League and the national anthem, the Divided States of America are exhibiting a very unhealthy level of polarization and mistrust.

The progressive forces of identity politics started this poisoning of America's favorite spectator sport last year by making a hero of Colin Kaepernick for refusing to stand for "The Star-Spangled Banner" before games. They raised the stakes this year by turning him into a progressive martyr because no team had picked him up to play quarterback after he opted out of his contract with the San Francisco 49ers.

The NFL is a meritocracy, and maybe coaches and general managers thought he wasn't good enough for the divisions he might cause in a locker room or among fans. But the left said it was all about race and class.

All of this is cultural catnip for Donald Trump, who pounced on Friday night at a rally and on the weekend on Twitter with his familiar combination of gut political instinct, rhetorical excess, and ignorance. "Wouldn't you love to see one of these NFL owners, when somebody disrespects our flag, to say, 'Get that son of a bitch off the field right now, out, he's fired. He's fired,'" Mr. Trump said Friday.

No doubt most Americans agree with Mr. Trump that they don't want their flag disrespected, especially by millionaire athletes. But Mr. Trump never stops at reasonable, and so he called for kneeling players to be fired or suspended, and if the league didn't comply for fans to "boycott" the NFL.   5

He also plunged into the debate over head injuries without a speck of knowledge about the latest brain science, claiming that the NFL was "ruining the game" by trying to stop dangerous physical hits. This is the kind of rant you'd hear in a lousy sports bar.

Mr. Trump has managed to unite the players and owners against him, though several owners supported him for President and donated to his inaugural.* The owners were almost obliged to defend their sport, even if their complaints that Mr. Trump was "divisive" ignored the divisive acts by Mr. Kaepernick and his media allies that injected politics into football in the first place.

Americans don't begrudge athletes their free-speech rights—see the popularity of Charles Barkley[1]—but disrespecting the national anthem puts partisanship above a symbol of nationhood that thousands have died for. Players who chose to kneel shouldn't be surprised that fans around the country booed them on Sunday. This is the patriotic sentiment that they are helping Mr. Trump exploit for what he no doubt thinks is his own political advantage.

American democracy was healthier when politics at the ballpark was limited to fans booing politicians who threw out the first ball—almost as a bipartisan obligation. This showed a healthy skepticism toward the political class. But now the players want to be politicians and use their fame to lecture other Americans, the parsons of the press corps want to make them moral spokesmen, and the President wants to run against the players.

The losers are the millions of Americans who would rather cheer for their   10
teams on Sunday as a respite from work and the other divisions of American life.

(2017)

---

1   *Charles Barkley*   African American retired NBA player who, on the day this editorial was published, criticized Trump on the CBS program *NFL Today*.

Questions

1. Another article in this anthology, Jonathan Capehart's "Taking a Knee with Colin Kaepernick and Standing with Stephen Curry against Trump," defends a view opposing that adopted in this piece. Read that article and consider the following questions:

   a. Kaepernick's explanation of his protest is quoted in Capehart's article. In your view, does anything in Kaepernick's statement contradict the suggestion that his protest "disrespect[s] the national anthem"? Why or why not?

   b. The *Wall Street Journal* article suggests that players who kneel during the anthem "are helping Mr. Trump exploit" Americans' patriotism (paragraph 8). How does Capehart counter this point? Which view do you find most compelling?

2. The editors appear to object to the actions both of Kaepernick and of Trump. Of the two, who is more strongly condemned in this piece? How can you tell?

3. This piece criticizes Kaepernick for "inject[ing] politics into football" (paragraph 7). To what extent do you agree with the implication that football was apolitical before the controversy surrounding Kaepernick arose?

4. Identify some words and phrases in this article that signal the authors' location on the political spectrum.

BIOGRAPHICAL NOTES

Anzaldúa, Gloria (1942–2004)
Poet and scholar Gloria Anzaldúa was a leading figure of twentieth-century feminist scholarship. Her best-known book, *Borderlands/La Frontera: The New Mestiza* (1987), is an academic work drawing upon her experiences as a Chicana lesbian; she was also the co-editor of *This Bridge Called My Back: Writings by Radical Women of Color* (1981), an influential collection of feminist writing.

Awad, Edmond (unknown)
Edmond Awad was born in Syria, where he obtained his BA; he earned his MA and PhD, both focused on multi-agent computer systems, at Masdar Institute in the United Arab Emirates. In 2015, the year he completed his PhD, he became a Postdoctoral Associate at MIT Media Lab. Awad has received mass media attention for his co-development of websites that solicit responses to ethical dilemmas for statistical analysis; one site, Moral Machine, poses dilemmas regarding self-driving cars, while another, MyGoodness, poses dilemmas regarding charitable giving.

Baldwin, James (1924–87)
Born and raised in New York City, African American writer James Baldwin left America for Paris at the age of 24, and he remained an expatriate for most of the rest of his life. His 1955 essay collection *Notes of a Native Son* (now an established classic) was followed by numerous other collections—notably, *Nobody Knows My Name: More Notes of a Native Son* (1961) and *The Fire Next Time* (1963). His novels include *Go Tell It on the Mountain* (1953), *Giovanni's Room* (1956), and *Tell Me How Long the Train's Been Gone* (1968).

Barthes, Roland (1915–80)
Roland Barthes was a French social and literary critic known for his influential writings on semiotics and structuralism. His written works include *Mythologies* (1957), *Elements of Semiology* (1967), *The Empire of Signs* (1970), and *The Luminous Room* (1980).

Boudway, Ira (unknown)
Ira Boudway is an American Bloomberg Businessweek reporter who focuses on sports.

Brennan, William (unknown)

American journalist William Brennan's writing appears in magazines including *The Atlantic, The New Yorker*, and *Pacific Standard*.

Capehart, Jonathan (1967–)

A Pulitzer Prize-winning journalist, Jonathan Capehart has served on the editorial boards for the *New York Daily News* and *The Washington Post*. He has also been a researcher for *The Today Show*, a columnist at Bloomberg News, and a speechwriter and policy advisor for Michael Bloomberg's successful 2001 campaign for mayor of New York City. Capehart also makes frequent appearances on MSNBC programs.

Coyote, Ivan (1969–)

Ivan Coyote is a Canadian storyteller, performer, filmmaker, and prolific author of fiction, non-fiction, and poetry. They (Coyote's pronouns are they/them) are a popular public speaker and an occasional commentator on transgender issues, including a widely viewed TED Talk on the need for gender-neutral bathrooms.

Gilchrist, Kristen (unknown)

Kristen Gilchrist's research explores government, media, and community responses to missing/murdered Aboriginal women in Canada. A Canadian PhD candidate at Carleton University, Gilchrist is also an activist and non-Indigenous ally. She co-founded Families of Sisters in Spirit, an organization dedicated to providing support for the families of missing/murdered Aboriginal women, in 2005.

Heller, Nathan (unknown)

An American journalist and film critic, Nathan Heller is a staff writer at *The New Yorker* and a contributing editor at *Vogue*. While working at *Slate* magazine, Heller was a finalist for a National Magazine Award for essays and criticism.

Klein, Naomi (1970–)

A Canadian journalist, scholar, and social activist, Klein is known for her environmentalism and criticism of corporate capitalism. Her work has appeared in such publications as *Harper's Magazine, Rolling Stone, The Nation*, and *The Guardian*. Her book *No Logo: Taking Aim at the Brand Bullies* (2000) has been translated into more than 28 languages, and her bestselling *Shock Doctrine: The Rise of Disaster Capitalism* (2007) was awarded the Warwick Prize for Writing. She is also a co-author of *The Leap Manifesto* (2015), a call to Canadians to pass legislation limiting fossil fuel consumption and to fully implement the United Nations Declaration on the Rights of Indigenous Peoples.

Kross, Ethan (unknown)
Director of the University of Michigan Self-Control and Emotion Laboratory, Ethan Kross is also a Professor of Social Psychology at the University of Michigan-Ann Arbor.

Lalami, Laila (1968–)
A Moroccan-American writer, Laila Lalami is best known for her novel *The Moor's Account* (2014), which was a finalist for the Pulitzer Prize and was long-listed for the Man Booker Prize. Lalami, who moved from Morocco to America in 1992 and began to publish her work shortly thereafter, is known for her literary and social criticism as well as her several works of fiction. She is currently a professor in the Department of Creative Writing at the University of California, Riverside.

Lester, Caroline (unknown)
American journalist Caroline Lester's writing has appeared in such publications as *The New Yorker*, *The Atlantic*, and *The New York Times*. She is also an audio producer whose work has been carried by broadcasters such as The New Yorker Radio Hour, PRI's The World, and the BBC World Service.

Li, Yiyun (1972–)
Award-winning Chinese American novelist and short story writer Yiyun Li is a professor of Creative Writing at the Lewis Center for the Arts at Princeton University. Her novels include *The Vagrants* (2009), *Kinder than Solitude* (2014), and *Where Reasons End* (2019). She published her first nonfiction book, the memoir *Dear Friend, from My Life I Write to You in Your Life*, in 2017.

Love, Bettina (unknown)
Scholar and educator Bettina Love is an Associate Professor of Educational Theory & Practice at the University of Georgia. Her published academic work includes numerous articles and the book *Hip Hop's Li'l Sistas Speak: Negotiating Hip Hop Identities and Politics in the New South* (2012). In that book, she articulates a vision of Hip Hop pedagogy, a concept she has put into practice with such projects as the Hip Hop civics curriculum GET FREE and the after-school program Real Talk: Hip Hop Education for Social Justice.

Nama, Adilifu (1969–)
Adilifu Nama, an Associate Professor of African American Studies at Loyola Marymount University, specializes in film and comics studies. His published works include *Black Space: Imagining Race in Science Fiction Film* (2008), *Super Black: American Pop Culture and Black Superheroes* (2011), and *Race on the QT: Blackness and the Films of Quentin Tarantino* (2015).

Nussbaum, Emily (1966–)

Emily Nussbaum, 2016 winner of the Pulitzer Prize for Criticism, has been the television critic for *The New Yorker* since 2011. She has also worked as a writer and editor for *New York* magazine and as Editor-in-Chief of *Nerve* (one of the first digital-only magazines). Her first collection of essays, *I Like to Watch: Arguing My Way Through the TV Revolution*, was published in 2019.

Rankine, Claudia (1963–)

Claudia Rankine was born in Kingston, Jamaica, and earned degrees from Williams College and Columbia University. Her published work, which straddles the boundary between poetry and non-fiction prose, includes *Nothing in Nature Is Private* (1995), *Don't Let Me Be Lonely: An American Lyric* (2004), and *Citizen: An American Lyric* (2014), which received a National Book Critics Circle Award. Rankine joined the faculty at Yale University in 2016.

Robinson, Eden (1968–)

A graduate of the University of British Columbia's MFA program in creative writing, Eden Robinson is a member of the Haisla and Helitsuk First Nations. In 1997 her debut short story collection, *Traplines* (1996), won Britain's Royal Society of Literature's 1997 Winifred Holtby Prize for the best regional work by a Commonwealth writer. Robinson's novel *Monkey Beach* (2000) is set in the Kitamaat territory, on BC's central coast, where she was raised. Her other books include *Blood Sports* (2006), *The Sasquatch at Home: Traditional Protocols and Modern Storytelling* (2011), *Son of a Trickster* (2017), and *Trickster Drift* (2018).

Silko, Leslie Marmon (1948–)

Leslie Marmon Silko's poetry, essays, and novels are influenced by the Pueblo storytelling tradition she learned in childhood from her aunt, grandmother, and great-grandmother on the Laguna Pueblo Reservation in New Mexico. Her novel *Ceremony* was released in 1977 to critical acclaim. Among her other books are the poetry and short-story collection *Storyteller* (1981) and the short-story and essay collection *Yellow Woman and a Beauty of the Spirit: Essays on Native American Life Today* (1997). Her memoir *The Turquoise Ledge* was released in 2010.

Smith, Zadie (1975–)

The daughter of a Black Jamaican mother and a white English father, Zadie Smith was raised in North London and began her writing career while a student at Cambridge University. The great success of her first book, *White Teeth* (2000), established her reputation as an important writer of fiction; her subsequent novels include *On Beauty* (2005), *NW* (2012), and *Swing Time* (2016). In 2018 she published *Feel Free*, a collection of essays, and her first collection of short fiction, *Grand Union: Stories*, was released in 2019. Smith is a professor of Creative Writing at New York University.

Staples, Brent (1951–)
American journalist Brent Staples is an editorial writer for *The New York Times*; he has also written and reported for the *New York Times Book Review* and *The Chicago Sun-Times* and contributed to the *Columbia Journalism Review* and the *Los Angeles Times*. His books include the memoir *Parallel Time: Growing Up in Black and White* (1996) and *An American Love Story* (1999).

Tovar, Virgie (1982–)
Self-described fat feminist Virgie Tovar is an author and lecturer on fat discrimination and body image. She edited the anthology *Hot & Heavy: Fierce Fat Girls on Life, Love & Fashion* in 2012; her manifesto, *The Right to Remain Fat*, was released in 2018. She has taught at the University of California at Berkeley, contributed to publications such as BuzzFeed and Forbes, and hosted "The Virgie Show" for CBS radio.

Wainaina, Binyavanga (1971–2019)
A Kenyan satirist and short story writer, Wainaina Binyavanga won the Caine Prize for African Writing in 2002. He was the founding editor of the influential literary magazine *Kwani?*, and his work appeared in *The New York Times*, *Granta*, *The Guardian*, and *National Geographic*. He was also an expert on African cuisines, and collected more than 13,000 traditional and modern African recipes. He is best known for *One Day I Will Write about This Place* (2011), a memoir about his youth in Kenya, and for essays such as "How to Write about Africa" (2005) and "I Am a Homosexual, Mum" (2014).

Waldman, Katy (unknown)
A staff writer at *The New Yorker*, Katy Waldman is an American sociocultural critic. In 2018, she received an American Society of Magazine Editors award for journalists under thirty.

Wallace, Carvell (unknown)
American writer and podcaster Carvell Wallace's work has appeared in publications including *The New Yorker*, *GQ*, *The Guardian*, and *New York Times Magazine*. His podcast about race in America, *Closer Than They Appear*, debuted in 2017. A popular-culture journalist who often interviews high-profile subjects, he is the coauthor of basketball player Andre Iguodala's memoir *The Sixth Man* (2019).

Worra, Bryan Thao (1973–)
Bryan Thao Worra is a Laotian American writer and activist. His publications include *The Tuk Tuk Diaries: My Dinner with Cluster Bombs* (2003), *On the Other Side of the Eye* (2007), *Touching Detonations*, *Winter Ink* (2008), *BARROW* (2009), and *Demonstra: A Poetry Collection* (2013).

Zhang, Jenny (1983–)
Chinese American author Jenny Zhang released her debut collection of short fiction, *Sour Heart*, in 2017. She has also published two collections of poetry: *Dear Jenny, We Are All Find* (2012) and *Hags* (2014).

PERMISSIONS ACKNOWLEDGMENTS

Anzaldúa, Gloria. "How to Tame a Wild Tongue," from *Borderlands/La Frontera: The New Mestiza*, Fourth Edition. Aunt Lute Books, 2012. Reprinted with permission.

Awad, Edmond, et al. Figure 2: "Global Preferences," from "The Moral Machine Experiment" in *Nature* 563 (24 October 2018): 59–64. Reprinted by permission from Springer Nature; copyright © 2018.

Baldwin, James. "If Black English Isn't a Language, Then Tell Me, What Is?" Copyright © 1979 by James Baldwin; copyright renewed. Originally published in *The New York Times*, July 29, 1979. Collected in *James Baldwin: Collected Essays*, published by Library of America. Used by arrangement with The James Baldwin Estate.

Barthes, Roland. "Soap-Powders and Detergents," and "Toys," from *Mythologies*, translated by Annette Lavers. Translation copyright © 1972 by Jonathan Cape Ltd. Reprinted by permission of Hill and Wang, a division of Farrar, Straus and Giroux.

Boudway, Ira. "NBA Refs Learned They Were Racist, and That Made Them Less Racist," from *Bloomberg.com*, February 7, 2014. Used with the permission of Bloomberg L.P. Copyright © 2017. All rights reserved.

Brennan, William. "Julie Washington's Quest to Get Schools to Respect African-American English," from *The Atlantic*, April 2018. Copyright © 2018 The Atlantic Media Co., as first published in *The Atlantic Magazine*. All rights reserved. Distributed by Tribune Content Agency, LLC.

Capehart, Jonathan. "Taking a Knee with Colin Kaepernick and Standing with Stephen Curry against Trump," from *The Washington Post*, September 24, 2017. Copyright © 2017 The Washington Post. All rights reserved. Used under license.

Coyote, Ivan. "Tomboys Still," pages 101–06 from *Tomboy Survival Guide*. Arsenal Pulp Press, 2016. Copyright © 2016 by Ivan Coyote. Reprinted with the permission of Arsenal Pulp Press.

The Economist. "Facebook Is Bad for You—Get a Life!" from *The Economist* print edition, August 17, 2013. Republished with permission of The Economist Group Limited, via Copyright Clearance Center, Inc.

Color Insert

Coney Island street art. Courtesy of Pest Control Office, Banksy, Coney Island, 2018.

GNC Total Lean advertisement. Photo courtesy Virgie Tovar.

Portrait of Virgie Tovar copyright © Andria Lo.

A large billboard showing Colin Kaepernick stands on top of the building housing the Nike store at Union Square Wednesday, Sept. 5, 2018, in San Francisco. Associated Press/Eric Risberg.

Hafkenscheid, Toni. Photograph of *Mixed Blessing* by Rebecca Belmore. Reprinted with the permission of Toni Hafkenscheid.

Tracey Emin (1963–). *My Bed*, 1998. Copyright © Tracey Emin / SOCAN (2019). Photo copyright © Tate.

Mamie Till Mobley. The body of Emmett Till, shown before an open casket funeral. From *The Chicago Defender*.

Young Emmett Till wears a hat. Bettmann Collection via Getty Images.

A group of Central American migrants climb the border fence between Mexico and the United States, near El Chaparral border crossing, in Tijuana, Baja California State, Mexico, on November 25, 2018. Pedro Pardo/AFP/Getty Images.

Serena Williams reacts after winning a point against Kaia Kanepi, of Estonia, during the fourth round of the U.S. Open tennis tournament, Sunday, Sept. 2, 2018, in New York. Associated Press/Andres Kudacki.

INDEX

From the Publisher

A name never says it all, but the word "Broadview" expresses a good deal of the philosophy behind our company. We are open to a broad range of academic approaches and political viewpoints. We pay attention to the broad impact book publishing and book printing has in the wider world; for some years now we have used 100% recycled paper for most titles. Our publishing program is internationally oriented and broad-ranging. Our individual titles often appeal to a broad readership too; many are of interest as much to general readers as to academics and students.

Founded in 1985, Broadview remains a fully independent company owned by its shareholders—not an imprint or subsidiary of a larger multinational.

For the most accurate information on our books (including information on pricing, editions, and formats) please visit our website at www.broadviewpress.com. Our print books and ebooks are also available for sale on our site.

broadview press
www.broadviewpress.com

This book is made of paper from well-managed FSC® - certified
forests, recycled materials, and other controlled sources.

PCF